How Toys Work

Springs

Siân Smith

Chicago, Illinois

www.capstonepub.com
Visit our website to find out more information about Heinemann-Raintree books.

To order:
☎ Phone 800-747-4992
🖳 Visit www.capstonepub.com to browse our catalog and order online.

Edited by Dan Nunn, Rebecca Rissman, and Sian Smith
Designed by Joanna Hinton-Malivoire
Picture research by Mica Brancic
Production by Victoria Fitzgerald

Originated by Capstone Global Library Ltd
Printed and bound in China by South China Printing Company Ltd

16 15 14 13 12
10 9 8 7 6 5 4 3 2 1

Library of Congress Cataloging-in-Publication Data
Smith, Siân.
    Springs / Siân Smith.
        p. cm.—(How toys work)
    Includes bibliographical references and index.
    ISBN 978-1-4329-6583-9 (hb)—ISBN 978-1-4329-6590-7 (pb)
    1. Springs (Mechanism)—Juvenile literature. 2. Toys—Juvenile literature. I. Title.
    TJ210.S57 2013
    621.8′24—dc23   2011041312

Acknowledgments
The author and publisher are grateful to the following for permission to reproduce copyright material: Alamy p.15 (© Paul Weller); © Capstone Global Library Ltd pp.10, 11, 13, 16, 19 (Tudor Photography), 18, 20, 21 (Lord and Leverett); © Capstone Publishers pp.6, 9, 12, 17, 22c, 23 bottom, 7 main (Karon Dubke); istockphoto p.14 (© Ken Kan); Shutterstock pp.4 (© anki21), 4 (© BestPhotoPlus), 4 (© Nikolai Tsvetkov), 4 (© originalpunkt), 5 (© Losevsky Pavel), 8 (© Julián Rovagnati), 22a (© Andy Z.), 22b (© Ales Liska), 22d (© pio3), 23 top, 7 inset (© HomeStudio).

Cover photograph of slinky toys reproduced with permission of Alamy (© Yiap Views). Back cover photograph of wind up toys reproduced with permission of © Capstone Global Library Ltd (Lord and Leverett).

We would like to thank David Harrison, Nancy Harris, Dee Reid, and Diana Bentley for their assistance in the preparation of this book.

Every effort has been made to contact copyright holders of material reproduced in this book. Any omissions will be rectified in subsequent printings if notice is given to the publisher.

Contents

Different Toys

There are many different kinds of toys.

Toys work in different ways.

Springs

Some toys use springs to work.

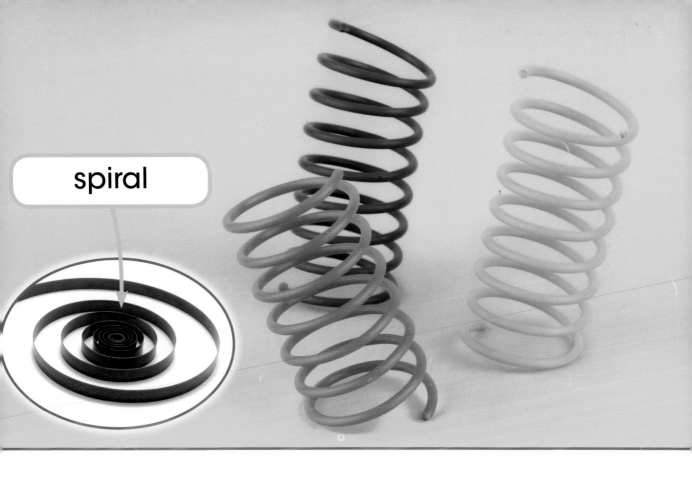

spiral

A spring is shaped like a spiral.

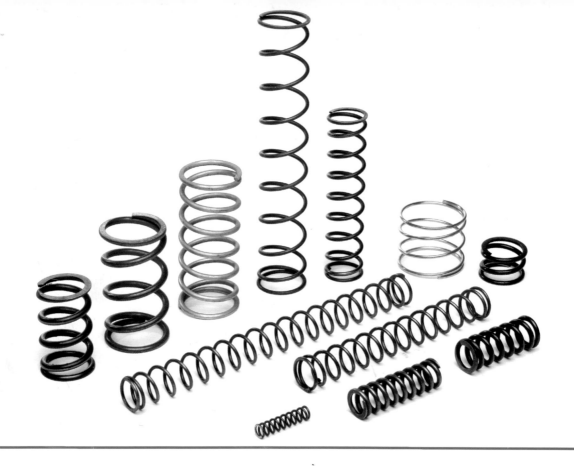

Springs can be made of metal.

spring

A jack-in-the-box uses a spring
to work.

Pushes and Pulls

You can stretch a spring by pulling it.

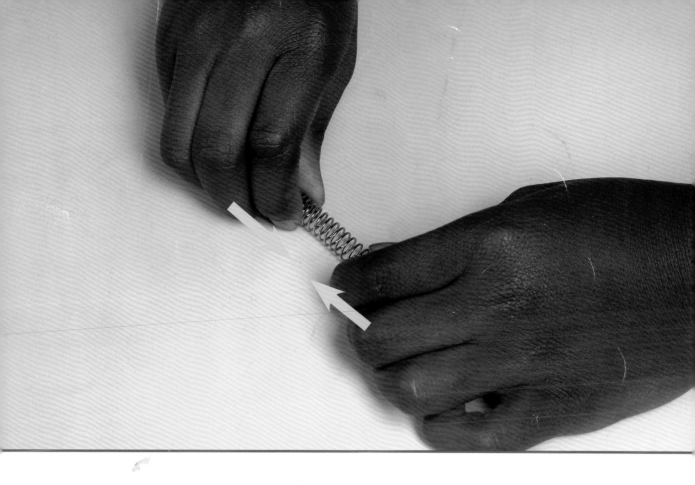

You can squeeze a spring by
pushing it.

The spring pushes or pulls back again.
It tries to go back to its normal shape.

These pushes and pulls can make
toys move.

More Toys with Springs

Some toys bounce on springs.

This toy bounces on a spring.

spring

Some springs make balls move.

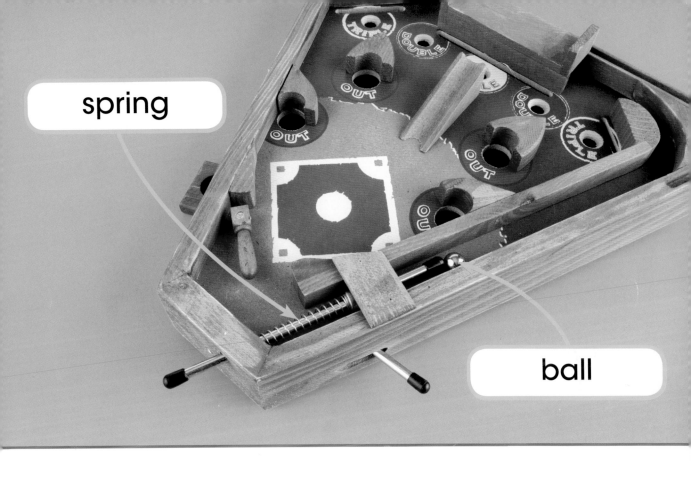

spring

ball

This spring makes a ball move.

Wind-Up Toys

Wind-up toys have springs inside.

When you wind up the toy, you
squeeze the spring.

spring

The spring pushes out as it goes
back to its normal shape.

This makes the toy move along.

Quiz

a

b

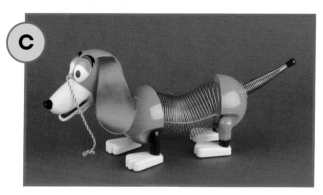

c

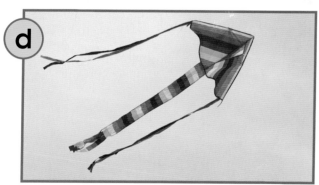

d

Which one of these toys uses a spring to work?

Answer on page 24

Picture Glossary

 **spiral** shape like a curl that winds around and around

 **spring** most springs are made of metal. A spring is shaped like a spiral.

Index

Answer to question on page 22: Toy c uses a spring to work.

Notes for Parents and Teachers

Introduction

Show the children a collection of toys. One or more of the toys should work by using a spring. Ask the children if they can spot the toy or toys with springs. Can they think of any other toys that use springs? Do they know what springs can do?

More information about springs

Explain that most springs are made out of metal, because this makes them very strong. But springs can also be made out of other materials, such as plastic. Most springs are helix shaped, but for younger children it is easier to describe them as shaped like a spiral that curls around and around. They can create their own spring shape by wrapping a strip of paper around a pencil. When we push or pull a spring, we change its shape. The spring pushes or pulls back as it returns to its original shape. We use these pushes and pulls from springs to make things move.

Follow-up activities

If possible, take apart a simple clockwork toy so that the children can see the spring inside. They could go on to invent and draw their own toy that uses a spring or springs. For more advanced work on simple machines, children can work with an adult to discuss and play the games at: www.edheads.org/activities/simple-machines.

OLD MAN HAWKEYE

FORTY-FIVE YEARS AGO, THE WORLD'S SUPER VILLAINS ORGANIZED UNDER THE RED SKULL AND COLLECTIVELY WIPED OUT NEARLY ALL OF THE SUPER HEROES. FEW SURVIVED THE CARNAGE THAT FATEFUL DAY, AND NONE OF THEM UNSCATHED. THE UNITED STATES WAS DIVIDED UP INTO TERRITORIES CONTROLLED BY THE VILLAINS, AND THE GOOD PEOPLE SURVIVE IN THESE WASTELANDS AS BEST THEY CAN. AMONG THEM LIVES A FORMER HERO WHO'S GIVEN UP ON THAT WAY OF LIFE. HE IS CLINT BARTON, BUT SOME KNOW HIM AS...

OLD MAN HAWKEYE

AN EYE FOR AN EYE

WRITER... **ETHAN SACKS**

ARTIST... **MARCO CHECCHETTO**

COLOR ARTIST... **ANDRES MOSSA**

LETTERER... **VC's JOE CARAMAGNA**

COVER ARTIST... **MARCO CHECCHETTO**

EDITOR... **MARK BASSO**

EXECUTIVE EDITOR... **NICK LOWE**

NOTE: THIS STORY TAKES PLACE FIVE YEARS BEFORE THE EVENTS OF THE ORIGINAL *OLD MAN LOGAN*.

COLLECTION EDITOR... **MARK D. BEAZLEY** | ASSISTANT EDITOR... **CAITLIN O'CONNELL**
ASSOCIATE MANAGING EDITOR... **KATERI WOODY** | SENIOR EDITOR, SPECIAL PROJECTS... **JENNIFER GRÜNWALD**
VP PRODUCTION & SPECIAL PROJECTS... **JEFF YOUNGQUIST** | SVP PRINT, SALES & MARKETING... **DAVID GABRIEL**
BOOK DESIGNER... **JAY BOWEN**

EDITOR IN CHIEF... **C.B. CEBULSKI** | CHIEF CREATIVE OFFICER.. **JOE QUESADA**
PRESIDENT... **DAN BUCKLEY** | EXECUTIVE PRODUCER.. **ALAN FINE**

1. AN EYE FOR AN EYE

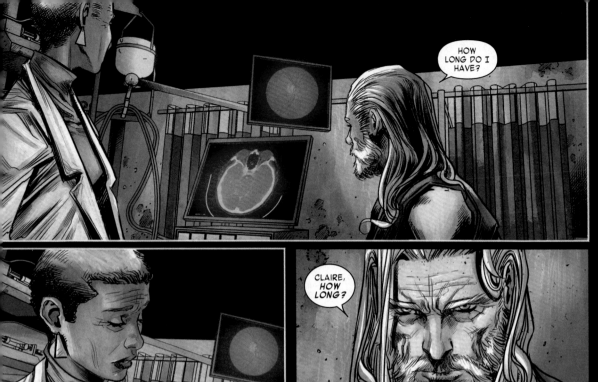

HOW LONG DO I HAVE?

CLAIRE, HOW LONG?

I DON'T KNOW FOR SURE. MONTHS. MAYBE WEEKS.

MY ADVICE? THERE'S SOMETHING YOU WANT TO SEE, SOMETHING YOU WANT TO DO...

"...DO IT NOW."

DIDN'T EXPECT TO SEE YOU HERE, CLINT.

I HAVE A PRESENT FOR YOUR BOY--

--IT'S AN XBOX, AND IT'S GOT A LONG-LIFE BATTERY, TOO. CUTTING-EDGE. WELL, IT WAS BACK WHEN THEY WERE STILL MAKIN' 'EM.

DON'T TELL ME, ULTRON-8--MY GOOD-FOR-NOTHING EX-HUSBAND JUST WALKED IN WITH MY ALIMONY.

SPIDER-SENSE FROM YOUR DAD'S SIDE OF THE FAMILY?

NAH, I CAN SMELL THE BOOZE FROM OVER HERE.

MY SCANNERS SHOW HIS WALLET INDENTATION IS FLATTER THAN PROJECTIONS, TONYA.

I BROUGHT SOME OF WHAT I OWE...BUT THE JOB DIDN'T GO AS PLANNED.

YOU COULD'VE JUST SENT THE MONEY. WHY ARE YOU *REALLY* HERE?

I JUST WANTED TO SEE MY DAUGHTER BEFORE...WELL, BEFORE...

IF YOU WANT TO SPEAK TO ASHLEY, SHE'S IN HER ROOM.

JUST MAKE IT QUICK. SHE ALREADY GOT HERSELF IN TROUBLE FOR FIGHTING, AND I DON'T WANT YOU TO FILL HER HEAD WITH MORE NONSENSE.

"WATER....!"

2. UNINVITED GUESTS

"...AND *WHERE* I CAN FIND HIM."

OUTSIDE HAMMER FALLS.

EYE CANDY

EYE CANDY

WHAT'S THE MATTER, MR. ORB, YOU DON'T LIKE WHAT YOU SEE? WE CAN GET THE DUDE PLAYING SUB-MARINER TODAY...IF THAT'S MORE YOUR FLAVOR.

NO... IT'S JUST... I THOUGHT I RECOGNIZED SOMEONE...

OH, GOD! NO! GUARDS! GUARDS--

--KEEP THAT MAN AWAY FROM ME!

"HE WENT BY THE PROFESSIONAL NAME OF 'RONIN.'"

RONIN?

THAT'S WHAT THE BROKER WHO FIXED ME UP CALLED HIM.

NOW, PLEASE LET MY WIFE GO. SHE'S SUFFERED ENOUGH.

RONIN

MINOR AVENGER INACTIVE YEARS BEFORE THE EVENT.

SPECIFICATION

87.09

HAMMER HEART RATE ELEVATED. POSSIBLY LYING.

IS THAT GARLIC AND PAPRIKA I'M SENSING THAT MAKE THIS BRISKET SO GOOD?

I...WHAT... YES, GARLIC AND PAPRIKA... GARLIC AND PAPRIKA.

I KNEW IT!

OF COURSE, I CAN'T TASTE THAT GARLIC AND PAPRIKA. I REGISTER THE CHEMICAL COMPOSITION OF THE MEAT, BUT I DON'T KNOW WHAT IT *TASTES* LIKE--

IT'S BEEN A LONG TIME SINCE I TASTED OR *FELT* ANYTHING.

MAKE NO MISTAKE, IF AND WHEN I KILL YOU AND YOUR WIFE, I WOULDN'T FEEL ONE BIT OF REMORSE.

I'D JUST SIT AND FINISH THE REST OF THIS BRISKET AFTER I'M DONE.

BUT THAT ARCHER...

HE'S SOMETHING ELSE. I RECKON I'LL FEEL SOMETHING WHEN I SEE THE LIFE DRAIN FROM HIS BODY.

SO, POINT ME TO--

3. THE **PRICE** OF ADMISSION

EXCUSE ME.

HARD TO SEE THAT, RIGHT?

NO OFFENSE, LADY, BUT YOU'RE PROBABLY BETTER OFF UNDER THAT BLINDFOLD.

WELL, SORRY, "SEEING" BEING JUST A FIGURE OF SPEECH IN MY CASE--

OPEN UP AND LET ME IN! PLEASE!

RAP RAP RAP

WHAT PART OF THE "CLOSED" SIGN WAS CONFUSING TO YOU?

I *NEED* MY WHEELS, TONYA.

I HAVE THE MONEY I OWE YOU...

LOOK, I DON'T HAVE TIME FOR CRAZY. CLOSED IS CLOSED.

PLEASE, I GOTTA GET OUT OF HERE...THE #$%& THAT WENT DOWN AT THE CLUB...

HE MIGHT BE AFTER ME, TOO!

WAIT-- *WHO* IS AFTER YOU? WHAT HAPPENED AT THE CLUB?

SUSPECT

VICTIM

CLINT BARTON A.K.A. HAWKEYE

ERIK JOSTEN A.K.A. ATLAS

KNOWN ASSOCIATES IN THUNDERBOLTS

CAN WE MOVE THE BODY NOW, MARSHAL? IT'S BAD FOR BUSINESS.

NOBODY'S BUYING STUFF AT THE GIFT SHOP ACROSS THE ROAD HAVING TO LOOK AT THAT ON THE WAY IN. THIS IS A FAMILY PLACE.

YEAH, YEAH, HE'S ALL YOURS.

COMPUTER-- GET ME A LIST OF THE SURVIVING THUNDERBOLTS.

4. ALL IN A DAY'S WORK

DOOMBOT FACTORY, KREE HAVEN.

MONDAY.

TUESDAY.

HMMMMMMM

...NAH, DON'T INVITE *JENKINS*... DUDE CREEPS ME OUT...

WEDNESDAY.

OOPS!

BUMP!

CLINK

OH, I'M SORRY, DID I MAKE YOU *DROP* SOMETHIN', ABE?

THURSDAY.

BEEP BEEP BEEP

HMMMMMM

...HEARD HE WAS ONCE A SUPER VILLAIN... THEN A HERO...THEN A BAD GUY AGAIN...

FRIDAY.

HMMMMMM

SATURDAY.

HMMMMMM

...DUMBASS WENT BY THE NAME MACH-X AND RAN WITH THE THUNDERBOLTS...

WHAT THE HELL IS A THUNDERBOLT? I HEARD HE CALLED HIMSELF THE BEETLE.

WHATEVER. BOTH ARE DUMB.

SUNDAY.

HMMMMMMM

Dearest Melissa, I'm sorry ?

Melissa Gold
c/o Sanctuary of the Silent Sisterhood

Melissa Gold
c/o Sanctuary

MONDAY.

...HEY! I'M TALKING TO YOU, ABE JENKINS! YOU KEEP WORKING EXTRA SHIFTS, YOU MAKE US LOOK BAD...

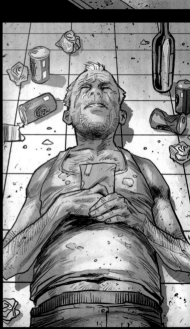

TUESDAY.

HMMMMMMM

QUITTING TIME CAME EARLY TODAY, ABE JENKINS...

5. DESPERATE TIMES

6. STRENGTH IN NUMBERS

HEY, WHAT ARE YOU DOING? IT'S MY CAR!

AFTER WATCHING YOU MISS WITH AN ARROW, YOU THINK I'D LET YOU DRIVE?

SO WHAT'S YOUR "PLAN" TO SAVE THOSE KIDS?

GET THE VENOMS TO CHASE US, OF COURSE.

AND HOW ARE YOU GOING TO GET ALL OF THEM TO FOLLOW US?

HEY, MADROXES! REMEMBER ME? THE GUY WHO KILLED ALL YOUR BROTHERS?

THIS TIME, I BROUGHT ENOUGH ARROWS TO #$%& UP THE REST OF YOU!

RAWLLL! AFTER HIM!

THAT SHOULD DO IT.

SMASSSHHH

GOING TO KILL YOU SSSLLOOOWWWLY. MAKE YOU SSSUFFER...

SHRRREEDDD

MY BEAUTIFUL CAR...!

AAARRRGGGHH... YOU ALIEN #$%&, THEY JUST SEWED MY SHOULDER BACK TOGETHER!

KATE...JUST KEEP...URK... HONKING THAT HORN...ATTRACT ATTENTION...

SLUNCH

HONK! HOOOONK!

AH, NO YOU DON'T.

TOOK YOU LONG ENOUGH.

FORTUNATELY FOR YOU, BULLSEYE HASN'T MOVED OUT OF POSITION.

THERE WAS A BIT OF A SETBACK EN ROUTE, TASKMASTER. IT WOKE UP EARLY WITHOUT ITS CONTROLLER BOOTED UP AND KILLED THREE GUARDS.

WE MAY HAVE PROGRAMMED TOO MUCH "ANGRY" IN ITS MENTAL PARAMETERS.

IT TOOK EVERY TRANQUILIZER WE HAD TO SEDATE IT BEFORE--

WELL, WAKE HIM UP AGAIN--

--AND FOR ALL OF OUR SAKES, MAKE HIM EVEN *ANGRIER.*

"'CAUSE *THE WINTER SOLDIER* AIN'T THE ONE I'M MOST WORRIED ABOUT."

"I TOLD YOU YEARS AGO TO STAY THE #$%& AWAY FROM ME..."

#1 VARIANT BY CLAYTON CRAIN

#1 VARIANT BY STEVE McNIVEN, JAY LEISTEN & MORRY HOLLOWELL

#1 VARIANT BY GREG LAND, JAY LEISTEN & FRANK D'ARMATA

#1 VARIANT BY RON LIM & RACHELLE ROSENBERG

#1 AVENGERS VARIANT BY BARRY KITSON & MATT YACKEY

#2 HULK VARIANT BY TERRY DODSON **&** RACHEL DODSON

#3 MIGHTY THOR VARIANT BY OLIVIER COIPEL & JASON KEITH

THE BIBLE AS BOOK
THE REFORMATION

THE BIBLE AS BOOK
THE REFORMATION

Edited by
ORLAITH O'SULLIVAN

Assistant Editor
ELLEN N. HERRON

THE BRITISH LIBRARY
& OAK KNOLL PRESS
*in association with The Scriptorium:
Center for Christian Antiquities*
2000

First published 2000 by
The British Library
96 Euston Road
St Pancras
London NW1 2DB

Published exclusively in North and South America by
Oak Knoll Press
310 Delaware Street
New Castle
DE 19720

in association with
The Scriptorium: Center for Christian Antiquities
PO Box 770
Grand Haven
Michigan 49417-0770

British Library Cataloguing-in-Publication Data
A CIP record is available from The British Library

Library of Congress Cataloging-in-Publication Data

The Bible as book : the Reformation / edited by Orlaith O'Sullivan, assistant editor Ellen
N. Herron.
    p. cm.
  Includes bibliographical references and index.
  ISBN 1-58456-025-8
    1. Bible – Translating – Europe – History – 16th century – Congresses. 2. Bible –
Versions – History – 16th century – Congresses. 3. Bible – Use – History – 16th
century – Congresses. 4. Reformation – Europe – Congresses. I. O'Sullivan, Orlaith.
II. Herron, Ellen N.
BS454.B5 2000
220'.09'031 – dc21
                                                                    00-039138

        ISBN 1-58456-025-8 (Oak Knoll)
        ISBN 0-7123-4675-9 (British Library)
Designed by John Trevitt
Typeset in England by Norman Tilley Graphics, Northampton
Printed in England by St Edmundsbury Press, Bury St Edmunds

CONTENTS

v

Contents

CONTRIBUTORS

WILLIAM S. CAMPBELL, *University of Wales, Lampeter*

DAVID DANIELL, *University of London*

RICHARD DUERDEN, *Brigham Young University*

SUSAN FELCH, *Calvin College*

ANDREW HADFIELD, *University of Wales, Aberystwyth*

FRANCIS HIGMAN, *University of Geneva*

GUIDO LATRÉ, *Katholicke Universiteit Leuven*

DAVID NORTON, *Victoria University of Wellington*

ANDREW PETTEGREE, *University of St Andrews*

TATIANA C. STRING, *University of Bristol*

ORLAITH O'SULLIVAN, *The Scriptorium: Center for Christian Antiquities*

DAVID WRIGHT, *University of Edinburgh*

LIST OF ILLUSTRATIONS

(reproduced between pages 38 and 39)

List of Illustrations

PREFACE

THIS COLLECTION of essays originated at a conference on the Bible in the Reformation, held at Hampton Court, Hereford, in May of 1997. It was the third of the series 'The Bible as Book', sponsored by the Van Kampen Foundation and The Scriptorium: Center for Christian Antiquities. My thanks to all the scholars who presented papers. Every successful conference is the result of a group effort, and ours was no exception: thanks to Kayleen Bobbitt, and Herb and Kiko Zimmermann for their contributions. Special thanks are due to Scott Pierre and Karla Van Kampen-Pierre for their superb organizational skills and generous hospitality, and to Robert and Judith Van Kampen, for their indefatigable commitment and support.

To all the contributors to this volume, my heartfelt thanks for your prompt replies to my many requests. To Professor David Daniell, who arranged the speakers' papers, and presided over the conference in 1997, I offer humble thanks; I hope that you share my view of this volume as a tribute to your vision of Reformation studies and your commitment to the field. Deepest thanks to Ellen Herron, my co-editor, for her sharp eye, insightful comments, and her work preparing the bibliography. Thanks to my colleagues Professor Bastiaan Van Elderen and Dr Herbert Samworth, and especially to Lois Goossen, who saved the day (as usual). I am also indebted to David Way, John Trevitt, and the staff at the British Library for their guidance and expertise.

Finally, on a personal note, my thanks to Bruce, for everything.

Orlaith O'Sullivan

INTRODUCTION

Orlaith O'Sullivan[1]

THE CALL-TO-ARMS of the early Reformation – *sola scriptura* – needed two things in order to function: access to the biblical texts in their original languages; and the availability of the Bible in a language comprehended by the populace. The work of the Reformers focused simultaneously on both of these areas, and this volume offers several perspectives on that work, from theories of translation to the preparation and control of the biblical texts through various means. The early Reformers saw the Bible as the key to the Kingdom of Heaven, but there were also further nuances to this relationship. The Early Modern era was a time of crisis in many ways for the Bible; it was tested and theorized, and exploited for political and other ends. Yet that time was also one of blossoming, a time when lay people developed an intimate, personal relationship with the Word, a time when some began to assume the full burden of the comprehension and interpretation of that Word.

Trained as a humanist, Martin Luther sought to increase access to the earliest versions of the biblical text, and established textual studies during the 1520s in the University of Wittenberg. Philip Melanchthon joined Luther there, becoming his distinguished professor of Greek. Scholarly Jews were assembled as Hebrew advisers, a group Luther came to call his *sanhedrin*, from the Jewish name for a supreme council. In preparing his German Bible, Luther must have carefully considered the nature of the canon of Scripture: he himself admitted to hating the books of Esther and II Maccabees, and had famously dismissed James as an epistle of straw. Other Reformers had similar concerns, particularly concerning the Song of Songs and the Book of Revelation. Yet despite this they all, without exception, printed the entire canon in their biblical publications. The reason for keeping the Bible in its entirety points to what was for the Reformers the key to its comprehension: the relationship between the Law and the Gospel. The Old and New Testaments cross-referred often, and in order to understand the true nature of God, all books of both Testaments were necessary, ideally in their first languages. The Reformers' interest in the original biblical texts soon resulted in a series of Hebrew and Greek Bibles; by the time that Theodore Beza had completed his editions of the Greek New Testament later in the century, the Bible had its proper basis in the original languages.

For the second condition necessary for *sola scriptura* – that of the people's Bible – the printing press proved to be the crucial factor. The production of cheap editions of the Bible, intended for private study, was essential for the transmission of the biblical text in the vernacular. While massive endeavours such as the Complutensian Polyglot of 1522 were of great significance to European biblical scholarship, the volumes were expensive and scarce, and were in monetary and intellectual terms well beyond the reach of the average lay person. While even students of Oxford and Cambridge – well

I

known for their complaints of poverty – could afford Erasmus' 1516 New Testament, it was still in Latin and Greek; only the vernacular editions of the Bible would fill that void in the spiritual life of lay people.

The self-interpreting quality so crucial to the Reformers' Bible was, however, inherently problematic. With a complete vernacular Bible, every man and woman with the ability to read or to listen could have access to the biblical text, and could interpret the Bible unsupervised. This release of power brought with it the possibility of reinterpreting the Bible in every generation; the area of biblical scholarship has remained vibrant ever since. However, such interpretations, as every church and religious movement came to learn, led to division.

William Campbell provides a detailed analysis of one such interpretation, that of Martin Luther on Romans, which remained unpublished until 1908. Although an accurate grammatical understanding of the Hebrew and Greek texts was important, Luther's primary stress was that the interpreter of the Bible should seek first and foremost the literal sense intended by its author, the Holy Spirit. In our consideration of the ground-breaking work embarked upon during the sixteenth century, we are fortunate to be reminded by Campbell that no innovation occurs in a vacuum, but instead represents a progression from or reaction to earlier traditions. Campbell examines Luther's relationship with Augustine, and illuminates the nuances of what the earlier scholar meant to the later. Luther came to regard Augustine as his main ally in the fight against the Pelagian tendencies of Scholasticism, which interpreted the Word through the philosophy of Aristotle. Augustine's concept of the perfectibility of human nature was 'too optimistic' for Luther, and he therefore 'embraced an Augustinianism more severe and thoroughgoing than Augustine himself'. Luther's interpretative approach was entirely Christological: 'every word in the Bible pointed to Christ'. The themes of Romans – the righteousness of God and of man, and justification by faith – were for Luther pervasive, unifying themes throughout scripture. Those who did not understand that had not been inspired by the Holy Spirit.

One of the areas that the Reformers were forced to reconsider in the wake of the inspiration argument was that of language and linguistics. The Bible translations of the sixteenth century often began with an optimistic faith in the mimetic transparency of language: the Word was like a liquid, that could be contained in many vessels, or like a medicine, that could be contained in many boxes. One of the most common comparisons was that of clothing: Latin was considered a rich velvet, while English was coarse cloth. With this is mind, translation only involved changing 'oute of Romayne gownes […] into Engyshe Liuerayes'.[2] It was not long before the deficiencies of such a theory came to light. Not only did the various translations take on different nuances and shades, but in the vernacular the Bible became radically destabilized. The early Reformers began their work in the hope that each lay person could attain a personal relationship with the Lord, but in actuality each lay person, through the process of reading, created a Bible of their own, with its own meanings. Conformity to Lutheranism, Calvinism, or Roman Catholicism could only be ensured through guiding the reader, and many of the articles in this volume address the ways in which the Biblical text was controlled, and framed in such a way that guided its readers towards a specific interpretation.

In her article 'The Bible Translations of George Joye', Orlaith O'Sullivan traces Joye's progression from the belief that 'the simple sely word' of God can speak for itself, to a belief in the need for a textual apparatus and overt instruction for his readers. Francis Higman examines the reading aids contained in Genevan Bibles, and relates them to the attempt by the Genevan Church to educate the lay person to the level of minister solely through private reading of the Bible. The centres of organized education could not keep up with the rapid expansion of Calvinism, and so a new kind of Bible developed through the printing presses of Geneva. In contrast to the Lutheran Reformation, which ended up discouraging unsupervised Bible study, Calvinist regions encouraged it through the production of texts such as the magnificent Barbier-Courteau Bible (1559), which provided a host of study aids to further the reader's understanding of the Word. The volume was not meant to aid a theology student in his studies, but was intended to constitute the entire course. Although this and similar texts emanated from the doctrine of *sola scriptura*, they silently modified its definition to 'only the *true* scripture'. This difference is crucial, for the reading aids supplied – summaries, prefaces, maps, tables, marginal notes, and dictionaries – all sought to restrain free interpretation of the Bible. In Germany, interpretation had been controlled through use of the catechism, with good reason: 'In an approved Lutheran catechism one could not find a false idea. This was certainly not true of the Bible.'[3] However, in Calvinist regions with rapidly growing congregations, encyclopedic Bibles were produced, preempting any heretical musings by providing a thoroughly Calvinist handbook to understanding the Word.

What is interesting about the process of guiding readers is that the same text may be used, but through marginal notes may be presented in many different ways. Many Bible editions were declared heretical not because of their scriptural renderings, but because of their glosses and prefaces; the biblical text itself was not considered suspect. One of the recurring themes of the conference in 1997 was the attitude of the Reformers towards the various versions of Scripture. The sixteenth century – with its emphasis on the 'new', humanist Latin, Hebrew and Greek – is always thought of as marking the downfall of the Vulgate, but in fact the Reformers' citations of Scripture are, first, often from the Vulgate, and second, often inaccurate.

Susan Felch, in her 'The Role of the Vulgate in the Work of Anne Lock', reveals that one of the Psalm paraphrases generally thought to epitomize Protestant literary culture is in fact based on the Vulgate. Having established Anne Lock's credentials as a well-educated woman 'with impeccable Protestant credentials', Felch embarks on an examination of the sources for her paraphrase of Psalm 51 (1560), and reveals that, out of all the versions available to Lock at the time, Lock drew on the Vulgate as her primary source and inspiration. More striking is Felch's further assertion, that Lock's preference for the Vulgate was unremarkable in her own time.

David Wright investigates the second point – that of inaccurate quotation. He undercuts the modern scholar's tendency to slavishly compare syllables of various translations by revealing that John Knox did not cite the Bible in an accurate manner. Wright points out that the severity of John Knox's insistence on the 'express' Word of God contrasts sharply with the impreciseness of the biblical quotations in his writings; this casual method of quotation, perhaps from memory, is common among English Reformers. Consequently, the identification of the specific editions used by Knox as sources is almost impossible. Not only various English versions, but also French and Latin biblical texts continued to influence Knox's writings, even after the publication of the Geneva Bible. Wright concludes that Knox was primarily an oralist, for whom the Bible existed as a vital presence in his mind, and was not to be limited to one specific edition.

David Daniell discusses the life and translations of William Tyndale, and traces the progression from Tyndale's first New Testament (1525), which was heavily dependent on Luther, to his later revisions, which changed in accordance with Tyndale's greater knowledge of Hebrew. Daniell highlights the contribution of Tyndale to the Bible in English, and to the English language itself. Tyndale's most characteristic feature is that of clarity; for the many English people coming to the Bible for the first time in the sixteenth century, the clear, simple renditions he provided were beyond value. Tyndale did not cease in his scholarly efforts, but continued to work on revisions of his text until his arrest in 1535.

In the year preceding the martyrdom of Tyndale, the *editio princeps* of the English Bible was printed by Miles Coverdale, the first complete Bible to be published in English. Guido Latré considers the long-argued issue of the place of printing of this Bible, and argues for Antwerp as its origin. He draws on evidence from one of the woodcuts – an illustration of the Tabernacle – which contains several words which appear to be in the Dutch language spoken around Antwerp at that time. Latré also tackles the problem of identifying a printing house, and drawing on typographical details, and biographical accounts of both Coverdale and de Keyser, designates the latter as the printer of the 1535 Bible.

One of the recurring points of the conference was that the Bible was not interpreted, translated, printed, or read in a vacuum. Richard Duerden examines the discourse of translation in the sixteenth century, which he argues was 'much more political and material than is dreamt of in theory'. He asks the question 'Can modernity read the Renaissance Bible?', arguing that the early biblical translations cannot be studied in the context of aesthetics and linguistics alone. Duerden addresses the issues of ideology, authority, and power that resonate through the translations, tracing the development of ideas of fluency, clarity, and naturalness of style. The early debates concerning translations dwelt not on the idea of equivalency, but on authority and ideology. As Scripture had previously been used to assert the authority of the Catholic Church, so it came, in the course of the English Reformation, to be used to realign loyalties to Henry VIII. As Duerden observes: 'Scripture is no mere depiction, description, or representation of reality; it is a force which alters reality by causing power to shift.' Tyndale placed himself and the Reformers in the position of restoring lost authority to kings; under Queen Elizabeth this relationship was inverted, and political authority instead established the authority and the availability of Scripture. Monarchy and Scripture enjoyed a symbiotic relationship, with one advancing the other. Duerden's investigation into some of the motivating forces behind Bible translations and the furore stirred up by them gives us an interesting perspective from which to consider all the subjects touched on in this volume. The Bible not only offered comfort and spiritual guidance, it offered power, which could be appropriated for political and other ends. It therefore needed not only to be available, but to be controlled.

The role played by illustrations in the matrix of power and authority is explored in several of the articles. The outcry against images in the early decades of the Reformation leaves scholars of today with the puzzling task of deciphering how the theological intricacies of the evangelical movement managed to reach the mass populace, of which a high percentage was illiterate. One thing is apparent from the trials of the time: oral reading and teaching of the Bible – both in sermons and in private reading groups – was a key factor in the spread of Protestantism. However, it is also clear that the visual aspect of Bible production had a part to play.

Tatiana C. String and Andrew Pettegree both discuss illustrations produced in the first generation of the German Reformation that served to communicate core messages of the new faith, such as justification by faith, or the true nature of the Roman Church. In her article 'Politics and Polemics in English and German Bible Illustrations', String uses selected woodcut images of the Antichrist in the Apocalypse cycle in English and German Reformation Bibles to examine the value of visual images in the dissemination of Reformist ideology. The visual medium would seem the most obvious way to deliver ideological message in a clear, straightforward manner. However, the iconography found in German Bibles is often complicated, and furthermore appears only in the more expensive, lavish productions. According to String, the visual references to the papal power were 'hardly likely to be self-evident to those of meaner education'. It is more likely that these illustrated Bibles were intended for a particular social circle, and did not function to disseminate ideas in a genuine mass movement.

Nevertheless, there was certainly a place for biblical art. For example, the identification of the pope as Antichrist was commonplace in Reformist polemic at that time; its motivation was drawn from both the political and the religious arenas. In early German Bibles the conflation of the imagery of the pope with the Antichrist by artists such as Lucas Cranach and Hans Holbein was carried out to great effect. However, in the Bibles of Tyndale and Coverdale the significance is overlooked, although they shared the same ideological concerns as those of Luther. One of the conclusions drawn from this evidence is that there did not exist in England the same close relationship between writer, illustrator, and printer as was to be found in Germany. Only the title-pages of English Bibles were specifically conceived to communicate political and theological messages; the illustrations appear to have been haphazardly chosen.

Andrew Pettegree examines the development of one of the great title-page illustrations of the Protestant Bible: 'The Law and the Gospel', which imaged the stark contrast between the old Law and the new Law of Christ. Humanity is justified not by adherence to the old law of Judaism, but by faith. He explores the nature and function of this woodcut, beginning with Lucas Cranach in the first generation of the German evangelical movement. The image reached its apex as a ideological tool in Luther's Bible of 1541, and went on to achieve great popularity in a largely Calvinistic society through the printing house of Gellius Ctematius in Emden. Pettegree explores its presence in Dutch and English Bibles, both Protestant and Catholic, and concludes that the lack of theological clarity in the employment of illustrative materials seems to be part of a more general pattern. Importantly, as with String's research, the evidence suggests that neither printers or Reformers were as uniformly calculating as has been presumed by later scholarship.

Andrew Hadfield examines early colonial writings, and finds in them a clear imprint of the Geneva Bible's reading of history, and its eschatological mindset. In his 'The Revelation and Early English Colonial Ventures', he assesses the impact of the apocalypticism of John Bale and the Geneva Bible's Revelation of John on those authors who sought to promote English colonial ventures in the Americas in the final decades of the sixteenth century. The European power struggle between England and Spain was imaged in terms of a pre-apocalyptic conflict between the forces of Christ and the Antichrist; English Protestantism would have to convert the native Americans to the true religion if it was to halt the progress of Catholic Spain. Within this apocalyptic framework, the identities of the English Protestant Church and nation were expanded, and the English colonizers became participants in a play of awesome proportions, fighting for Christ's true church. However, as Hadfield demonstrates through texts and images of the period, in the course of judging the nature of the Spanish and the native Americans the colonizers looked inward to their own nature and society, with the result that the colonial tracts produced were often paradoxical and uneasy.

The volume concludes with David Norton's article, which was prompted by a Rudyard Kipling short story in which Shakespeare majestically polishes off a draft of the King James Version. Norton imagines the process of translation quite differently. Basing his interpretation on the extant evidence concerning the functioning of the Revised Version New Testament committee in the 1870s, and the scant details available of the 1611 translation committees, Norton recreates the history of the rendering of a single verse for the King James Version, following its progression from the first committee through to the printing press. He impresses on us the force of character that went into each line; the translation decided upon was as much about committee politics as it was about accuracy. Luther's declaration that 'God is in every syllable' seems a far cry from the petty backbiting and the human capacity to err witnessed in these reconstructions.

What starts to emerge is a very different picture of the Reformation, populated by people with human concerns and failings. When we consider the findings of many of these papers, one wonders exactly to what extent we have oversimplified or mis-interpreted the history of the Reformation: Reformers relied on the Vulgate, and quoted inaccurately in any case; the Bible was deliberately appropriated to ends which were other than theological; Luther's theology was later developed in ways he never intended; Bible illustrations were not often consciously employed to convey ideological messages, and the same pictures thought to sum up the Protestant cause were also used in Catholic texts – we need to ask ourselves what, if anything, the people of the Reformation thought of these things.

The underlying theme of the conference was the future of Reformation studies. This volume suggests that we need broader perspectives, coupled with a greater attention to detail. Much is known of the progress of Reformation theology among the well-educated, but the mechanism of the dissemination of ideas to the masses is another story. More research is needed on the biblical study aids, to map their development during the growth of the various churches. Were the printers of Bibles operating from religious fervour or from commercial motives: was the *Gesetz und Gnade* title-page chosen for its clear espousal of the doctrine of justification by faith, or from purely monetary considerations, because of its associations with other best-selling Bibles? Furthermore, the network by which, having been printed, Bibles were circulated to so many households throughout Europe has yet to be clearly delineated. Another obvious lack is that of editions of original texts from the period. The vernacular biblical

Introduction

translations produced in the sixteenth century are worthy of close study, as are the polemical writings of the Reformers, saturated as they are with Scripture. In addition, the effect of the vernacular Bible on native languages warrants further research, considering the great extent to which it is infused in legal, literary, medical, linguistic, and education writing throughout the century.

As a final thought, I would like to reiterate the observation of David Wright: 'how limiting a perspective it can be to view the Reformation Bible as a scholarly, literary text rather than as the flaming and searing sword of the Spirit, wielded in living combat for the souls of men and women and for the heart of the Church.' So also it is limiting to view the Reformation as a series of editions of the Bible, or a list of martyrs of various faiths, or a sequence of religious ordinances – each perspective can only offer a restricted view of the period. This volume concerns itself with both the theoretical and the practical, the broader picture and the details of the Reformation; I hope that its cumulative effect does justice to the intricate, staggering historical period it seeks to represent and understand.

NOTES

1 Prof. David Daniell delivered the plenary address at the conference in 1997, and the thoughts and concerns there expressed have infused this introduction. Many thanks to David for the support and advice offered throughout the production of this volume.
2 Richard Foster Jones, *The Triumph of the English Language: A Survey of Opinions Concerning the Vernacular from the Introduction of Printing to the Restoration* (Stanford, CA: Stanford University Press, 1953), p. 21.
3 Richard Gawthrop and Gerald Strauss, 'Protestantism and Literacy in Early Modern Germany', *Past and Present*, 104 (1984), 31-55 (p. 39).

EQUIVALENCE OR POWER?

AUTHORITY AND REFORMATION BIBLE TRANSLATION

Richard Duerden

I N 1540 the prolific French translator and printer Étienne Dolet wrote 'the earliest treatise on translation in a modern European language', *La maniere de bien traduire d'une langue en aultre.*[1] In it he offered five principles for translating well: (1) understanding perfectly the author's meaning and matter; (2) knowing perfectly both languages; (3) rendering not slavishly, word for word, but following the intention, sentence for sentence; (4) trusting the vernacular languages and common usage over latinisms; and (5) arranging words with sweetness, observing harmony and figures of speech.[2] But two years later, for errors in certain words in his translations and paraphrases, as well as for printing forbidden books in the vulgar tongue (such as the New Testament), Dolet was convicted of heresy, despite his insistence that he was a faithful child of the Church. He petitioned King Francis, who granted him a royal pardon, yet within another two years he was arrested again and charged with blasphemy and sedition, primarily because he had wrongly translated a single sentence concerning the immortality of the soul in a dialogue attributed to Plato. (His sentence read '*Apres la mort tu ne seras plus rien du tout*' – the last three words had no direct source in the dialogue.)[3] In 1546 he was hanged and burned at the stake. His sentences – that is, both the one he translated and the sentence of death that resulted from it – remain puzzling, not only because adding colloquial emphasis to a sentence in a pseudo-platonic dialogue could lead to a charge of blasphemy, but because such trust for the common language could motivate an additional charge of sedition. Charged with heresy, blasphemy, and sedition for a colloquial rendering of a non-Christian text, Dolet discovers for us that accuracy and aesthetics were not after all the full measure of translations in that period. In the sixteenth century, the reception of translations and the attacks on and defences of those translations create in practice a discourse on translation much more political and material than is dreamt of in the theory.

We still prefer to discuss early translations of the Bible as if they were rendered in a separate realm of aesthetics and language alone. In our modern treatises on the translations of the sixteenth century, particularly in our discussions of early English Bibles, we too have talked primarily about philological accuracy and stylistic beauty in the texts, while all about and through those texts swirl the perils and promises of conviction – both kinds – and of ideology, authority, and power. Modernist assumptions about the objectivity of texts or the superstitiousness of religion will not help us to read early modern discourse, but the critique of modernism which has been called post-modernism can shake us from those assumptions and teach us to see in those texts the struggle and aspirations which give them another kind of eloquence. Reading the translators of early modern England, while attending not only to clarity and beauty but also to ideology and authority, we can attend not only to what the translations *say*, but also to what they *do*: the cultural and social acts they perform.

What makes a good translation? Modern translation studies emphasize accuracy of representation: equivalence, fidelity, clarity, and sometimes style or aesthetics.[4] But such criteria are relatively absent from sixteenth-century discussions of translation. Despite translators' awareness of such philological and aesthetic concerns as those Dolet enumerated, their emphasis actually rests on such ideological and institutional concerns as those Dolet experienced. William Tyndale and Thomas More, Miles Coverdale and Henry VIII, Gregory Martin and William Fulke – their writings may mention issues of language, but they dwell on issues of power.

MODERNITY: EPISTEMOLOGY, HERMENEUTICS, TRANSLATION

Can modernity read these texts? They are written under assumptions handed down from Aristotle and the Scholastics, that knowledge is not just information, but requires integration and harmony with experience. Political knowledge is therefore the highest kind, since it requires combining all other kinds of knowledge and keeping them together, functioning well. For instance, in his *Apologie for Poetry* (1595) Philip Sidney urges that all other sciences are 'directed to the highest end of the mistres Knowledge, by the Greekes called *Arkitecktonike*, which stands (as I thinke) in the knowledge of a mans selfe, in the Ethicke and politick consideration, with the end of well dooing and not of well knowing onely'.[5] For the Christian Middle Ages, all knowledge found its harmony and governance in the Church. However, with modernism emerged a fragmentation of knowledge. As early as Occam's bracketing of God off from the world of inquiry, modernism began its turn away from a concept of knowledge governed by ethical and institutional harmony and towards a concept of knowledge governed by certainty. Rather than asking 'How does what I know harmonize with what we do?', modernism asks 'How do you know?' To find certainty, modern reason looks not towards the harmony or mutual functioning of knowledges, but towards the accuracy of each form of knowledge as a picture of the world. Knowledge is no longer so connected with social action; knowledge is a depiction, a mental image judged by its accuracy and clarity.

What gives knowledge or reason their legitimacy? Ancient and medieval thinkers decided that ethical and religious experience legitimate reason; they lend it their authority. Modernism insists that only reason itself can legitimate reason; true ideas, after Descartes, are clear and distinct ideas. Post-modernism has responded that reason is in trouble: it may not appeal to something higher, and yet it cannot be its own foundation;[6] it is influenced on all sides by such practical concerns as modernism sought to bracket off: ethics, politics, ideology, will.

A similar story of the gradual shift from active knowledges to passive and reflective kinds of knowledge can be told with the Bible itself as protagonist. Hans Frei's *The Eclipse of Biblical Narrative* (1974) explains how, as we moved into the modern period, from about 1650 on, we ceased to think of the Bible as narratives embodying meaning and started thinking of it as a history referring to external events and facts, as a reflection or shadow of something else more real than the story itself.[7] In effect, we decided that fact deserves more attention than truth. We lost the sense that the Bible is narrative and, moreover, that the Bible does not just describe a history which is elsewhere in time and space, the Bible *renders* that history, and gives access to it. Having surrendered those kinds of awareness, critical reflection on the Bible instead thought of the Bible as description or representation of something distant, and separated reference and meaning, focusing primarily on the accuracy of the representation, confusing fact with truth, and bracketing the ethical, rhetorical, spiritual import of the text. Frei's study of hermeneutics challenges the concept of representation, suggesting that it may be an inadequate way of describing and understanding how texts work; in other words, paradoxically, 'representation' is an inaccurate representation. The problem with the notion of representation grows larger and more complex with each century, until the very mess convinces us to rethink textuality not as reflection or reference to a separate objective reality but as discourses which constitute reality and history for us, even as they do indeed communicate in various literal ways ideas about reality and history.

As with epistemology and hermeneutics, so with translation: in early modern England, the legitimacy of a translation was determined primarily in the realm of social, ethical, and religious experience. Modern translation theories, however, test a translation by its aesthetics and its accuracy. Lawrence Venuti's history of translation theory runs parallel to those I have just outlined of philosophy and biblical hermeneutics.[8] Starting in the mid-seventeenth century, theories of translation came to emphasize 'fluency', or clarity and naturalness of style in the target language. This dedication to a faithful translation in smooth and effortless language serves the illusion of transparency, the myth that one text is a clear and accurate representation of another, while by this 'discursive sleight of hand' it 'masks the political interests it serves' and ignores or reduces the otherness of the foreign culture.[9] Post-modern translation studies are returning to pragmatic tests: the social authority of source texts and how it is constituted, the power and interests served or subverted in the work of translation, the impact of a translation in the target culture.

Having dismissed authority, power, and ideology from the sphere of knowledge as illegitimate interlopers, we moderns find ourselves dismissing much, even most, of what we find in early modern texts. Can modernity read the Renaissance Bible? Reading these early modern, even pre-modern, texts from my modern location, I find myself haunted by these words from *Of Grammatology* (1976): 'No model of reading seems to me at the moment ready to measure up to this text – which I would like to read as a *text* and not as a document.'[10] Having bracketed off so much of culture and textuality, modernity misses too much when it reads. But fate smiles wryly. The figures feared as destroyers of tradition and authority – Derrida, Althusser, Foucault, etc. – are the most helpful hermeneuticists in three centuries for us who want to read the Renaissance Bible as a discourse in a culture, because they direct us to a new set of assumptions about discourse which help us see the Renaissance Bible not only as a repository of truths, but as a vehicle of power.

Richard Duerden

A HERMENEUTICS OF SUSPICION

For example, in 1582 Gregory Martin evaluated the English Bibles of the previous half century in *A Discoverie of the Manifold Corruptions of the Holy Scriptures*. His table of contents and chapter headings list his arguments, none of them philological. Rather, he argues that the Protestant translations contradict authoritative doctrine; they run 'Against Apostolical Traditions', 'Against sacred Images', 'Against Priest and Priesthod', 'Against Purgatorie', etc., and therefore demonstrate 'That the Protestants translate the holy Scriptures falsely of purpose, in favour of their heresies'.[11] The corruptions he discovers have little to do with deviations from the source languages, and everything to do with deviations from ecclesiastical authority. Purposely avoiding discussion of Greek and Hebrew, which is 'only for the learned', Martin defends 'the true and authentical Scripture, I mean the vulgar Latin Bible'.[12] The flaw in the English Bibles, he says, is that they refuse to 'be tried by the auncient Latin translation, which is the text of the fathers and the whole Church'; they insist instead on a principle, 'that the Scriptures are easie and plaine and sufficient of themselves to determine every matter'.[13] Martin's concern with the accuracy of the translations is subordinated to the larger issues of convention, community, and legitimation by the authority of the institution; the authority of principle, such as *sola scriptura*, he considers the high road to heresy. Principles merely mask a schismatical agenda: the translators, he says, follow not the Greek and Hebrew, but their own wilfulness, 'and consequently are obstinate Heretikes'.[14] Ideology rather than philology explains the translators' errors: 'it could not be negligence at the first or ignorance, but a plaine heretical intention'.[15]

Four hundred years before Paul Ricoeur coined the phrase, Gregory Martin, like Thomas More and others before him, was practising 'the hermeneutics of suspicion', reading through the words of a text towards the implied agenda of its producers.[16] Modern commentators never quite hide their distaste for the intolerant partisanship in Thomas More's voluminous dispute with William Tyndale, but More is a very apt reader of ideological implications. Those three words, elder (rather than priest), congregation (rather than church), and love (rather than charity), in Tyndale's New Testament do advance the interests of the Protestants.[17] More does not see Tyndale's New Testament as a rendering of a single book, the Bible, from one language to another; he believes Tyndale has produced a different book:

It is quod I to me great meruayll / that any good crysten man hauyng any drop of wyt in his hede / wold any thyng meruayll or complayne of the burnynge of that booke yf he knowe the matter. Whyche who so callyth the newe testament calleth it by a wronge name / excepte they wyll call it Tyndals testament or Luthers testament. For so had Tyndall after Luthers counsayle corrupted and chaunged it frome the good and holsom doctryne of Cryste to the deuylysh heresyes of theyr owne / that it was clene a contrary thyng.[18]

As Derrida has argued, 'the first translation, if it has the force of an event, becomes an original'.[19] We might say that Thomas More sees the Tyndale New Testament as an original in a double sense, as not only a new text distinct from holy scripture and thenceforth seeking its own survival, but as an origin or well-spring of heresy and even a source of a new discursivity. More sees this novelty not as the work of an individual, as we have tended to do – after all, More believes that inasmuch as individual identity and significance derive from adherence to a community, no valid work is truly individual[20] – he sees it rather as the work of an interest group or faction, and, more to his point, the wrong faction: 'the confederacye betwene Luther and hym / is a thynge well knowen and playnly confessed / by suche as haue ben taken and conuycted here of heresye comynge frome thens / and some of them sent hyther to sowe that sede aboute here'.[21] He does not argue that the English New Testament is a false and inaccurate translation and therefore may cause schism; he believes the opposite, that, because the translation is a work of schism, it is 'false' and even 'peryllous' (p. 285).

For Thomas More, Tyndale's work cannot be considered apart from its context – Tyndale's location and the conditions of its production. If Tyndale is a heretic, no amount of philological ability will make the text acceptable; ideology and language form a single inter-text. So, as each person is in-dividual, indivisible, from a community, so each 'fault' in Tyndale's translation will be synechdochic, connected with many others: 'euery one … is more than thryes thre in one' (p. 285).[22] Because ideology, institution, and language are so intricately implicated in each other, More observes not that it is just difficult but that 'it is daungerous to translate yᵉ texte of scrypture out of one tonge into another' (p. 315).

AUTHORITY AS CREDIBILITY OR AS POWER

William Tyndale proves Thomas More's point. Scripture is dangerous to the authority of the institution, and an English Bible introduces plurality where there was unity. However, to understand the danger, we must revise our notion of the authority of scripture. Authority has developed two additional widely encompassing senses: speaking of authority we mean either (1) credibility, an epistemological matter, or (2) the power to influence or compel belief or action, a political matter. Most libraries have shelves of books written in the last two hundred years on the authority of scripture, but they address a question of authority different from that posed by the sixteenth century. When modernity asks about the authority of the Bible, it means credibility-authority; it asks, 'Can you believe it?' But when the sixteenth century asked about the authority of the Bible, it meant power-authority; it asked, 'What does it lead people to do?' It asked not what epistemological status the Bible has, but what power it has, and who has the right to wield it.

Of the criteria I have mentioned for judging a translation, this one, authority, looms largest in early modern disputes over Bibles, yet is least remarked in modern discussions of them. Both the sixteenth-century and the modern discussions include several criteria – authority, ideology, accuracy, clarity – but the proportions of emphasis have changed dramatically. Modernist assumptions about translation lay greatest emphasis on accuracy, almost as much on clarity and readability, less but still some emphasis on ideological neutrality, and not much on authority; modern translation theory has focused upon the ideal of equivalency as a means to the end of credibility. The early modern disputes dwell on authority, almost as much on ideology, occasionally mention accuracy, and sometimes but rarely discuss clarity; the early translators and their detractors were concerned with power as a means to the end of social and individual transformation.

Official discourse on translation in the early sixteenth century focused on the ways in which English scripture might affect the balance of power or, perhaps, how it might upset the desired imbalance of power among monarchy, church, and people. Henry VIII gathered the leading divines of Oxford and Cambridge to evaluate the first English Bibles and other texts and, following their deliberations, issued a royal proclamation on 22 June 1530, which prohibited the possession of 'the New Testament or the Old translated into English, or any other book of Holy Scripture so translated' as well as 'any other book being in the English tongue and printed beyond the sea, of what matter soever it be'.[23] The reason for this prohibition was a fear of sedition. The proclamation warns not only of heretical subversion of the Church, but also of lawless subversion of the State: 'pestiferous English books, printed in other regions' have been spread in the realm

to the intent as well to pervert and withdraw the people from the Catholic and true faith of Christ, as also to stir and incense them to sedition and disobedience against their princes, sovereigns, and heads, as also to cause them to condemn and neglect all good laws, customs, and virtuous manners, to the final subversion and desolation of this noble realm, if they might have prevailed.

An earlier proclamation, of 6 March 1529, likewise prohibits unlicensed books because 'perversion of Holy Scripture ... soweth sedition among Christian people'.[24]

The concern over sedition continued in a proclamation of April 1539 which warns about using Scripture 'to subvert and overturn as well the sacraments of Holy Church as the power and authority of princes and magistrates, and in effect generally all laws and common justice' and therefore restricts the exposition and public reading of the English Bible to university graduates and licensed preachers.[25] By the late 1530s, however, the political force of English scripture was seen as a power to be channelled rather than dammed; if scripture could realign loyalties, then it could also reaffirm loyalty to the king. A proclamation of 1541 reiterates an earlier injunction ordering that every church should provide a copy of the Great Bible for parishioners and explains the official motive: 'to the only intent that every of the King's majesty's loving subjects, minding to read therein' might 'learn thereby to observe God's commandments, and to obey their sovereign lord and high powers'.[26]

A full range of the senses of the term 'authority', from the verity of texts to the legitimate or usurped exercise of power, appears in William Fulke's survey of a century of Bible translation, *A defense of the sincere and true translations of the holie scriptures into the English tong* (1583), which was written in response to Gregory Martin. Fulke generally answers Martin's charges of heretical intent by either turning the tables, charging 'papists' with equal though opposite biases, or by offering philological reasons for the fidelity of the English translation to the ancient languages. He answers Martin argument by argument and proceeds through the details word by word, instance by instance; but if anything underlies the arguments and unites the details, it is denial of the Church's authority by appeal to scripture's authority (or, less often, by appeal to political authority). At times 'authority' means the credibility and antiquity of the books of scripture; Fulke says the Protestant translators 'with due reverence do acknowledge them all and every one to be of equal credit and authority, as being all inspired of God'.[27] 'Authority' also means the power to command or determine, especially when such power is usurped or illegitimate, and a single sentence can put this and the previous senses into competition: 'But the papists, arrogating to their pope authority to allow or refuse any book of holy scripture, and affirming that no scripture hath authority but as it is approved by their church, do bring all books of the holy scripture into doubting and uncertainty with such as will depend upon their pope and popish church's authority' (p. 9).

This contest of authorities can also pit scriptural credibility against political obedience, as Fulke warns Queen Elizabeth: 'under colour of the authority of holy scriptures, they seek to infect the minds of the credulous readers with heretical and superstitious opinions, and to alienate their hearts from yielding due obedience to your majesty' (p. 5). Political authority, on the other hand, can establish the authority and even availability of scripture, particularly scripture in English, whose credibility is less sure and is therefore in need of support; Fulke thanks the Queen, 'under whose high and christian authority your people have so many years enjoyed the reading of the holy books of God in their native language'.[28] Yet scripture's authority, in return, can augment royal authority as the people read it, 'by which they may be stirred up more and more in all dutiful obedience, not only to be thankful unto your majesty, as it becometh them, but also to continue their most earnest and hearty prayers to Almighty God for this your most godly and happy regiment over them' (p. 6). Neither Fulke nor any of the other disputants over scripture is particularly careful to discriminate the various senses of authority: power (legitimate or usurped) to compel obedience; conferred power or right by association with or delegation from a greater source; control or influence over belief; testimony, statement, or text capable of settling a dispute. It is precisely this interplay of political, spiritual, epistemological, and rhetorical authorities that marks early modern arguments over vernacular scripture. The various kinds of power may reinforce each other symbiotically, or they may clash destructively.

SUBVERSION BY APPROPRIATION

The Reformation debate over scripture in English included a subtext: the question of power. Power was won or exercised – in part – through textual and rhetorical strategies manipulating the authority attributed to scripture: claiming scriptural authority, denying the Church's or the reformers' claim to it, symbolically offering it to rulers or ministers. 'Discourses are objects of appropriation', Foucault observes,[29] and the Bible was a discourse many sought to appropriate. Such discursive forms of power

> can be bent to any purpose. The successes of history belong to those who are capable of seizing these rules, to replace those who had used them, ... and redirect them against those who had initially imposed them; controlling this complex mechanism, they will make it function so as to overcome the rulers through their own rules.[30]

The early translators were not unconcerned with an accurate rendering from Greek, Hebrew, or Latin; philological concerns are among the first they mention. However, their concerns with accuracy seem always to tell us more about their humility than about their motives. They briefly and modestly invite correction, then at length, and passionately, they emphasize concerns with authority. Tyndale, in the prologue to the Cologne fragment, his first attempted printing of the English New Testament, begins by 'exhortynge instantly and besechynge those that are better sene in the tongs then y / and that have hyer gyfts of grace to interpret the sence of the scripture' to peruse and amend his translation.[31] But next, in hinting at 'the causes that moved me to translate', he emphasizes what an English New Testament will do, implying that it will challenge and confront a corrupted institution as 'lyght destroyeth dercknes / and veritie reproveth all manner lyinge' (p. 1). Similarly, in his 1534 New Testament, he first reassures his readers of his diligent revision to bring the text nearer to equivalence with the Greek, mentioning that he has added glosses for hard places, and inviting correction (though somewhat more defensively this time); then, once again, he explains that he translates in order to outmanoeuvre 'false prophets and malicious hypocrites' who have 'taken away the key of knowledge'.[32] The metaphor of keys as symbols of authority was a common one in Tyndale's earlier writings, notably in *The Obedience of a Christian Man* (1528). Here, and in his preface to the New Testament, scripture itself is, metaphorically, the site of authority – 'the kingdom of heaven, which is the scripture and word of God, may be so locked up, that he which readeth or heareth it, cannot understand it' – and Tyndale's own work of translation is 'distributing ... the true key to open it withal'.[33]

William Tyndale mentions equivalence, how well Greek or Hebrew may pass into English, but he does so only briefly in the preface of an entire book on whether or not the Bible undercuts established authority. The objections to his English New Testament culminated in the charge 'that it would make the people to rebel and rise against the king'.[34] In response, Tyndale wrote *The Obedience of a Christian Man* to set his readers straight on the political role of vernacular scripture. The Prologue opens,

For as moch as oure holy prelates and oure gostly religious, which ought to defende Gods worde, speake evyll of it, ... yt it causeth insurrection and teacheth the people to disobeye their heedes and governers, and moveth them to ryse agenst their princes, and to make all comen, and to make havoke of other men's goodes. Therfore have I made this litle treatyse that folweth contayninge all obedience that is of God.[35]

Immediately the book enters a power dispute centring on vernacular scripture, and an opposition develops between the powerful 'powerlessness' of scripture and the powerless power of Rome. Tyndale's preface 'unto the Reader' starts the book with encouragement for those who read the translated Bible despite laws making it treason; the reader may find comfort knowing that persecution proves he or she is reading 'the true worde of God, Which worde is ever hated of ye worlde' as opposed to

the Popes doctrine ... which (as thou seist) is so agreable unto ye worlde, and is so receaved of the world or which rather so receaveth the worlde and the pleasures of the worlde, and seketh no thinge but the possessions of the worlde, and auctorite in the worlde, and to beare a rule in ye worlde, and persecuteth ye worde of God, and with all wilynes driveth the people from it, ... and moveth the blynde powers of ye world to sley with fyre, water, and swerde all that cleve unto it. (fol. iiʳ)

The 'hypocrites' always have the world's powers on their side, but 'the nature of Gods worde is to fyght agenst ypocrites' (fol. iiiʳ). Tyndale's strategy throughout the treatise is to reverse the relations of power by wielding God's word: to strip the Church of assumed authority and to keep true power where he thinks it belongs – with scripture and king.

The Obedience is a rhetorical gesture toward the king and magistrates of England, encouraging them to cut off papal power in the realm and to trust what their subjects will learn from holy writ in the mother tongue. Constant reference to the Bible defines relationships of subjects and rulers in all degrees of dominion: familial, master/slave, landlord/tenant, judicial, magisterial, ecclesiastical. But the proportions of treatment clearly show two cruxes: the powers of the king and of the pope, affirmed or denied by scripture. Scripture shows 'that the kinge is in this worlde without law and maye at his lust doo right or wronge and shall geve acomptes but to God only' (fol. xxxii^v), and that the true Christian is obedient and unresisting.[36]

From scripture Tyndale constructs an ordered realm, but his other great task with the rod and staff of God's Word is destructive: to dispossess Rome of scripture, which it claims to hold as its own, and thereby to pull down papal authority. For 'auctorite' which is not 'of men,' one would go to 'the scripture whose knowlege (as it were a keye) letteth in to God,' but one cannot, for they have bound it 'with gloses and tradicions' (fols liiii^v-lv^r, liiii^r). Accusations fly during a long digression rebutting Bishop Fisher's claims for the pope's authority, then Tyndale gets to his point: 'But let us returne at the last unto oure purpose agayne. What is the cause that laye men can not now rule … ?' It is that the pope has taught Christians 'to dreade not God and his worde, but hymselfe and his worde' (fol. lxvii^v). Secular magistrates are hindered in their rule because scripture is withheld.

Tyndale thus places himself and other reformers in the position of restoring lost authority to kings by preaching from holy writ (fol. lxxxiiii^v). The final challenge, then, is to establish who has rights to scripture, and thus authority: 'We, will they saye, are the Pope, Cardinals and Bisshopes all auctorite is ours. The scripture perteyneth unto us and is our possession. … Whence therfore hast thou thine auctorite will they saye' (fols cxi^v-cxii^r). Here Tyndale turns the tables on the prelates to deny their claim to ownership and to assert his own: 'The old pharises had the scripture in captivite lykewise … [but ye speak] not Gods worde, nor anythinge save your awne lawes made clene contrary unto Gods worde. … For the scripture is Gods and thers that beleve and not the false prophetes' (fol. cxii^r). Tyndale seizes authority from the Church by claiming possession of scripture. Spiritually – and rhetorically – the control of the text has passed to the translators, who offer its authority to the king.

The appropriation of power from Rome, and its bestowal on the king in the form of vernacular scripture, becomes a convention in England after Tyndale. By repetition the gesture is stylized, as ritualized as other bestowals of authority such as ordination or coronation. And in fact the bestowing of a Bible became the climax of the rite for the ordering of Anglican ministers, and became a contested or climactic point in the coronation pageants of Mary and Elizabeth.[37]

Coverdale repeats the pattern set by Tyndale. In his prologue to the first complete English Bible, he confesses to lacking the sort of philological expertise that a translator like Dolet would soon insist on: 'Considering how excellent knowledge and learning an interpreter of scripture ought to have in the tongues, and pondering also mine own insufficiency therein, and how weak I am to perform the office of a translator, I was the more loath to meddle with this work.'[38] Modesty, however, does not blunt the edge of his assault on the Church. In dedicating his translation to Henry VIII, Coverdale urges that the immediate current purpose of English scripture is to subvert the authority of the Church. Moreover, he insists that the ecclesiastical hierarchy have suppressed scripture so that they will not be dethroned. The papacy is guilty of the suppressing, keeping secret, and burning of the word of faith, lest the light thereof should utter his darkness; lest his own decretals and decrees, his own laws and constitutions, his own statutes and inventions, should come to none effect; lest his intolerable exactions and usurpations should lose their strength; lest it should be known what a thief and murtherer he is in the cause of Christ, and how heinous a traitor to God and man, in defrauding all christian kings and princes of their due obedience; lest we, your grace's subjects, should have eyes in the word of God. (p. 5)

As a source and sign of authority, an English Bible does not only destroy, it enables. While it undermines the current ecclesiastical power, it also underwrites monarchical authority:

Forsomuch now as the word of god is the only truth that driveth away all lies, and discloseth all juggling and deceit, therefore is our Balaam of Rome so loath that the scripture should be known in the mother-tongue; lest, if kings and princes, specially above all over, were exercised therein, they should reclaim and challenge again their due authority, which he falsely hath usurped so many years, and so to tie him shorter; and lest the people, being taught by the word of God, should fall from the false feigned obedience of him and his disguised apostles unto the true obedience commanded by God's own mouth; as namely, to obey their prince. (p. 5)

Scripture is no mere depiction, description, or representation of reality; it is a force which alters reality by causing power to shift. Translation is therefore not just a restatement in new terms of an original meaning, a restatement which may be more or less equivalent to the original; it is, much more, the freeing or unleashing of a force. With eighteen verbs listing the social acts this force performs, Coverdale is explicit about the practical impact of vernacular scripture:

The only word of God, I say, is the cause of all felicity: it bringeth all goodness with it, it bringeth learning, it gendereth understanding, it causeth good works, it maketh children of obedience; briefly, it teacheth all estates their office and duty. Seeing then that the scripture of God teacheth us everything sufficiently, both what we ought to do, and what we ought to leave undone, whom we are bound to obey, and whom we should not obey; therefore, I say, it causeth all prosperity, and setteth everything in frame; and where it is taught and known, it lighteneth all darknesses, comforteth all sorry hearts, leaveth no poor man unhelped, suffereth nothing amiss unamended, letteth no prince be disobeyed, permitteth no heresy to be preached; but reformeth all things, amendeth that is amiss, and setteth everything in order. (p. 10)

Therefore, scripture can offer increased authority to Henry VIII, to whom Coverdale dedicates his translation:

the scripture, both in the old testament and in the new, declareth most abundantly, that the office, authority, and power given of God unto kings is in earth above all other powers: let them call themselves popes, cardinals, or whatsoever they will, the word of God declareth them (yea, and commandeth them under pain of damnation), to be obedient unto the temporal sword. (p. 6)

The rhetorical act of Coverdale's dedicatory preface, then, culminates in the symbolic bestowal of scripture and its authority upon Henry VIII:

considering your imperial majesty not only to be my natural sovereign liege lord, and chief head of the church of England, but also the true defender and maintainer of God's laws, I thought it my duty, and to belong unto my allegiance, when I had translated this Bible, not only to dedicate this translation unto your highness, but wholly to commit it unto the same; to the intent, that if anything therein be translated amiss, (for in many things we fail, even when we think to be sure,) it may stand in your grace's hands to correct it, to amend it, to improve it, yea, and clean to reject it, if your godly wisdom shall think it necessary. (p. 11)

Henry thus joins in the work of translation as he 'applieth all his study and endeavour' 'to set forth' God's Word in English and give it 'free course throughout all christendom, but specially in your realm' (p. 4). Reciprocally, the translations join in the work of monarchy as they legitimate Henry's kingship and supremacy. Monarchy advances scripture; scripture advances monarchy.

In the discourse of the reformers who provided the early translations, 'Bible' ('scripture', 'God's Word', etc.) must be understood in more than one dimension. Bible is not only a text providing doctrines for belief or topics for exegesis; 'Bible' is also a trope which functions to signify a disparity in power – it expresses the force of a desire for authority. It signifies 'the way things ought to be' combined with 'a speaker's right and obligation to challenge the way things are'. We miss much in the reformers' discussions of the Bible if we fixate on questions of content rather than on questions of function. The Bible does things for those who invoke it. For reformers who insist on truth, yet find that the state of the church or of society conflicts with their beliefs, the trope 'scripture' allows an alternative reality to which their beliefs can fully correspond; the trope 'scripture' allows coherence in the face of contradiction. And when reformers invoke scripture, they signal not only the coherence of their discourse, but the authority by which they enter the discussion. Scripture, then, is a trope of authority (in two senses, using 'of' with both the genitive and objective forms): 'scripture' is a trope with authority (that is, it is a trope having authority), and scripture tropes authority; it is a trope which figures authority in a new way. 'Scripture' changes who can enter discourse, and it changes the kind of attention they can demand. Therefore, it is incomplete to say this or that reformer translates, writes about, or interprets scripture. Scripture is not only the passive recipient of the translator's action; scripture is an agent within the discourse. Scripture enables, informs, determines, and marks who can write and what acts their writing can call for.[39]

Some may think that, by taking a post-modern angle on these texts, I have defended all the wrong things on both sides of the Reformation disputes: More's fear of Tyndale's translation, Tyndale's authoritarian politics, etc. Some of what they thought or did I too still find reprehensible: burning Bibles and their readers, virulently insulting each other, cringing before political authority – but even what is reprehensible should be comprehensible. What I have intended, though, is a work of charity towards those writers: to make us less prejudiced towards their stances, to argue that their reasons had reason, to make the way they think accessible again, as it has not been since we became modern. I prefer reading them with some help from post-modern critique; not only do they become more intelligible, but their complexity and paradoxes, their interest for us and the challenges they pose, become more apparent.

We can move beyond modern criteria for judging the impact of translations because the translators and their detractors worked within assumptions not bounded only by clarity and equivalence. Their criteria are more numerous, more pragmatic, and more effectual than ours have been. Because Tyndale and other Protestant reformers insisted on the Bible alone as authority, they may be and have been considered, anachronistically, as fundamentalist. But that is not how contemporaries like More, Henry VIII, and Martin knew them. They saw the translators not as paring down, but as multi-plying religious discourse. Into a world structured as a unity, the translation of the sacred text introduced plurality, a multiplicity of contesting texts, interpretations, practices, and authorities both sacred and secular. And when they objected to Tyndale's translation, Tyndale responded by deconstructing their desire for unity, noting that the sacred language of the Vulgate was always already translated. ('Saynt Jerom also translated the bible into his mother tonge: why maye not we also?')[40]

The discourse of the Bible translators is more complex than we have noticed. The reformers confront us with paradox: they are subversive and they are fundamentalist; in both their aims and in their effects, they delegitimate institutions and they support nascent absolutism; they are insurgents casting off colonial rule, and they are national-istic; they insist on a single authority, *sola scriptura*, and they introduce plurality into both the language and the interpretation of it. As both they and their detractors knew, their translations would not only be clear enough to be read by ploughboys, but would change ploughboys' allegiances and realign the balances of power in Europe.

NOTES

1 Susan Bassnett, 'The Meek or the Mighty: Reappraising the Role of the Translator', in *Translation, Power, Subversion*, ed. by Roman Alvarez & M. Carmen-Africa Vidal (Clevedon, UK: Multilingual Matters, 1996), p. 14. Valerie Worth, *Practising Translation in Renaissance France: the Example of Étienne Dolet* (Oxford: Clarendon Press, 1988), p. 51, calls it 'the first work in French which claims to offer a full theoretical analysis of the act of translation'.

2 Étienne Dolet, *La maniere de bien traduire d'une langue en aultre* (Lyon: 1540; facsimile repr. Geneva: Slatkine, 1972), pp. 11-16. For a selection, in English, see *Translation/History/Culture: A Sourcebook*, ed. by Andre Lefevere, (London: Routledge, 1992), pp. 27-8.

3 Thus the sentence was read by the Faculty of Theology of Paris, who judged Dolet. In Dolet's translation, the sentence read 'et quand du seras decedé, elle n'y pourra rien aussi, attendu que tu ne seras plus rien du tout'. R. C. Christie, *Étienne Dolet: the Martyr of the Renaissance*, rev. edn (Niewkoop: B. De Graaf, 1964), p. 461, cf. pp. 415-21, pp. 460-4; Worth, pp. 80-1; Bassnett, p. 14.

4 The following statements are typical and even influential: 'The traditional concepts in any discussion of translations are fidelity and license – the freedom of faithful reproduction and, in its service, fidelity to the word', Walter Benjamin, 'The Task of the Translator', in *Illuminations* (New York: Schocken, 1969), pp. 77-8); 'The question of equivalence is central to all translation theory. It is our word for describing the victory of translation', Willis Barnstone, *The Poetics of Translation: History, Theory, Practice* (New Haven & London: Yale University Press, 1993), p. 233; 'What is generally understood as translation involves the rendering of a source language (SL) text into the target language (TL) so as to ensure that (1) the surface meaning of the two will be preserved as closely as possible but not so closely that the TL structures will be seriously distorted', Susan Bassnett-McGuire, *Translation Studies* (London: Routledge, 1991), p. 2.

The primary concern with fidelity, and sometimes with style, carries over into discussions of early English Bible translation. Again, the following are typical: 'It would not perhaps be too gross a generalization to suggest that the aims of the sixteenth-century Bible translators may be collocated in three categories:

(1) To clarify errors arising from previous versions, due to inadequate SL manuscripts or to linguistic incompetence.

(2) To produce an accessible and aesthetically satisfying vernacular style.

(3) To clarify points of dogma and reduce the extent to which the scriptures were interpreted and re-presented to the laypeople as a metatext' (Bassnett-McGuire, p. 49); 'the most ambitious part of this book is its attempt to analyse the stylistic relationships between the original and its translation', Gerald Hammond, *The Making of the English Bible* (Manchester: Carcanet, 1982), p. 14; 'Most readers, including myself, make judgements about the quality of various English Bible translations. These judgements are often offered in terms of prose style. Yet quite often they have no direct reference to the source or to questions of the fidelity of a given translation. Nor, given the fact that they are liable to be expressed with some moral indignation, is it more than possible that they are merely aesthetic judgements. This discussion focuses on questions of prose style, particularly with reference to the King James Bible. But it also looks at the questions of what value is put upon prose style, and where such value is located', David Lawton, *Faith, Text and History: The Bible in English* (New York ; London : Harvester Wheatsheaf, 1990), p. 66. Of course, studies in linguistic and stylistic equivalence have often been sensitive and brilliant, for example, David Daniell, *William Tyndale: a Biography* (New Haven & London: Yale University Press, 1994); or George Steiner, *After Babel: Aspects of Language and Translation*, 2nd edn (Oxford: University Press, 1992), which focuses on understanding, meaning, and knowledge without attention to concerns of politics or ideology.

Recently, however, academic discussion of translation has widened its scope to include the intersection of 'translation, power, subversion', as the title of one promising recent collection has it (Alvarez & Vidal (n. 1 above)). In that collection, Theo Hermans notes the change: 'Translation used to be regarded primarily in terms of relations between texts, or between language systems. Today it is increasingly seen as a complex transaction taking place in a communicative, socio-cultural context' between 'active social agents', each with political, cultural, religious, or other ideological interests ('Norms and the Determination of Translation: A Theoretical Framework', in Alvarez & Vidal, p. 26). So also Bassnett-McGuire announces, 'Translation Studies is branching out in new ways, because the emphasis on the ideological as well as the linguistic makes it possible for the subject to be discussed in the wider terms of post-colonial discourse' (Bassnett-McGuire, p. xiv). See also *Translation, History and Culture*, ed. by Susan Bassnett & Andre Lefevere (London: Cassell, 1990), and *Rethinking Translation: Discourse, Subjectivity, Ideology*, ed. by Lawrence Venuti (London: Routledge, 1992).

5 Sir Philip Sidney, 'An Apologie for Poetrie', in *Elizabethan Critical Essays*, ed. by G. Gregory Smith (Oxford: Clarendon Press, 1904), I, 161.

6 Jean-François Lyotard, *The Postmodern Condition: A Report on Knowledge* (Minneapolis: University of Minnesota Press, 1984).

7 Hans Frei, *The Eclipse of Biblical Narrative: A Study in Eighteenth and Nineteenth Century Hermeneutics* (New Haven & London: Yale University Press, 1974).

8 Lawrence Venuti, *The Translator's Invisibility: A History of Translation* (London: Routledge, 1995).

9 Ibid., pp. 57, 65, 68.

10 Jacques Derrida, *Of Grammatology*, trans. by Gayatri Spivak (Baltimore: Johns Hopkins University Press, 1976), p. 149.

11 Gregory Martin, *A Discoverie of the Manifold Corruptions of the Holy Scriptures* (Rhemes: J. Fogny, 1582), STC 17503, *English Recusant Literature 1558-1640*, vol. 127 (Menston, Yorkshire: Scolar Press, 1973), sig. b vi^v.

12 Ibid., preface, par. 32, 35.

13 Ibid., par. 48, 42

14 Ibid., par. 39.

15 Ibid., ch. 1, p. 6.

16 Paul Ricoeur, *Freud and Philosophy: An Essay on Interpretation* (New Haven & London: Yale University Press, 1970), p. 32.

17 Thomas More, 'A Dialogue Concerning Heresies', in *The Complete Works of St Thomas More*, ed. by Thomas M. C. Lawler, Germain Marc'Hadour, & Richard C. Marius, vol. 6, part 1 (New Haven & London: Yale University Press, 1981), pp. 285-90.

18 Ibid., p. 285.

19 Jacques Derrida, 'Roundtable on Translation', in *The Ear of the Other: Otobiography, Transference, Translation*, trans. by Peggy Kamuf, ed. by Christie V. McDonald (New York: Schocken, 1985), p. 148. On the structure of an original, see pp. 121-2, 152.

20 Stephen Greenblatt, *Renaissance Self-Fashioning* (Chicago: University of Chicago Press, 1980), pp. 32-73, esp. pp. 60-1.

21 More, p. 288.

22 Cf. p. 293. More uses the same argument from motives and heretical connections to defend the judgements against Richard Hunne: More had heard testimony that Hunne was one of a network of heretics, the English Bible he read had to be faulty or naught, and so he and it were well burned (pp. 327-30).

23 *Tudor Royal Proclamations*, ed. by Paul L. Hughes & James F. Larkin, vol. 1 (New Haven & London: Yale University Press, 1964), pp. 193-7.

24 Ibid., p. 182.

25 Ibid., pp. 284-6.

26 Ibid., p. 297.

27 William Fulke, *A Defence of the Sincere and True Translations of the Holy Scriptures into the English Tongue, Against the Cavils of Gregory Martin* (London: H. Bynnemann, for G. Bishop, 1583), STC 11430, ed. by Charles Hartshorne, Parker Society 17 (Cambridge: University Press, 1843), pp. 8-9.

28 Ibid., p. 6. Ecclesiastical as well as secular position can be a source of this authority to legitimate and disseminate vernacular scripture; in reference to the Great Bible of 1539-40, Fulke says to Martin, 'That bible perhaps you mislike more than the other translations, because archbishop Cranmer allowed it by his authority' (p. 190).

29 Michel Foucault, 'What is an Author?', in *The Foucault Reader*, ed. by Paul Rabinow (New York: Pantheon, 1984), p. 108.

30 Foucault, 'Nietzsche, Genealogy, History', in *The Foucault Reader*, ed. by Rabinow, p. 86.

31 *The First Printed English New Testament, translated by William Tyndale*, facsimile, ed. by Edward Arber (London & Frome: Selwood Printing Works, 1871), p. 1.

32 'W. T. Unto the Reader', in *Tyndale's New Testament*, ed. by David Daniell (New Haven & London: Yale University Press, 1989), pp. 3-4.

33 Ibid.

34 John Foxe, *Acts and Monuments*, ed. by George Townsend (New York: AMS, 1965), V, 121.

35 STC 24446. William Tyndale, *The Obedience of a Christian Man and how Christen rulers ought to gouerne* (1528) ([Antwerp: H. Peeterson van Middelburch?] 1535), reproduced in *The English Experience* 897, facsimile repr. (Amsterdam: Theatrum Orbis Terrarum; Norwood, NJ: Walter J. Johnson, 1977), fol. xxi^r.

36 The only qualification of this obedience is stated, in passing, in a single phrase: 'in all thinge that is not to the dishonoure of God' (fols xliii^v, xlvi-xlviii). Only the Word can set limits to the obedience it enjoins.

37 *Two Liturgies with other Documents of King Edward VI*, ed. by Joseph Ketley, Parker Society 29 (Cambridge: University Press, 1844), p. 349; J. E. Neale, *Queen Elizabeth I* (Garden City,

NY: Doubleday, 1957), pp. 61-3; Norman L. Jones, *Faith by Statute: Parliament and the Settlement of Religion, 1559* (London: Royal Historical Society, 1982), p. 45; Sydney Anglo, *Spectacle Pageantry and Early Tudor Policy* (Oxford: Clarendon Press, 1969), pp. 329-30, 337-8, 349-51.

38 Miles Coverdale, 'Dedication and Prologue to the Translation of the Bible', *Remains of Myles Coverdale*, ed. by George Pearson, Parker Society 14 (Cambridge: University Press, 1846), p. 12.

39 On such rules controlling discourse, see Michel Foucault, *The Archaeology of Knowledge*, trans. by A. M. Sheridan Smith (New York: Harper & Row, 1972), especially ch. 4 and 6.

40 Tyndale, *Obedience*, fol. xv^v.

THE BIBLE TRANSLATIONS
OF GEORGE JOYE

Orlaith O'Sullivan

In a consideration of the translators who were instrumental in the development of the English Bible, the name of George Joye may not feature prominently. His relative anonymity in modern times belies the status he held among his contemporaries. Joye was considered to be one of the leaders of the Brethren abroad, and posed a threat serious enough to be attacked personally by Thomas More in the 1530s and by Stephen Gardiner, the Bishop of Winchester, in the 1540s. Furthermore, of the early Reformers, only William Tyndale translated more of the Bible into English. Between 1528 and 1535 George Joye was in exile in Antwerp, and from there he undertook the production of lay religious handbooks for those of the 'new learning'. He prepared for the English market two primers, two Psalters, Isaiah, Jeremiah, Lamentations, Proverbs, and Ecclesiastes. All were printed for the first time in the English language, and all were infused with an 'heretical' reforming spirit.

These first printed translations had an indelible effect on the Bible in English, an effect which has been largely overlooked or underestimated. It is only through consideration of the significance of Joye's works both to his contemporaries and to the theologians of the later Renaissance that we can begin to realize his importance. There is a tendency to absorb Joye's achievements under the aegis of Miles Coverdale, whose 1535 Bible relies heavily on Joye's earlier translations. The neglect of his translations has severely limited our understanding, not only of how the English Bible came into being, but also of how the process of translation was approached by the early Reformers. In tracing George Joye's influence and examining his semantic ideology, I hope to contribute to our understanding of the importance of these texts and of the fervent beliefs that sustained the English Brethren in their exile.

I

Joye's debut publication was an English primer, which probably appeared in 1529. It contained the first Psalms to be printed in the English language, and Joye followed this work with his translation of the entire Psalter. On 16 January 1530 the first printed book of Psalms in English (RSTC 2370) was issued from the press of Martin de Keyser in Antwerp. The title reads: *The Psalter of Dauid in Englishe purely and faithfully translated aftir the texte of Feline*. The 'texte of Feline' refers to a Psalter published in September 1529 by one 'Aretius Felinus', better known as Martin Bucer. The mention of the source text is significant in that it provides an indication of the speed at which Joye worked: he spent at most a little over three months translating the entire book.

25

Joye then moved on to other projects, returning to the Psalter four years later. In August 1534 the second English Book of Psalms was printed, again by Martin de Keyser: *Dauids Psalter/ diligently and faithfully translated by George Joye* (RSTC 2777). This time Joye based his work on the Latin Psalter of the Swiss Reformer Huldrych Zwingli, which had been published (posthumously) in 1532.

Immediately striking about these books are their dimensions: for example the 1530 Psalter measures under four inches in height. The physical appearance indicates the authorial intention: these were texts meant to be read privately and smuggled easily. The second noticeable feature is that the text is presented with verse divisions. The clarity this offers to the work would have been particularly beneficial to those coming to the Bible for the first time. In setting forth the text as such, George Joye was considerably ahead of his time; as David Norton points out, the first complete Bible to have such divisions was the Geneva New Testament of 1557.[1] The third characteristic of the Psalters is one of the most impressive: they are utterly without decoration. There are no woodcuts or illustrations of any kind in these texts; neither were there any in the primers produced by Joye. The plainness of these handbooks stands in stark contrast to the traditional books of hours and psalters, which were filled with artistic embellishments. This works against the traditional role of the lay handbooks, which included 'functioning in part as sacred objects'.[2] It may have been a simple lack of funds which prevented Joye from decorating his texts, but, irrespective of the motives behind their appearance, the stripping away of both the visual and the textual dross highlights the reforming spirit of *sola scriptura* instilled in the books: only the Word was to be prioritized.

This visual rusticity is paralleled in the style of the translation. In comparison to the smooth-flowing poetic language of the King James Version of 1611, Joye's Psalms have a rough quality to them. His vocabulary is colloquial, belonging to the dialect of a Bedfordshire man. Thus his Bible translations include words such as 'backsliders', 'slougherde', 'potsherd', 'retcheth', 'wambleth', and 'loaveth'. Some of these were taken over by Coverdale and subsequent editors, and survived through to the King James Version. The language is idiomatic and unelevated, dotted with native alliteration. For example, in his 1530 translation, Joye's Psalm 23 begins: 'The Lorde is my pastore and feder/ wherfore I shall nat want.'[3] The 1534 Zwinglian Psalter continues: 'He settith me in a goodly lusty pasture: and retcheth me forthe unto swete still runninge waters. ... Ye/ if I shuld go thorow the myddes of deth/ yet wyll I feare non yuel/ for thou arte with me/ thy staffe & thy shepe hoke counfort me.'

That Joye chooses to translate into parochial English, despite almost two decades spent in the University of Cambridge, comes as no great surprise. First, no standard English existed at this time, and the effort to raise the status of the language was only beginning to gain momentum. Second, the type of translation resembles the colloquial style found in the sermons of Joye's contemporaries, exemplified by the humanist chancellor of the university, John Fisher. Fisher's direct, uncomplicated translations of the Bible may have made an impression on men such as George Joye, John Frith, and William Tyndale at a crucial stage of their development: 'Aske and ye shall haue/ seke and ye shall fynde/ knocke and the gate shall be opened to you. ... This is my welbeloued sone in whome I haue moche plesure.'[4] In this respect, George Joye is John Fisher's heir: for example, compare Fisher's 'The herte of a synfull persone is lyke vnto the troublouse see whiche neuer hathe reste', to George Joye's 'The ungodly men are lyke a fearse swellinge see, whiche cannot reste'.[5]

Third, in asserting English dialect, Joye deliberately differentiated his writing from that of Sir Thomas More. Although More's prose descended into scatological vitriol at times, his language and style were essentially clerical and Latinate. This was seen by the Reformers, and still strikes some eminent scholars today, as 'rather artificially holy'.[6] The Reformers reacted to More's aureate language by employing the everyday English of the common people. Although implicit in the use of this straightforward style is the honesty of the Reformers' intentions, it remains nevertheless a style; it is a conscious fashioning of language, with an underlying ideology. The gap in language existing between reformer and conservative points to a theological gulf.

From the perspective of the Reformers, the Latin language served only to reinforce the hierarchy falsely established and maintained by the Roman Church. Christ and his apostles had preached and taught in the vernacular, but their words were now restricted to the Latin language, thus excluding the vast majority of the population from a personal comprehension of God's Word. The Reformers interpreted this as a 'Romish' plot to maintain the Roman Church's illegal authority through precluding the common people from understanding the true Church of Christ. William Tyndale writes of the clergy: 'to kepe us from knowleage of the trouth/ they doo all thinge in latyne/ They praye in latyne/ they Christen in latyne/ they blesse in latyne. they geue absolution in latyne only curse they in the englyshe tonge.'[7] Hugh Latimer remarks: 'They roll out the Latin language by heart, but in so doing they make the poor people of Christ altogether ignorant.'[8] Miles Coverdale voices a similar complaint, claiming that the Word was kept in Latin

lest, if kings and princes, specially above all other, were exercised therein, they should reclaim and challenge again their due authority, which he [Baalam of Rome] falsely hath usurped as many years … and lest the people, being taught by the word of God, should fall from the false feigned obedience of him and his disguised apostles unto the true obedience commanded by God's own mouth.[9]

At times the use of Latin kept knowledge of the Scriptures even from the clergy themselves. In his preface to the book of Isaiah, Joye comments that the prophet 'haue ben locked up longe in latyne so that the lay man (I dare say) understode hym not/ nor yet parauenture many that repute them selfe learned' (fol. A2ᵛ).

Because the Word was intended for an all-inclusive audience, it had to be in a language that was uncomplicated and straightforward. One of the most common accusations of the early Reformation concerns the 'wresting' of language. Both conservative and reformed factions were associated with reading the Bible out of context, contorting its meanings, and using rhetoric to embellish their sophistical, flawed arguments. The Reformers were accused of seeking only 'to abolishe with their fine tongues, their rhetoricall argumentes, their exclamacions and outcries'.[10] Bishop John Fisher comments:

The fair speech, the eloquence, the knowledge of languages/ these be but the veray hull of the scriptures. This hull these heretics have: But the veray pithe and substance of the seed is piked out of their hearts by these evil spirits/ that keep them in this carnality.[11]

Similar charges were launched at the conservatives. In one of his works against the

Bishop of Winchester, Stephen Gardiner, Joye associates this linguistic deceit with the first fall: 'The symple playne truthe knoweth no deceytful coloured sophems ne any perplexed persuasions wherby as the serpent deceiued Eue, so wold you deceiue the simple.'[12] The Church did not merely restrict knowledge through the use of Latin; even when the clergy did speak in the vernacular, they did so in a sophistical manner, in ornate rhetorical displays, confusing people with 'their thornye spinose disputacions fonde questions and withe their skoldinge cauillacions and sophisticall besye brawlinges'.[13] The Reformer Nicholas Ridley asked, 'what can crafty inventions, subtilty in sophisms, eloquence or fineness of wit, prevail against the unfallible word of God?'.[14] A simple English style, resembling 'the olde breife and playne speche of the scriptures', could appeal to an unlimited audience, and as it imitated the Word of God, so it was by its very nature more truthful than Latin.[15]

The early translators sought to empower readers to develop their own relationship with the Bible, to understand for themselves the Word of God. Similar to William Tyndale's intention to open up the Bible to each ploughman in England, George Joye believed that every person, be they 'neuer so simple & rude maye se & understand it clerly'.[16] However, unlike William Tyndale, who had always employed glosses, Joye initially shunned marginalia and any kind of editorial intrusions on the text. In his *An Apologye made by George Joye to satisfye ... w. Tindale* (1535, RSTC 14820), he declared: 'I wolde the scripture were so puerly and plyantly translated that it neded nether note/ glose nor scholia/ so that the reder might once swimme without a corke (fol. C7ʳ).' The preface to Isaiah exhorts its readers to 'Gather grete frute without any grete glose' (fol. A2ᵛ). Joye further explains this process in his preface to Jeremiah, where he argues that to the pure of heart the Scriptures will become clear. He who reads by directing 'his inwarde eye to beholde & knowe our heuenly father ... beleuinge perfitly to be iustifyed and saued by the grace of God the father through the merits only of Cristis dethe ... he readeth a right with grete fruite' (fol. A2ʳ).

With the language, style, and method of reading decided upon, there remained the process of translating. The mechanics of constructing meaning had been examined by the biblical humanists in the early decades of the century. Their underlying presumption was that the biblical language was (to use John Fisher's terminology) but 'the veray hull of the scriptures'; the 'pithe and substance of the seed' was something else entirely.[17] Theoretically, the pith could be contained in any hull. Language, as the mere 'accidents' of God's Word, bore no relevance to the actual meaning of the Bible. Whether read in Hebrew or Dutch or English, the true meaning of the Scriptures never varied. The language was irrespective to the essence of the Word, which could only be understood through the grace of the Holy Spirit. Miles Coverdale voices this belief in his dedication to the 1538 New Testament: 'The scripture and word of God is truly to every christian man of like worthiness and authority, in what language soever the Holy Ghost speaketh it.'[18] It was the domain of the Holy Spirit, who would communicate the meaning to those coming to the text 'with a pure heart'. This unproblematic approach was supported wholeheartedly by the Reformers, and it was not long before the deficiencies of a mimetic theory of language became manifest. Perhaps the worthiness and the authority of the Word remained unscathed after translation, but had the meaning also been left intact?

Due to the nature of language, translation is doomed to be an inexact and somewhat subjective process. The question eternally dogging translators is whether to translate word for word or sense for sense. The problems inherent in the former, in a stencil translation, were exemplified in the first Wycliffite Bible. The Lollard Bible was dependent on Latinate sentence construction, which was (and is still) seen to impede the 'natural' flow of the English language. One editor, John Lewis, described its translation as being 'rather too Verbal and not always good English'.[19] Through viewing language as a socio-historical product, the biblical humanists came to consider stencil translations as somewhat superficial, and instead prioritized sense-for-sense translations, which were 'explanatory rather than imitative'.[20] Joye's translations follow this development; often he gives two or three words to render one word in the source. For example, in Psalm 23 the lord is not 'my shepherd' but 'my pastore and feder'.[21] The extra words provided a fuller, more accurate rendering of the source, and, in his opinion, helped to make glosses redundant. This furthered Joye's aim to produce a self-contained, self-explanatory, independent text.

Despite the haste with which it was carried out, the effect of Joye's pioneering work on the Psalms (completed within a three-month period) is discernible to this day. Their popularity is attested by the reprints and by the incorporation of both translations and commentaries into later editions.[22] Miles Coverdale used both of Joye's Psalters as templates when preparing his Bible in 1535. The phrase 'three score years and ten' (Psalm 90) derives ultimately from Joye's 1534 Psalter, which reads 'The dayes of owre yeares are thre score and tenne'. Coverdale rearranged the wording slightly to produce: 'The dayes of oure age are iii. score yeares & ten.'[23] Compare the following selections:

My God/ my god: wherfore hast thou forsaken me? the wordes of my oute cryinge are ful farre from helthe. (Psalm 22.1, 1530 Psalter)
My God, my God: why hast thou forsaken me? the wordes of my complaynte are farre fro my health. (1535 Coverdale)

The Lorde is my light & my helthe: whome then shal I feare? (Psalm 27.1, 1534 Psalter)
The LORDE is my light and my health: whom then shuld I feare? (1535 Coverdale)

At times both of Joye's Psalters influenced Coverdale's work: for his translation of Psalm 126.5, Coverdale adopted the format of the 1530 Bucerian Psalter, and the vocabulary of the 1534 Zwinglian:

Thei that sue with teares: shall reape with gladnes. (1530 Psalter)
They that had sowen with teres haue reped with ioye. (1534 Psalter)
They that sowe in teeres, shal reape in ioye. (1535 Coverdale)

Joye's Psalms resound through those of the Bibles of the English Renaissance, and a substantial proportion of them survived into the King James Version. Take for instance, the end of *De Profundis*, Psalm 130.7-8:

Let Israel waite for the lorde: for with the lorde is there mercy & plentuous redempcion. And it is he that shall redeme Israhel; from all his wykedneses. (1530 Psalter)
let Israel trust in the Lorde, for with the Lorde there is mercy and plenteous redempcion. And he shal redeme Israel from al his synnes. (1535 Coverdale)
Let Israel hope in the LORD: for with the LORD there is mercy, and with him is plenteous redemption.
And he shall redeem Israel from all his iniquities. (KJV)

The crucial words – mercy, plenteous redemption, redeem – all derive directly from Joye. Quite simply, his Psalters permeated. When Nicholas Ridley, waiting for death, wrote *A Farewell to all his Friends* in 1559, he quoted Psalm 79.1: 'O Lord God, the gentiles, heathen nations, are come into thy heritage, they have defiled thy holy temple, and made Jerusalem an heap of stones.'[24] Although smoothed out, Joye's words of 1530 are recognizable: 'The haithen (oh god) are come into thyn heretage: thei have polluted thi holy temple/ and have broughte Hierusalem into an heape of stones.' Joye was also one of the sources used by Thomas Wyatt in preparing a metrical version of the Penitential Psalms, and by Anne Lock in her sonnet sequence.[25] His texts therefore not only influenced the first editions of the English Bible, but also contributed to the form that the Bible took as a source text.

II

On 10 May 1531 Joye's next translation *The Prophete Isaye* (RSTC 2777) went to press. His translation is immediate and direct: 'Heare heaven/ and listen erthe: for it is the Lorde that speaketh (fol. B1ʳ).' As with the Psalms, the vocabulary and format of Joye's work is recognizable in the *King James Version*:

Thi syluer is turned into drosse/ Thy wyne is marred withe water. (1.22, *Isaye*)
Thy silver is become dross, thy wine mixed with water. (KJV)

Howle ye therfore/ for ful nyghe is the daye of the lorde. (13.6, *Isaye*)
Howl ye; for the day of the lord is at hand. (KJV)

There are more significant and more famous renderings, in which Joye's word-order has been modified slightly but has basically survived intact:

The lorde therfor his owne selfe shall geue yow a token. Beholde/ a mayde shalbe with chylde and bringe forth a sonne and she shall call his name Immanuel. (7.14, *Isaye*)
Therefore the Lord himself shall give you a sign; Behold, a virgin shall conceive, and bear a son, and shall call his name Immanuel. (KJV)

Lyft up thy voyce lyke a trompet/ and tel my people their synnes/ tel the house of Jacob theyr offences. (58.1, *Isaye*)
Lift up thy voice like a trumpet, and shew my people their transgression, and the house of Jacob their sins. (KJV)

The wyne press (I tel yow) haue I troden al alone/ and of al the people was there not one with me. (63.3, *Isaye*)
I have trodden the winepress alone; and of the people there was none with me. (KJV)

The fact that so much of his work was passed on is something of an added bonus, because it was completely ancillary to Joye's aim. He sought simply to get the Word of God out to the people of England, unmediated and unimpeded. As a result of his belief in 'open' Scripture, problems of comprehension are attributed to the reader. In the preface to his translation of Jeremiah, *Jeremy the Prophete* (1534, RSTC 2778), Joye argues:

in the Prophetis sermons there is no siche hardnes & difficultye as some men complayneth of/

except the sloughisshe & sleapy reder nothinge excercysing himselfe in readinge diligently & reuerently the holy scriptures bringe it with him/ and so himselfe be the very cause why he bringeth awaye so lytel frute in reding them. (fol. A6ᵛ)

Yet although the onus is laid firmly on the reader, as transmitter of the text Joye does attempt to increase the harvest of 'grete fruit'. In *Isaye*, he includes 'A note for the clearer understandinge of the Prophete'. This organizes the book into sections, according to the monarch reigning at the time, and includes a comment on the worthiness of each monarch. During an account of the Passion in his second primer, *Ortulus Anime* (1530, RSTC 13828.4), the narrative is abruptly halted to accommodate a detailed explanation of the Hebrew system of hours. In providing a background for the Scriptures in this way, Joye is putting into effect the humanist view of language as a socio-historical product; he is contextualizing the immutable Word.

The most important way that Joye provides a context for the Scriptures is by demonstrating their contemporary relevance. The vernacular *Isaye*, we are told, is heaven-sent: 'God of his infinite goodnes hathe restored us his prophete Isaye speakinge playne englysshe' (fol. A2ᵛ). Isaiah's world is strikingly paralleled with that of Joye. The desperate state of the English people is seen to derive from their genealogy: as the spiritual heirs of Abraham, they have fallen into sinfulness, and are cut off from their prophet-saviour, forsaken for their unbelief. Joye informs his readers that Isaye 'was in lyke troublouse tyme & sinful worlde as we ar now: when destruccion & captiuite was at hande, & men wer fled bakwarde from the true worshype of god to the worshipping of stockes & stones' (fol. A2ʳ). Similarly in the preface to *Jeremy*, Joye asserts that the people of Judah and Jerusalem were guilty of the same sins, and suffered the same plagues and afflictions as the people of England do now. His translation is to function 'as a brason wall & piller of yerne to preche in englissh agenst this heuy monster of Rome & al his drasse' (fol. A5ʳ). By 1534 the time of 'destruccion & captiuite' had begun to pass away: Joye explains that whoever reads Jeremiah 48-51 'shal se there clerely the present face of the soden miserable fall of the Pope & his kingedome now at hande' (fol. A5ʳ).

Joye identified personally with both Jeremiah and Isaiah, both of whom were faithful believers whose fortune '(as be the chaunces of all trwe prechers before the worlde) was moste miserable and hard'.[26] Analogies between the tribulations of the Reformers and those of the Old Testament prophets were commonly drawn, but the figure of Jeremiah seems to hold particular significance for George Joye. Certain affinities spring immediately to mind: Jeremiah's work is infused with personal feeling and biographical detail, and like Joye he lived in a period that was chronically unstable both politically and spiritually. In addition, Jeremiah's evangelism dates from the instigation of Josiah's reforms, which were intended to purge the kingdom of idolatry. This reformation was seen by Jeremiah as the beginning of a return to the Lord. According to a letter of William Tyndale, in February 1533 George Joye 'printed two leaves of Genesis in a great form, and sent one copy to the king, and another to the new queen', accompanied by a request for permission to 'so go through all the Bible'.[27] Offering his two leaves of Genesis to Henry VIII and Anne Boleyn, Joye must have hoped for a similar return to the 'true' religion.

As with his *Isaye*, Joye's *Jeremy* commands a strong presence in the later translations, in terms of both structure and vocabulary:

Babylon shalbe taken. Beel shalbe confounded with shame. Merodach shalbe taken/ hir grauen images shalbe shamefully confounded/ and their Idolis shalbe taken. (50.2, *Jeremy*)
Babylon is taken, Bel is confounded, Merodach is broken into pieces; her idols are confounded, her images are broken into pieces. (KJV)

Before I fasshioned the in thy mothers wombe/ I knew the: and before thow wer borne/ I sanctified the: and ordined the to be a Prophete for the peple. (1.5, *Jeremy*)
Before I formed thee in the belly I knew thee; and before thou camest forth out of the womb I sanctified thee, and I ordained thee a prophet unto the nations. (KJV)

Certain of Joye's more colloquial renderings were however not transmitted; the theologians working under King James settled on more dignified translations:

And Moab in his vommyte shalbe clapped out with handis/ And shal be a laughing stocke to. (48.26, *Jeremy*)
Moab also shall wallow in his vomit, and he also shall be in derision. (KJV)

Beholde Lorde/ for I am sore scourged/ my bely rombleth/ my herte wambleth in me. (1.20, *Lamentacions of Jeremye*)
Behold, O LORD; for I am in distress: my bowels are troubled; mine heart is turned within me. (KJV)

That George Joye was actually allowed to return home in 1535 reflects the strong trend towards reform then current in England. His Bible translations had proven extremely influential, as publishers cashed in on the increasing demand for vernacular scripture. With the surge in popularity of English primers and collections of prayers, Joye's works were heavily relied on by London printers. Between the reprinting and the new editions of works such as the *Ortulus Anime* and the Psalters, and the obvious culling of passages from *Isaye* and *Jeremy*, Joye's works resonate throughout the vernacular religious publications of the period.

Around this time the printer Thomas Godfray published the books of Proverbs and Ecclesiastes, of which printing only one copy survives.[28] Although anonymous, Joye's hand is visible: his distinctive vocabulary is present containing words like 'bakslyders' (fol. A6[v]), and 'ydle slougherde' (fol. B2[r]). Joye's colloquial turn of phrase is well suited to the idiomatic wisdom: 'Better is a lytell with the fere of God than moch tresure with trouble (15.16).' The choice of these texts, less explicitly religious than Joye's earlier translations, is perhaps explained by the proverbial and speculative wisdom contained within them. The homely, colloquial teachings, extremely practical in any age, must have appealed to Joye, who perhaps felt similarly to Miles Coverdale: 'The Proverbs and the Preacher of Salomon teach us wisdom, to know God, our own selves, and the world, and how vain all things are, save only to cleave unto God.'[29]

In these books the advantages and disadvantages of Joye's prose style are amply demonstrated: while his pithy phrasing is often taken over by later translators and editors, much of Joye's parochial terminology and idiosyncratic vocabulary is not reproduced. The affinities between the Proverbs of the *King James Version* and the first printed translations are manifest:

Plesant spech is an honey combe/ the soules sewtnes and medicine to the bones. (16.24, *Prouerbes*)
Pleasant words are as an honeycomb, sweet to the soul, and health to the bones. (KJV)

The feare of god is the beginnyng of wysdome. (1.7, *Prouerbes*)
The fear of the LORD is the beginning of knowledge. (KJV)

The glorye of youth is theyr strength/ & the beauteful dignite of age is a graye heed. (20.29, *Prouerbes*)
The glory of young men is their strength: and the beauty of old man is the gray head. (KJV)

Euen in the myddes of great laughter lyeth sorowe: and the ende of mirth is calamyte. (14.13, *Prouerbes*)
Even in laughter the heart is sorrowful; and the end of that mirth is heaviness. (KJV)

The examples demonstrate that the rhythm of the earlier translation has been smoothed out, and that while Joye's wording is modified by transposition, it is not lost. This is not always the case: 'A blabby mouth shalbe smytten with his owne folyssh speche' (18.7) was understandably omitted. Nowadays, it is common to credit Miles Coverdale with the formation of the style of the gnomic books, as William Tyndale had established no precedent. In *The Making of the English Bible*, Gerald Hammond remarks that it is in the Prophetic and Poetic books of the Old Testament 'that we see Coverdale's creative translation at its freest, unaffected by any existing English version'.[30] However, in order to credit Miles Coverdale with the formulation of the style for these books, one must necessarily ignore George Joye's renderings, which in effect dismisses one of the foundation-stones of the vernacular English Bible.

III

Thus far, Joye's work on the Old Testament functioned in tandem with that of William Tyndale. Tyndale had covered the Pentateuch through to II Chronicles; Joye worked on Psalms through to Lamentations. However, although Joye's translations may have complemented those of Tyndale, his editing did not. The disputes that Tyndale and Joye had been engaging in quietly for years exploded into the public sphere with the infamous publication in August 1534 of an edition of Tyndale's New Testament, corrected by George Joye.[31]

Joye's editing extended beyond mere typographical corrections, and it was from this that the serious problems arose. The most significant alteration (as Joye recounts) was that 'my conscience compelled of the truthe of goddis worde caused me to englysshe thys word Resurrectio the life aftir this'.[32] His belief was that the souls of the dead lived; the purpose of the general resurrection was to rejoin the souls to their newly risen bodies. William Tyndale, on the other hand, believed that on doomsday both flesh and soul were to be given new life, and that until that time the souls of the dead slept. Joye left the word *resurrectio* untouched when it referred to the general resurrection, but otherwise he rendered it 'the life of them that be dead' or 'the life after this', what is now called the afterlife. Joye declared: 'I had as lief put the trwthe in the text as in the margent and excepte the glose expowne the text ... I had as lief leue sich fryuole gloses clene out.'[33] Joye therefore translated *resurrectio* according to its context, in order to minimize the confusion of the reader with either detailed glosses or the fluctuating meaning of the word. As Tyndale saw it, Joye had taken his text and unforgivably implanted in it a mistaken belief in the active state of souls after death.

Among other reasons, Joye's edition of Tyndale's New Testament is worthy of mention because it affected the course of events. Tyndale's revised edition, which had been promised for eight or nine years, appeared within three months of Joye's. The typographical errors were corrected, as in Joye's edition, and, ironically, on occasion Tyndale revised according to the discrepancies pointed out in Joye's condemned edition; he included certain phrases added by Joye, and also corrected certain of the glosses.[34] Joye's editing work therefore resulted in William Tyndale producing two editions of his New Testament a matter of months before his arrest. When Miles Coverdale came to prepare his 1535 Bible, he had a copy of Tyndale's original corrected text. Had there only been corrupt copies available, the Bible of 1535 would have appeared in a very different state. Furthermore, Joye's corrections and his translations of certain scriptural excerpts appended to the New Testament were used by the revisers working under King James.[35] Therefore apart from his direct influence on Tyndale, Joye's own work stands independently as another source for the *King James Version*.

After his clash with Tyndale, it was twenty years before George Joye embarked on another piece of biblical scholarship. By this time the Act of Six Articles and the upheaval which ensued had forced Joye into exile once more, and it was from Antwerp that he published *The exposicion of Daniel the Prophete* in August 1545 (RSTC 14823). As with *Isaye* and *Jeremy*, *Daniel* was seen to have a specific contemporary relevance for the Reformers. Through this book, the history of the world could be mapped out and given coherence; the present state of turmoil could be rationalized and placed in context. For Joye, the context required to make sense of the irreconcilable religious differences, the destitution of Christendom, the plague-ridden, poverty-crippled country of England, and the widespread violent unrest, was that a monumental phase of history was being entered into: the End was nigh. His exegesis of Daniel returns again and again to the subject, telling us 'These thinges be wryten for oure warninge ouer whom the ende of the worlde hangeth' (fol. K3[r]). Joye was in no doubt: 'the tyme is come that the iudgement or plage muste beginne at the house of god'.[36]

In Joye's opinion, the book of Daniel functioned as a microcosmic text, in which was mirrored the entire history of humankind: 'it is the very breif compendious some and reherceall of the storye of the hole worlde/ euen from the firste monarchye to the laste/ setting befor our eyes the cleare examples of the good and euil princes and rulers' (fol. A4[r]). Despite its impact on previous generations, Joye considered the book to have reached its time of ultimate significance, because 'now are the last dayes come/ as Daniel prophecieth ... wherin the emprour and kynges all as many as haue burned and yet burne men for the gospell be lyke to be greuously punisshed' (fol. E6[v]).

Ultimately, Joye's apocalyptic discourse served to offer reassurance to the 'simple sely flocke of chryst'.[37] The sufferings of the Reformers were elevated to the level of mythic narrative; through their pain the Brethren reproduced the torments of Christ himself. Of the anguish experienced by Jesus, Joye writes: 'The same rebukes iniuste vexacions and cruell persecucions do we suffer this daye.'[38] The best consolation for the Reformers was that they would suffer into the perpetual glory of God. Books such as *The exposicion of Daniel the Prophete* served to expand their perspectives, so that the exiled brethren could view their present trials within the larger context of the (fast approaching) spiritual afterlife: 'the more affliccion and persecucion the worde of the crosse bringeth to us, the more felicite and greter ioye abideth us in heuen'.[39] When viewed within the context of the blissful eternity awaiting them, the importance of the

Reformers' earthly sacrifices was greatly diminished. Joye tirelessly exhorted his fellow believers not to be troubled 'for feare of the losse, of our litle goodis and disquietinge of our mortall bodyes in this transitory lyfe'.[40] 'I tell you my frendes, be not afraid of them that slaye your bodies, and then can thei do nomore to you. ... They kyll our bodyes, but thei sende our soules into the handis of our heuenly father, and make our dethe preciouse in the syght of god.'[41]

Writing in a time when 'the Bible in English' has a stable identity, it is difficult to comprehend fully the implications of Joye's translations. Unfortunately, it is all too easy to work backwards, to compare Joye's versions with those that followed, and use the *King James Version* as the final yardstick with which to measure skill and influence. Despite Joye's obvious influence, the extent to which Miles Coverdale used (or did not use) Joye's works must not be the deciding factor in evaluating the worth of these texts. At times Coverdale deviated from Joye's work only to render the verse more awkward and stilted; but irrespective of Coverdale's ability, there is a fundamental flaw in a system of worth which is dependent on the extent to which Miles Coverdale or a seventeenth-century theologian approved of Joye's translations. Neither Coverdale nor the revisers of 1611 took over Joye's 'Pride goeth before a fall', yet this has remained with us, and could in fact suggest the existence and the legacy of an 'oral Bible', which developed and survived through sermons and popular literature.[42] Judging the translations by comparison alone completely neglects one of the most important elements in the extensive sphere of Joye's influence: the people who read and prayed with and took comfort in his works.[43] When he raced through his Bible translations, George Joye was not thinking of posterity. He was responding to the widespread desire of the laity to read for themselves the Word of God, and he was trying to reassure them that all this terrible persecution had in fact happened before, and that retribution had been meted out, and would be again.

The prologue to the second Wycliffite Bible asserts: 'although covetous clerks ... despise and stop holy writ as much as they can, yet the common people cry after holy write to know [kunne] it'.[44] Joye was fuelled by that need. *Isaye, Jeremy, Dauid's Psalter*: the names of these texts do not imply scholarly, academic exercises. George Joye spent much of his life on the run with his family; he had no time and no money. What sustained him was the belief that he was doing God's work in restoring David, Solomon, and Isaiah to the people of England, 'speakinge playne englysshe'.[45] The value of his Bible translations therefore, derives not only from their certain influence on the English Bible, but also from their resonating presence in the religious lives of the English laity of the sixteenth century. His work – had it never been used as a source by Miles Coverdale or anyone else – possesses its own inherent value and is its own achievement.

NOTES

1 David Norton, *A History of the Bible as Literature*, 2 vols (Cambridge: University Press, 1993), I, p. 169, footnote.
2 Eamon Duffy, *The Stripping of the Altars* (New Haven & London: Yale University Press, 1992), p. 231.

3 Due to the unavailibility of the de Keyser 1530 Psalter at the time of writing, all quotes are taken from Thomas Godfray's 1534 reprint of the 1530 Psalter.

4 John Fisher, *This treatyse concernynge the fruytfull saynges of Dauyd the kynge & prophete in the seuen penytencyall psalmes* (London: Wynkyn de Worde, 1508), fol. nn4^r.

5 John Fisher, fol. A3^r; *Ortulus Anime* (Antwerp: Martin de Keyser, 1530), fol. O6^r.

6 A phrase of David Daniell's from his *William Tyndale: A Biography* (New Haven & London: Yale University Press, 1994), p. 139.

7 *The Obedience of a Christian Man* (Antwerp: J. Hoochstraten, 1528), fol. 104^r. Tyndale also comments (fol. 74^v): 'It is verely as good to preach it to swyne as to men/ if thou preach it in a tonge they understonde not.'

8 'Certain Godly, Learned, and Comfortable Conferences, between the two Reverend Fathers and Holy martyrs, Doctor Nicholas Ridley, late bishop of London, and M. Hugh Latimer, sometime Bishop of Worcester', in *The Fathers of the English Church*, ed. by Legh Richmond, 8 vols (London: John Hatchard, 1807-12), IV, p. 86.

9 Dedication to 1535 Bible, *Remains of Myles Coverdale*, ed. by George Pearson (Cambridge: University Press for the Parker Society, 1846), p. 5.

10 *A notable Oration, made by John Venaeus a Parisien in the defence of the Sacrament of the aultare*, trans. by John Bullingham (London: John Cawood, 1554), fol. C3^v.

11 John Fisher, *A Sermon had at Paulis* (London: T. Berthelet, 1526), fol. F3^r.

12 George Joye, *The Refutation of the byshop of Winchesters derke declaration of his false articles* (London: John Herford, 1546), fol. f6^v.

13 George Joye, *Our sauiour Jesus Christ hath not ouercharged his chirche with many ceremonies* (Antwerp: Catherine Van Endhoven, 1543), fols C5^v-C6^r.

14 Nicholas Ridley, 'A Brief Treatise upon the Lord's Supper', in *The Fathers of the English Church*, IV, pp. 188-9.

15 Joye, *Refutation*, fol. Bb3^r. John Bale builds on the notion of Latin being a more deceitful tongue than English in his play *King Johan*, when Dissymulacyon boasts of the tricks he employs to win over the people:

> Thowgh I seme a shepe,   I can play the suttle foxe:
> I can make Latten   to brynge this gere to the boxe.
> Tushe, Latten ys alone   to bryng soche mater to passe;
> Ther ys no Englyche   that can soche profyghtes compass.
> And therfor we wyll   no servyce to be songe,
> Gospell nor pystell,   but all in Latten tonge.   (I, 715)

16 George Joye, *Jeremy the Prophete* (Antwerp: Catherine Van Endhoven?, May 1534), fol. A7^r.

17 Fisher, *Sermon*, fol. F3^r.

18 Dedication to the 1538 New Testament, Pearson, p. 26.

19 From the dedication to *The New Testament of Our Lord and Saviour Jesus Christ: Translated out of the Latin Vulgate by John Wiclif*, ed. by John Lewis (London: Thomas Page, 1731), p. ii.

20 Gerald Hammond, *The Making of the English Bible* (Manchester: Carcanet New Press, 1982), p. 30.

21 This was a common occurrence in the translation of Latin into English, which was commented upon by Gawin Douglas, in the preface to his 1553 translation of the *Aeneid*:

> Besyde Latyn, our langage is imperfite
> … thar bene Latyne wordes, mony ane
> That in our leid ganand, translation has nane
> Les than we mynnis, thare sentence and grauite
> And yit skant weil exponit …

Quoted in Richard Foster Jones, *The Triumph of the English Language: a Survey of Opinions Concerning the Vernacular from the Introduction of Printing to the Restoration* (California: Stanford University Press, 1953) p. 16.

22 For example, for the Matthew's Bible (1537), Joye's Bucerian commentaries were taken over almost *verbatim*.

23 For studies of the influence of Joye's Psalters see: Charles C. Butterworth, *The Literary Lineage of the King James Bible, 1340-1611* (Philadelphia: University of Pennsylvania Press, 1941), ch. 5; and C. Hopf, *Martin Bucer and the English Reformation* (Oxford: Blackwell, 1946), ch. 4.

24 *The Fathers of the English Church*, IV 38.

25 As pointed out by Susan Felch in her article in this volume.

26 Joye, *Jeremy*, fol. A5^{v}.

27 John Foxe, *Acts and Monuments*, ed. by Stephen R. Cattley (London: R. B. Seeley & W. Burnside, 1841), V, 132.

28 Although now existing in separate bindings, the books were originally intended to be in the same volume: George Joye, *The prouerbes of Solomon … Here foloweth the boke of Solomon called Ecclesiastes* (London: Thomas Godfray, *c.* 1535), RTSC 2752.

29 Prologue to 1535 Bible, Pearson, p. 18.

30 Hammond, p. 69.

31 The successful Worms edition of 1525 had been twice reprinted by the Van Endhoven press, in 1526 and in 1530. The textual corruptions multiplied with each successive edition. After the 1530 publication sold out, Catharine Van Endhoven asked William Tyndale if he would correct his translation; he refused, and after some hesitation, and a third version in an appalling condition, Joye agreed to edit the corrupt text. In August 1534 *The new Testament as it was written/ and caused to be written/ by them which herde yt* went to press.

32 George Joye, *An Apologye made by George Joye to satisfye (if it maye be) w. Tindale* (London: John Byddell, 27 February 1535), fol. A4^{r}.

33 Ibid., fols C6^{v}-C7^{r}.

34 For example, in Romans 12.13 Joye added *giuen to hospitalitie*. He also altered Tyndale's Matthew 1.18 *Mary was married to Joseph*, rendering it *Mary was betrothed to Joseph*. Tyndale took over both of these corrections, and also followed Joye's critique of certain glosses. Writing in 1731, John Lewis commented on the positive effect of Joye's New Testament: '*Joye* observed, that in this the first Edition the marginal Gloss upon I *John* iii. was, Love *is the* first *precept and cause of all other*: and on the other side, Fayth *is the first commandment, and* Love *the* seconde. The staring contradiction was now in this Edition thus prudently avoided: Faith *and* Love *is the* fyrste *commandement and all commaundementes, and he that hath them is in God, and hath his sprete.*' Lewis (cited above, n. 19), p. 21.

35 Joye's Song of Solomon appears to have been of particular influence: Tyndale 2.1 reads *I am the floure of the felde*; Joye renders this *I am the flower of Saron*, and the King James Version follows with *I am the rose of Sharon*. Similarly in 2.4: *his behauer to mewarde was louely* (Tyndale); *spred the baner of his loue ouer me* (Joye); *his banner over me was love* (KJV). For further details see Butterworth (cited above, n. 23), pp. 85-7.

36 George Joye, *A present consolacion for the sufferers of persecucion for ryghtwysenes* (Antwerp: S. Mierdman, September 1544), fol. D3^{v}.

37 George Joye, *George Joye confuteth/ Winchesters false Articles* (Antwerp: Catherine Van Endhoven, 1543), fol. c6^{r}.

38 *A present consolacion*, fol. C6^{r}.

39 Ibid., fol. B4^{r}.

40 Ibid., fol. B5^{v}.

41 Ibid., fols F7^{v}, F8^{v}.

42 In the 1535 Bible of Miles Coverdale Proverbs 16.18 reads 'Presumptuousness goeth before destruction, and after a proud stomach there foloweth a fall'; the King James Version renders the verse 'Pride goeth before destruction, and an haughty spirit before a fall.'

43 The extent of the comfort taken, not only in the contents of the Reformers' works, but also in the physical existence of the works themselves, is remarkable. It is evident in the case of one Stile, who was burned at Smithfield, as John Foxe recounts: 'With him there was burned also a book of the Apocalypse, which belike he was wont to read upon. This book when he saw fastened to the stake, to be burned with him lifting up his voice, "O blessed Apocalypse," said he, "how happy am I, that shall be burned with thee!"' Foxe (cited above, n. 27), V, 655.

44 *The Holy Bible, containing the Old and New Testaments, with the Apocryphal Books, made from the Latin Vulgate by John Wycliffe and his Followers*, ed. by Josiah Forshall & Frederic Madden, 2 vols (Oxford: University Press, 1850), I, 57.

45 George Joye, *The prophete Isaye* (Antwerp: Martin de Keyser, 10 May 1531), fol. A2$^\text{v}$. Likewise the revisers of the King James Version declared: 'we desire that the Scripture may speak like itself, as in the language of Canaan, that it may be understood even of the very vulgar.' *The Holy Bible: The Authorized or King James Version of 1611 now reprinted with the Apocrypha*, 3 vols (London: Nonesuch Press, 1963), I, p. xxvi.

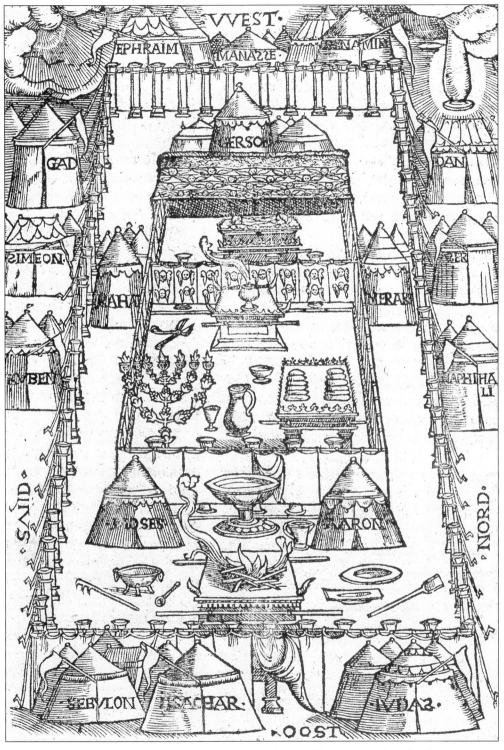

1. Postilla-woodcut of the Tabernacle in Coverdale's Bible, 1535, 2nd Book of Moses, ch. 40 (real size 187 × 130 mm)

2. Barbier-Courteau Bible (1559): Noah's Ark

7. *La Bible* (Antwerp: Martin Lempereur, 1530): Noah's Ark

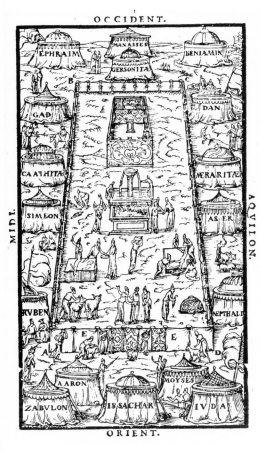

3. Barbier-Courteau Bible (1559):
Forecourt of the Tabernacle

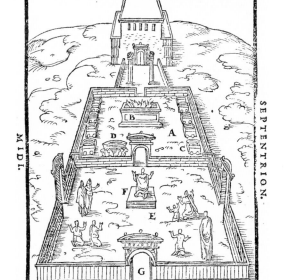

4. Barbier-Courteau Bible (1559):
Temple Forecourt

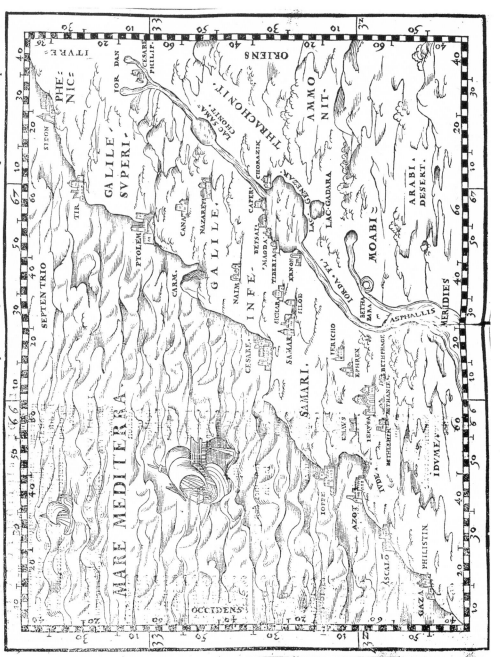

5. Barbier-Courteau Bible (1559): Map of the Holy Land

DISCOVRS PAR ORDRE DES ANnées apres la côuerfion de fainct Paul, monftrant le temps de la peregrination d'iceluy, & des epiftres efcrites aux Eglifes.

Annees. De la natiuité de IESVS Chrift.	Annees. De la côuerfion de S. Paul.	DISCOVRS PAR ORDRE DES ANnées apres la côuerfion de fainct Paul, monftrant le temps de la peregrination d'iceluy, & des epiftres efcrites aux Eglifes.	Annees. De l'empire de Tybere.
35	1	Paul perfecuteur, Act.7.8.9. Eft conuerti allant a Damas, Act.9.	De l'empire de Tybere. 20
36	2	De Damas il va en Arabe prefcher l'Euangile: Puis retourne en Damas où on le veut prendre, mais il efchappe par le moyen des fidelles qui l'auallent en bas en vne corbeille par deffus la muraille, Gal.1. Act.9.	21
37	3	De là vien en Ierufalem pour voir fainct Pierre, Gal.1. Act.9. 2.Cor.12.	22
38	4	Les Iuifs le voulant mettre à mort il fut mené en Cefaree, & de là enuoyé en Syrie, & en Tarfe de Cilice, A ces neufieme.	23
39	5	Galatiens premier chap.	De Caligula
40	6		
41	7		3
42	8	En apres il eft mené en Antioche par Barnabas, & là les difciples font premierement nommez Chreftiens.	4
43	9		De Claude
44	10	La famine predite par Agabus fous Claude Cefar, Act.11.	2
45	11	Sainct Iaques le maieur occis par Herodes, Act.12.	3
46	12	Paulus Proconful en Cypre, conuerti par fainct Paul, Act.13.	4
47	13	Sainct Paul prefche l'Euangile en Antioche de Pifidie, qui eft partie de Galatie, Act.13.&14.	5
48	14	De là il vient en Iconie où il demeure quelque temps, Act.13.&14.	6
49	15	Il guarit vn boiteux en Lyftre & y eft lapidé. Act.14.	7
50	16	Ayant ordonné des Anciens en l'Eglife, & vifite toute la Pifidie & Pamphilie, il retourne a Antioche.	8
51	17	En ce temps eft celebré le concile des Apoftres en Ierufalem, où fainct Paul affifté, & de là retourne en Antioche, où fainct	9
52	18	Pierre vint auffi, & S.Paul luy refifta en face, Act.15. Gal.2.	10
53	19	Sainct Paul va en Syrie & Cilice auec Siluanus pour confermer les Eglifes: Puis a Derbe & Lyftre, où il prend pour adioint	11
54	20	Timothee puis va en Macedone, & enfeigne en la ville nommee Philippes, Act.15.&16.	12
55	21	Il enfeigne a Athenes Act.17. Et de là efcrit aux Theffaloniciens.	13
56	22	Il demeure a Corinthe dixhuit mois, Act.18.Et là efcrit aux Romains.	14
57	23	Il retourne en Afie, a Ephefe, & de là en Cefaree: puis en Ierufalem, & de là en Antioche. Apres il vifite les Eglifes de Galatie	De Nero
58	24	& Phrygie, Act.18.	2
59	25	Il vient a Ephefe où il enfeigne deux ans & y laiffe Timothee, Act.19,&1.Timoth.1.	3
60	26	Il efcrit d'Ephefe la premiere aux Corinthiens, 1.Corinth 16.	4
61	27	Apres le tumulte, qui fut en Ephefe, appaifé, il vient a Troas, & de la en Macedone, & eftant a Philippes efcrit la feconde aux Corinthiens par Tite & S.Luc, 2.Corinth 2.&13.& Act.20.	5
62	28	De là il vint en Achaie & a Corinthe ainfi qu'il auoit promis, 1.Cor.16.&2.Corinth.12. Et a caufe des embufches qu'on luy faifoit, il retourna par Macedone en Troas vers Ariftarque & Timothee qui y eftoyent allez deuant, Act.20.	6
63	29	De Troas il vient en Affos, en Mytilene, autrement dite Lesbos, & de la a Milete, où il dit adieu aux Ephefiens, Act.20.	7
64	30	Act.10.de la vient a Rhodes, a Patare, a Tyr, a Ptolemais, a Cefaree, finalement en Ierufalem & y eft pris, Act.21.&22.	8
65	31	Eftant prifonnier eft mené a Cefaree au preuoft Felix, Act.23, où il demeure deux ans, Act.24.	9
66	32	Puis eft enuoyé a Rome prifonnier, Act.27.	10
67	33	Eftant és liens il efcrit aux Galatiens, aux Ephefiens, aux Philippiens.	11
68	34	Aux Coloffiens, a Philemon.	12
69	35	La feconde a Timothee.	13
70	36	Finalement eft decapité par le commandement de Neron.	14

6. Barbier-Courteau Bible (1559): Table of Paul's missionary career

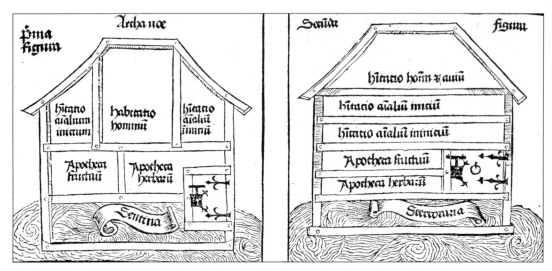

8. Nicholas of Lyra, *Biblie iampridem renovate pars prima* (Basle: Froben, 1501): Noah's Ark

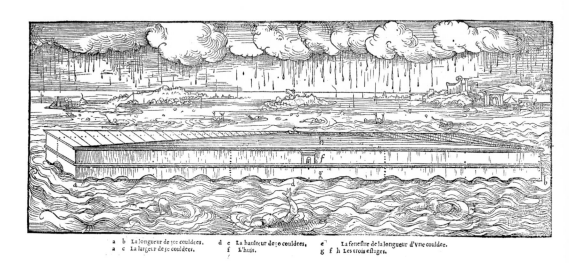

a b La longueur de 300 couldees.   d e La haulteur de 30 couldees,   e´   La fenestre de la longueur d'vne couldee.
a c La largeur de 50 couldees.   f L'huis.   g f h Les trois estages.

9. *La Bible* (Geneva: Robert Estienne, 1553): Noah's Ark

11. *La Bible* (Antwerp: Martin Lempereur, 1530):
Forecourt of the Tabernacle

10. Nicholas of Lyra, *Biblie iampridem renovate pars prima*
(Basle: Froben, 1501): Forecourt of the Tabernacle

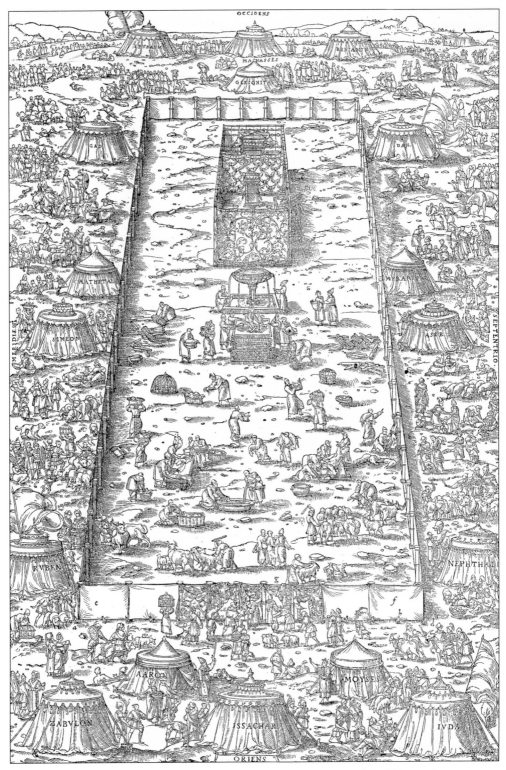

12. *La Bible* (Geneva: Robert Estienne, 1553): Forecourt of the Tabernacle

De Bibel in duyts

voortijts by Jacob Liesveldt wtghegaen na de alder oudtste/ e.ioe correcrste Copien die ghedzuckt zijn

Cum Gratia ¢ Pzeuilegio.

Nu oock laestmael wederom met grooter neerstichept ouerge- sien ende verbetert. An. M. D. lix.

2. Timoth. 3.

¶ Alle Schrift van God inghegheuen is oozbaerlick te leeren/tot straffinghe/tot beteringhe/tot onderwijsinge inder rechtueerdichept/dat een men- sche Gods zp volkomen ge- schickt tot alle goede wercken.

13. Title-page to Gellius Ctematius's edition to the Liesvelt Bible (1559)

14. Cranach, *The Law and the Gospel* (1528)

15. Woodcut depicting Cranach's *The Law and the Gospel* (1529)

16. Another version of *The Law and the Gospel* by Cranach (1529)

18. Title-page to the Luther Bible of 1533

17. Title-page to the Luther Bible of 1541

20. Luther's *Septembertestament* (1522):
the Beast of the Apocalypse

19. Luther's *Septembertestament* (1522):
the Harlot of Babylon

22. Luther's *Dezembertestament* (1522):

21. Luther's *Dezembertestament* (1522):

23. Tyndale's New Testament (1536):
the Harlot of Babylon

24. Coverdale's New Testament (1538):
the Harlot of Babylon

26. Coverdale's New Testament (1538):
the Beast of the Apocalypse (b)

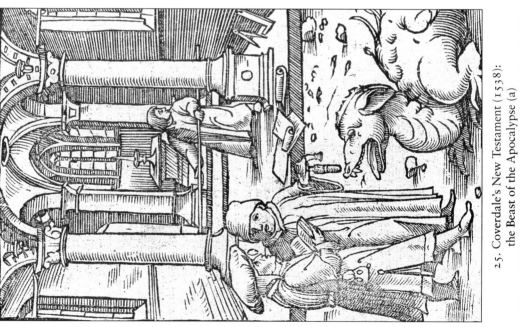

25. Coverdale's New Testament (1538):
the Beast of the Apocalypse (a)

27. Thomas Harriot, *Briefe and True Reporte* (1590): Adam and Eve in the Garden of Eden

He aged men of Pommeioocke are couered with a large skinne which is tyed vppon their shoulders on one side and hangeth downe beneath their knees wearinge their other arme naked out of the skinne, that they maye bee at more libertie. Those skynnes are Dressed with the hair on, and lyned with other furred skinnes. The yonnge men suffer noe hairr at all to growe vppon their faces but assoone as they growe they put them away, but when thy are come to yeeres they suffer them to growe although to say truthe they come opp verye thinne. They also weare their haire bownde op behynde, and, haue a creste on their heads like the others. The contrye abowt this plase is soe fruit full and good, that England is not to bee compared to yt.

B

28. Thomas Harriot, *Briefe and True Reporte* (1590): 'An ageed manne in his winter garment'

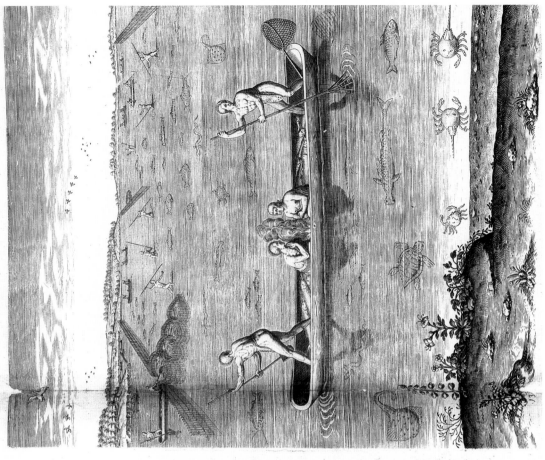

XIII.

Their manner of fishynge in Virginia.

Hey haue likewise a notable way to catche fishe in their Riuers. for whear as they lacke both yron, and steele, they faste vnto their Reedes or longe Rodds, the hollowe tayle of a certaine fishe like to a sea crabb in steede of a poynte, wcht with by night or day they stricke fishes, and take them opp into their boates. They also know how to vse the prickles, and pricks of other fishes. They also make weares, with setinge opp reedes or twigges in the water, which they soe plant one within a nother, that they growe still narrower, and narrower, as appeareth by this figure. Ther was neuer seene amonge vs soe cunninge a way to take fish withall, wherof sondrie sortes as they fownde in their Riuers vnlike vnto ours. which are also of a verye good taste. Dowbtlesß yt is a pleasant sighte to see the people, somtymes wadinge, and goinge somtymes sailinge in those Riuers, which are shallowe and not deepe, free from all care of heapinge opp Riches for their posterite, content with their state, and liuinge frendlye together of those thinges which god of his bountye hath giuen vnto them, yet without giuinge hym any thankes according to his desarre, So sauage is this people, and depriued of the true knowledge of god. For they haue none other then is mentionned beforein this worke.

30. Thomas Harriot, *Briefe and True Reporte* (1590): A Pictish Man

32. Thomas Harriot, *Briefe and True Reporte* (1590):
A Daughter of the Picts

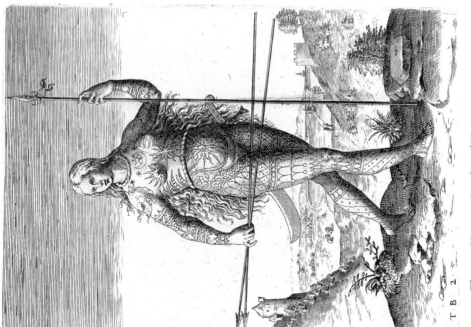

31. Thomas Harriot, *Briefe and True Reporte* (1590):
A Pictish Woman

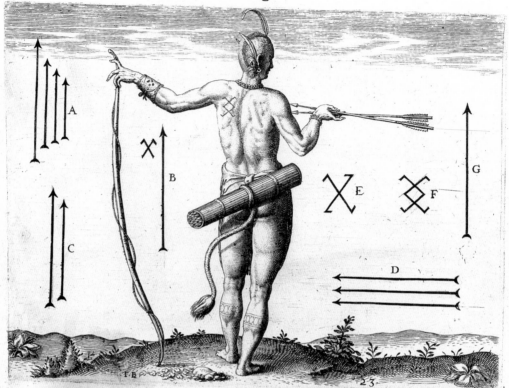

He inhabitãts of all the cuntrie for the most parte haue marks rased on their backs, wherby yt may be knowen what Princes subiects they bee, or of what place they haue their originall. For which cause we haue set downe those marks in this figure, and haue annexed the names of the places, that they might more easelye be discerned. Which industrie hath god indued them withal although they be verye simple, and rude. And to confesse a truthe I cannot remember, that euer I saw a better or quietter people then they.

The marks which I obserued a monge them, are heere put downe in order folowinge.

The marke which is expressed by A. belongeth tho Wingino, the cheefe lorde of Roanoac.

That which hath B. is the marke of Wingino his sisters husbande.

Those which be noted with the letters, of C. and D. belonge vnto diverse chefe lordes in Secotam.

Those which haue the letters E. F. G. are certaine cheefe men of Pomeiooc, and Aquascogoc.

33. Thomas Harriot, *Briefe and True Reporte* (1590): The Marckes of sundrye of the Cheif mene of Virginia

unto all the nations   M.   W. mg. In Greek Logos which

from Jer".   M.   means also reason

48 Scr. — 또 — And   M.   that there be a mg. } 7 7

N. join ἀρξάμενοι with v 48. 5 M   Ho. that ὁ θεός be rendered

N. mg. Or nations. Beginning   GOD. (Caps. } 2 M

from Jer" ye are to }M   3 W. mg. Or made. That which

49 Ἐξαποστέλλω] send forth M   hath been made was life in him }M

clothed   } 7   St. mg. Or it   1 M

Ie. from on high with power 2 M   Ho. came into being   4 M

50 Scr. — ἕως] πρός.   M   through   } 8 8

towards v to   M   Sal. mg. Or by   wd

51 he parted from them & was M   Chairman gave casting vote

Ho. borne up   } 7 8   for by in text, though in mg.

Ho. mg. S.a.a. on. & was carried   V. mg. Or came into being 5 M

up into heaven   }M   V. that hath been made   M

52 Ho. mg. S.a.a. on. worshipped him & M   Br. not one   wd

53 Scr. — αἰνοῦντες καὶ] — praise M   4 the darkness   M

Scr. a mg.   6 7   W. overcame it not (3) 8 7

Sa — ἀμήν] — Amen   M   mg. Or apprehended it not M

Par. 12, 35, 43, 49, 53.

12.50 pm (2)

John.

St. that we consider the titles 4 M

34. A page from Samuel Newth's notes from the first and provisional revision
for the Revised Version

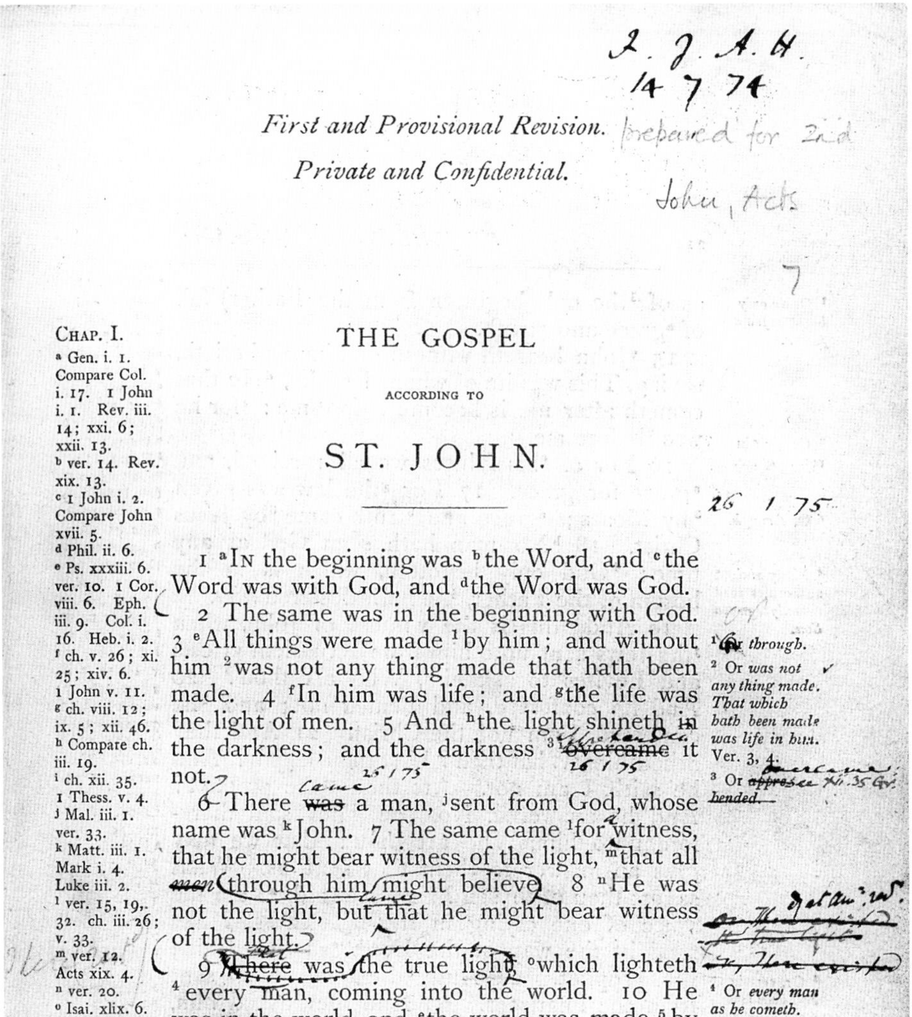

[handwritten: 2. J. A. H. 14 7 74 prepared for 2nd John, Acts 7]

THE GOSPEL

ACCORDING TO

ST. JOHN.

[handwritten: 26 / 75]

CHAP. I.
ᵃ Gen. i. 1.
Compare Col.
i. 17. 1 John
i. 1. Rev. iii.
14; xxi. 6;
xxii. 13.
ᵇ ver. 14. Rev.
xix. 13.
ᶜ 1 John i. 2.
Compare John
xvii. 5.
ᵈ Phil. ii. 6.
ᵉ Ps. xxxiii. 6.
ver. 10. 1 Cor.
viii. 6. Eph.
iii. 9. Col. i.
16. Heb. i. 2.
ᶠ ch. v. 26; xi.
25; xiv. 6.
1 John v. 11.
ᵍ ch. viii. 12;
ix. 5; xii. 46.
ʰ Compare ch.
iii. 19.
ⁱ ch. xii. 35.
1 Thess. v. 4.
ʲ Mal. iii. 1.
ver. 33.
ᵏ Matt. iii. 1.
Mark i. 4.
Luke iii. 2.
ˡ ver. 15, 19,.
32. ch. iii. 26;
v. 33.
ᵐ ver. 12.
Acts xix. 4.
ⁿ ver. 20.
ᵒ Isai. xlix. 6.
1 John ii. 8.
ᵖ ch. xvi. 32.
�q ch. xiii. 1.
ʳ 1 John v. 1.
ˢ 1 John iii. 1.
ᵗ ch. xi. 52.
ᵘ 1 Pet. i. 23.
ᵛ ch. iii. 6.
ʷ James i. 18.
ˣ Rom. i. 3.
1 Tim. iii. 16.
Heb. ii. 14.
ʸ Rev. xxi. 3.
ᶻ Luke ix. 32.
ch. ii. 11.
2 Pet. i. 16, 17.

1 ᵃIn the beginning was ᵇthe Word, and ᶜthe Word was with God, and ᵈthe Word was God. 2 The same was in the beginning with God. 3 ᵉAll things were made ¹by him; and without him ²was not any thing made that hath been made. 4 ᶠIn him was life; and ᵍthe life was the light of men. 5 And ʰthe light shineth in the darkness; and the darkness ³overcame it not.

6 There was a man, ʲsent from God, whose name was ᵏJohn. 7 The same came ¹for witness, that he might bear witness of the light, ᵐthat all men through him might believe. 8 ⁿHe was not the light, but that he might bear witness of the light.

9 There was ᵒthe true light ᵒwhich lighteth ⁴every man, coming into the world. 10 He was in the world, and ᵉthe world was made ⁵by him, and the world knew him not. 11 He came unto ᵖhis own, and �q they that were his own received him not. 12 But as many as received him, ʳto them gave he ⁶power ˢto become ᵗchildren of God, *even* ᵐto them that believe on his name: 13 which were born, ⁿnot of ⁷blood, ᵛnor of the will of the flesh, nor of the will of man, but ʷof God.

14 And ˣthe Word ˣbecame flesh, and ⁸ʸdwelt among us, (and ᶻwe beheld his glory, the glory

F f

¹ Or *through.*
² Or *was not any thing made. That which hath been made was life in him.* Ver. 3, 4.
³ Or *apprehended.*

⁴ Or *every man as he cometh.*
⁵ Or *through.*

Gr. *his own things*

⁶ Or *right.*

Or, *begotten.*

⁷ Gr. *bloods.*

⁸ Or ʸ *had his tabernacle.*

35. F. J. A. Hort's copy of the first and provisional revision, with his manuscript notes

WILLIAM TYNDALE, THE ENGLISH BIBLE, AND THE ENGLISH LANGUAGE

David Daniell

In 1525, England was two generations behind the rest of Europe in printing. We know the names of over one thousand printers in continental Europe up to 1500; London had three: one reasonably good, Caxton, but two – de Worde and Pynson – who were in no way capable of matching the quality of work across the Channel.

In 1525, England was also two generations behind Europe in the area of printed vernacular complete Bibles. There had been such in German since 1466, and in French, Italian, Catalan, Czech, and Dutch since the 1470s; the Spanish and Portuguese translations followed before 1500. All these, of course, were from the Latin Bible. By the time of Luther's ground-breaking 1522 September Testament from the original Greek, there had been in Germany eighteen separate editions of translations of the whole Latin Bible in the vernacular.

Obviously, the two sets of statistics belong together. Printed vernacular Bibles made the market. The English Church was uniquely afraid of what vernacular Bibles there were, the 'Lollard' manuscript translations from the Vulgate produced in the 1380s under the inspiration of John Wyclif. The Constitutions of Oxford of 1407-9 forbade the making or owning of such translations, and men and women were still being burned alive for possession of such 'Lollard' material well over a hundred years later.

My subject is the pioneering work of William Tyndale, who in Germany and the Low Countries in the 1520s and 1530s translated into English the New Testament from Greek twice, and half of the Old Testament from Hebrew, and printed his translations in little pocket-books, which were then smuggled into England. He was a scholar and translator of genius; his work went directly into the King James Bible almost one hundred years later in 1611, and is still influential in translations even today. Through that King James Bible, which dominated the English-speaking world for 350 years, Tyndale has reached more people than Shakespeare. He gave the English language a plain prose style of the very greatest importance, at a time in the first decades of the sixteenth century when English was of little significance, with no apparent future. Tyndale's Bible translations are of towering, and often neglected, importance.

A brief sketch of his life will help our understanding of his work. A Gloucestershire man from a prosperous family, born in a village by the river Severn overlooking the hills of Wales, he spent a dozen years at Oxford, and possibly a short time at Cambridge just after Erasmus had been teaching Greek there. He returned to Gloucestershire and was ordained priest. He had with him Erasmus's new Latin translation of the New Testament from the original Greek, his *Novum instrumentum* of 1516. Erasmus printed the

Greek alongside his Latin, making his volume a special contribution to the European Reformers' work of getting back to New Testament roots. Tyndale, reading the Greek, found his vocation – famously, of bringing the Scriptures to 'the boy that driveth the plough'. A fine Greek scholar, as he could demonstrate, he offered his services to Erasmus's friend Cuthbert Tunstall, then Bishop of London, but was rebuffed. He set up in Cologne, and was printing his first New Testament when he was betrayed and fled up the Rhine. In Worms in 1526 he successfully completed his New Testament, and copies were smuggled to England. Somewhere in Germany he learned Hebrew (virtually unknown in England), and in 1530 he printed in Antwerp his Pentateuch, the first translations ever made from Hebrew into English. In 1534 he revised his New Testament, and finished the historical books of the Old Testament. In 1535 he was tricked into arrest, and imprisoned in a cell in Vilvorde Castle outside Brussels for sixteen months. Early in the morning of 6 October 1536 William Tyndale was taken out, and in a grand ceremony strangled and burned.[1]

Tyndale's first attempt at an English Bible was in the productive high-quality print-shop of Peter Quentell in Cologne in 1525. Cologne, then the largest city in Germany, had been the centre of north-west German printing for half a century, led by Heinrich Quentell, who supplied local universities with scholastic texts. Heinrich's grandson Peter again specialized in orthodox Catholic texts.[2] One of his authors was the anti-Lutheran John Dobneck (Cochlaeus), who was in 1525 seeing through his press his *De Petro et Roma, adversus Velenum Lutheranum*. Cochlaeus' strategy was to try to persuade leading English figures to write prefaces to his anti-Lutheran books. He had contacts at the English court. He either discovered, or made, Quentell's print-shop workers drunk, and heard from them that there were 'two Englishmen lurking there, learned, skillful in languages, and fluent' who were printing a Lutheran New Testament in English, already advanced as far as the letter K.[3] One of these men was William Tyndale (the other was William Roye). Cochlaeus reported his findings, and the Cologne senate issued a prohibition against Quentell. Cochlaeus himself tried to impound the work, but was just too late. The two Englishmen, with the printed sheets (as far as a Prologue and Matthew 22), got away. The sheets were later to circulate in England, to make the first printed Lutheran documents in English: a single set survives, in the Grenville collection of the British Library, a precious document.

Cochlaeus was so impressed with himself that he printed three separate accounts of those events, in 1533, 1538, and as late as 1549. His description of Tyndale's New Testament as 'Lutheran' is wholly accurate. Closely imitating Luther's 1522 New Testament in black-letter Bastard (*Schwabacher*) fonts, quarto page lay-out, preliminaries, longish Prologue, and style and content of marginal notes in rotunda, this Testament would indeed have been Luther in English. (It is in its way charming, with a delightful opening full-page woodcut of St Matthew dipping his pen in an inkpot held by a young angel.) That the super-orthodox Peter Quentell was printing the 'heretical' translation, at some risk to himself, must tell us something about his confidence in sales in England (there would be none on the Continent, as the English language was not commonly known), even though he would have known that the translation was contraband.

Something will be said below about the similarities to Luther's famous first, 'September', Testament. First we should consider three matters: the ignorance of the whole Bible of the English people in 1525; where Tyndale learned Hebrew, specifically whether it was with Luther's '*sanhedrin*' in Wittenberg; and quite how influential Luther was in Tyndale's making of this, and subsequent, translations.

Of course the English people, though uniquely in Europe deprived of vernacular Bibles, knew Bible stories. From sermons, from stained glass and tapestry hangings, from the cycles of 'mystery' plays performed annually in York, Coventry, and elsewhere, they would know of the Creation, Adam and Eve, Noah and the ark, Abraham and Isaac, Jonah and the whale, the Annunciation, the birth of Jesus, some of his parables, his death and resurrection, Pentecost and the Last Judgement. Great and significant as these stories are, however, they are a fraction of the whole Bible. This they were forbidden to know. Faced with a clamour for a Bible in English, the best that Chancellor Thomas More could suggest was that small sections – say, half of the book of Joshua – might be loaned to carefully selected people: on pain of death, they were not to get together so that someone could see the whole Bible in English.[4]

Obviously, More and the senior churchmen were afraid that if the lay people could read the Bible, they would 'get the wrong idea' – they might find in it what the Church did not want them to find, for example, justification by faith and not by works in Romans 5, 7, and 8. Such central New Testament doctrines need the whole Bible, as the Bible properly must be understood as a whole; and you cannot write a play about the Epistle to the Romans. Fatally, such lay men and women might also find that profitable Church practices were not in the Bible at all, like the doctrine of purgatory, which was a twelfth-century invention, nor the necessity of 'mortuaries' (that is, the right of the priest, at a death, to demand the most valuable item of a household as a gift). The Bible knows no Pope. Less obviously, it remains mysterious why the English Church alone in Europe was so repressively severe, burning people alive for possessing even a fragment of a 'Lollard' English Bible: much work remains to be done here. That there was a hunger in England for the whole Bible in English can be easily demonstrated, not least through noting the high print-run figures of and risks taken by the German and Flemish printers of English Bibles. Add to that the later evidence of a multitude of Bible-reading groups in towns and villages of England; and add again those moving stories of the inquisition of humble men and women by Church commissioners, where the interrogators were startled by the depth and breadth of the Bible knowledge of their prisoners – even though, sometimes, those prisoners could not read. True, that was somewhat later in the century, when, thanks to Tyndale, whole Bibles in English were freely available. From the end of the reign of Henry VIII in 1547, the English people began to be what they were until about the Second World War, a people of the Book. That was Tyndale's doing: before him, the darkness was almost total.

Tyndale was an exceptional scholar: some are coming to believe that he was a greater scholar than even Erasmus. His Latin was the good, new, humanist Latin, learned in Oxford. His Greek, also learned in Oxford, was good: he offered to Cuthbert Tunstall as a model of his skills in Greek his translation of an oration of Isocrates – the Greek is difficult. He was, as we know from Buschius, a German scholar of the time, fluent in eight languages. Indeed, Buschius seems to think that his native language was German. We can see Tyndale translating from German, French, Spanish, Italian, Greek, Hebrew, Latin, and so on (some believe he knew Welsh). A mystery is where he learned Hebrew. It was certainly not in England. Although the idea of trilingual colleges (teaching Latin,

Greek, and Hebrew) was current, at that time in England only two men in Cambridge knew Hebrew, and neither had any interest in translation. John Foxe in his *Acts and Monuments* says that Tyndale went for a while to Cambridge after his long time at Oxford. Though there is no other supporting evidence, it is remotely possible (but, as we shall see, unlikely) that Tyndale studied under Robert Wakefield, England's first Hebraist, who was, in 1520, back in Cambridge from Louvain.

It is most likely that Tyndale learned Hebrew in Germany, where there were rabbinical schools in several cities (including Worms), and where Johannes Reuchlin had published his important Hebrew grammar and dictionary *De rudimentis hebraicis* (1506) around the time that Tyndale was going up to Oxford. Reuchlin met considerable hostility from churchmen who maintained that the Bible was originally in Latin (interestingly, he failed to get support from Erasmus) but he made Hebrew studies possible in northern Europe. Tyndale could have bought a Hebrew Bible in Germany: for scholarly work at his level he would have benefited greatly from the magnificent Complutensian Polyglot, published from Alcala in Spain (*Complutum* in Latin) in 1522: this would have given him the Hebrew Bible, comparative texts in Latin and Greek, a supporting grammar and dictionary, and Targums, that is, Aramaic commentaries and paraphrases.

For access to these splendid volumes, he would probably have needed a university library. There is an old tradition that Tyndale was for a while at Wittenberg with Martin Luther. No evidence has survived, although sixty years ago his biographer Mozley claimed to find him in the Wittenberg records as 'Daltici'.[5] The notion that he was closely confederate with Luther was put about by his enemies in England as a political smear. On the other hand, Luther was gathering his Hebrew scholars around him at the right time, and at the beginning, Tyndale's dependence on Luther's New Testament translation and prologues was great. People like to sentimentalize about Luther and Tyndale discussing together many points of translation, perhaps even fantasizing Tyndale arriving with 'Hi, Mart: call me Bill.' But Luther would have had no cause to know the English language, that obscure and remote dialect of German spoken in an off-shore island. He had other things to do than welcome an eccentric and desperately poor Englishman in serious trouble with the English authorities – this was just at the time when he was too occupied with disputes with German leaders even to concentrate on winning back the support of Henry VIII, after having called him *stolidem regem* ('stupid king') and *stultum regem* ('dense king'), among other things.[6] The strongest evidence suggests that Tyndale learned Hebrew after 1526 and before 1530. When he printed his revised New Testament in 1534, he began his Prologue with an explanation of some changes. He had discovered 'the Hebrew phrase or manner of speech left in the Greek words'. This, now commonplace in New Testament scholarship, was disseminated by Tyndale, and clearly dates his learning Hebrew after his first New Testament. He printed his Pentateuch in 1530, in Antwerp, where he had been at least from 1528, when his first doctrinal books appeared there.

The fragment printed in Cologne in 1525 has been described as 'Luther in English'. Anyone familiar with Luther's splendid 1522 Testament sees the resemblance at once. Though Tyndale's book is a small quarto, against Luther's handsome folio, he has the same page layout, similar woodcuts, parallel marginal texts, and an introductory list of New Testament books which is identical in order and layout – Matthew to III John are numbered 1-23, and, unnumbered and set apart as less canonical, are Hebrews, James, Jude, and Revelation (this judgement was not one in the end that Tyndale supported). What there is of the translation can be found to rely heavily on Luther: for example, where Luther in Matthew 2 has *'Auff dem gebirge hat man ein geshrey gehoret'*, Tyndale equally inverts to 'On the hills was a voice heard'. Where the Greek in Matthew 9 has 'Have mercy on us, son of David', Tyndale has 'O thou son of David have mercy on us', exactly following Luther's *'Ach du sohn David, erbarm dich unser'*. I offer only two instances here, but dozens of such faithful followings can be found. The ninety marginal notes are often direct translations of Luther. There are more to the page than in any other text of Tyndale (the 1526 Worms New Testament has none at all: the 1530 Genesis only six). Sixty such marginal notes are slight adaptations of Luther, thirty are Tyndale's own. All Tyndale's are purely elucidatory (e.g. in Matthew 3, 'Locusts are more than our grasshoppers'). In addition, Tyndale removes the occasional anti-papal and anti-clerical stabs of Luther.

Strongly Lutheran is Tyndale's Prologue, which is Luther's *Vorrhede* to his 1522 New Testament translated, altered, cut, and above all added to. Tyndale has expanded Luther's seven pages to fourteen, developing the main points of what the Old Testament and New Testament are, what 'Gospel' and 'Law' mean (following Paul), and what is sin. Tyndale on his own is revealed as a formidable scholar of Paul, and master of New Testament theology. His prologue ends with five pages not found in Luther's Testament, but powerfully Lutheran in its harsh tone of exposition of our bondage to Satan. It seems that doctrinally and stylistically it is a faithful translation of something of Luther (and just possibly not translated by Tyndale himself). An original has not yet been found: the fifty-eight large volumes of Luther in the Weimar edition are somewhat daunting.

When Tyndale is on his own he is building his text out of Scripture, sometimes slightly paraphrased. The feeling is that as he writes he is quoting from memory. It takes a moment to ask 'Memory of what?' There was no modern English translation of Paul – he, Tyndale, made the first. Three things need saying at once: first, quite often his quotations do not match his own 1526 translation; second, they sometimes match the earlier late-middle-English manuscript 'Lollard' translations made under Wyclif, and sometimes most definitely do not; and third, it may be, from those two facts, that we are finding here the first evidence of a common pool among English Reformers of memorized English phrases translated from Erasmus's Greek New Testament of 1516, used in preaching and exposition.

Tyndale's first completed New Testament was made with Peter Schoeffer in the small, and safely Lutheran, city of Worms in late 1525 or early 1526. It is very different from the Cologne fragment. Though still in neat black-letter *Schwabacher*, it is now an octavo pocket-book. There is no Prologue, and there are no marginal notes – it is all simply a bare text, with small illuminated initials at the start of each book. At the end are three pages 'To the Reader' and three pages of errata.

Not a prolific printer, Schoeffer had apparently only issued four books before Tyndale's (one of which was on mining), between 1513 and that in 1526: he went on to specialize in a small way in Protestant German Bible material.[7] Cochlaeus reported that this New Testament had a print-run of six thousand. We know that copies, smuggled to England down the Rhine in bales of cloth, were being sold openly by

'Master Garrett, Curate of All Hallows in Honey Lane London' by February 1526.[8] The Bishop of London, under pressure from Cardinal Wolsey (whose vigorous anti-Lutheran campaign was part of his wish to be the next Pope) forcibly collected all he could, and burned them at a public occasion at St Paul's. The Bishop preached a sermon at the burning denouncing Tyndale's work as containing 'two thousand errors'. That is, Tyndale was translating from the Greek, and showing up the inferior Vulgate text. That bishop, Cuthbert Tunstall, who had helped Erasmus to find manuscripts for his printed Greek New Testament, would have known his own hypocrisy: but Wolsey's pressure, and influence with the King, were intense.

Tyndale's translation, as a rendering of the Greek, was in fact excellent, often inspired. The extraordinary quality of the English, in its Saxon clarity and timelessness, and range of effects, was quite unknown in any other writer in English in 1526 (people frequently remark how modern Tyndale feels). Many thousands of phrases went unchanged into King James's 1611 Authorized version 85 years later: 'with men, this is impossible, but with God all things are possible'; 'the powers that be'; 'the last enemy that shall be destroyed is death'; 'work out your own salvation with fear and trembling'; 'it is a fearful thing to fall into the hands of the living God'; 'behold, I stand at the door and knock'; 'O wretched man that I am, who shall deliver me from this body of death ?'; 'For here we have no continuing city, but we seek one to come.' Only two textually complete copies of this first 1526 New Testament survive, one discovered only in 1996.[9] In 1994, Tyndale's quincentenary, the British Library bought the rather finely decorated copy, for a hundred years owned by Bristol Baptist College, for over one million pounds, more than they have spent on any other volume.

The burning affected Tyndale deeply. From that event we can date his attacks on bishops and the Church hierarchy. He had earlier grieved that there was nowhere in England, uniquely in Europe, where a vernacular Bible could be produced;[10] he knew that his enemies in the English Church, combing his Testament for error, would, as he put it, denounce him as a heretic if he failed to dot an 'i'.[11] Such spectacular, co-ordinated, organized destruction by the English Church of God's word, to prevent lay men and women reading and understanding it and finding salvation, was to him devastating.

After the burning, a lesser man would have given up. Tyndale learned Hebrew. Some time in January 1530 there began to appear in England, smuggled in now from Antwerp, copies of a well-made little book, *The first book of Moses called Genesis*. The Prologue was headed 'W.T. To the Reader', the first time Tyndale's presence was stated in his translations. Genesis could be bought alone, or with the other four books of the Pentateuch. Each had a Prologue, and Exodus had eleven full-page woodcuts. The colophon states 'Hans Luft at Marlborow', one of the forged addresses already becoming common, indeed necessary, for the printing of Reforming books, and until recently thought to be Johannes Hoochstraten of Antwerp, now known to be Tyndale's regular Antwerp printer, Martin de Keyser. (The real Hans Luft of Wittenberg was Luther's highly successful printer.) De Keyser also used other false addresses, including 'Adam Anonymous, Basel'. (Other Reformed printers suggestively located themselves in 'Utopia', or , for fully Lutheran pieces, even 'Rome, at St Peter's court'.)

This Genesis must have smitten its readers between the eyes: instead of 'Fiat lux, et lux erat' which the Church had for a thousand years, or, for those few with access to a

Lollard manuscript, 'Be made light, and made is light', Tyndale gave us 'Let there be light, and there was light'.[12]

Exodus and Deuteronomy, for the first time in English Bible printing, are in roman fonts. The five individual prologues and the differing fonts suggest that the five books were issued separately as well as together. Each has marginal notes, though these are neither so frequent (only 6 in Genesis) nor so 'vicious' as report has erroneously handed down.[13] In Exodus at chapter 33 is 'The pope's bull slayeth more than Aaron's calf'. In Numbers 23, against Balam saying, 'How shall I curse God?', Tyndale's note has 'The pope can tell how'. But almost all these Pentateuch notes, a total of 132, are Tyndale the Hebrew scholar elucidating, helpfully.

To study this Pentateuch of Tyndale with, laid out on the desk, a Hebrew Bible, the ancient Greek translation known as the Septuagint, Luther's German version, and the Latin Vulgate, is to watch Tyndale the translator ferreting out meaning and making, above all, clarity in English. It used to be said that Tyndale knew no Hebrew, but merely put Luther into English – indeed, it is still said. It is nonsense. Tyndale is translating Hebrew, often with brilliance. True, he knew Luther's Hebrew translation very well, and took help from him in matters of grammar and vocabulary, as he did from the Septuagint. Tyndale believed passionately that Hebrew went exceptionally well into English, and expressed it strongly in his *Obedience of a Christian Man* of 1528:

And the properties of the Hebrew tongue agreeth a thousand times more with the English than with the Latin. The manner of speaking is both one, so that in a thousand places thou needest not but to translate it into the English word for word, when thou must seek a compass [go round about] in the Latin, and yet shall have much work to translate it well-favouredly, so that it have the same grace and sweetness, sense and pure understanding with it in the Latin, as it hath in the Hebrew. A thousand parts better may it be translated into the English, than into the Latin.[14]

Tyndale understood the variety and range in the Hebrew scriptures, and turned them into an English which still speaks strongly, and has endured for almost five hundred years. Here is the opening of Genesis 3:

But the serpent was subtler than all the beasts of the field which the Lord God had made, and said unto the woman. Ah sir, that God hath said, ye shall not eat of all manner trees in the garden. And the woman said unto the serpent, of the fruit of the trees in the garden we may eat, but of the fruit of the tree that is in the midst of the garden (said God) see that ye eat not, and see that ye touch it not: lest ye die.

Then said the serpent unto the woman: tush ye shall not die. But God doth know, that whensover ye should eat of it, your eyes should be opened and ye should be as God and know both good and evil. …[15]

Each Prologue in Tyndale's Pentateuch is of interest, the first giving us a few rare sentences of autobiography about the reasons he left Gloucestershire, and then England. The Prologue to Deuteronomy begins:

This is a book worthy to be read in day and night and never to be out of hands. For it is the most excellent of all the books of Moses. It is easy also and light and a very pure gospel, that is to wete, a preaching of faith and love: deducing the love to God out of faith, and love of a man's neighbour out of the love of God.[16]

These are characteristic sentences of Tyndale in their plain directness.

Before and after that 1530 Pentateuch he published five doctrinal monographs, including the important and still little-known books *The Parable of the Wicked Mammon* and *The Obedience of a Christian Man*, both from the press of Martin de Keyser in 1528, and his brief (eighty thousand words) *Answer* to the gallons of vitriolic ink (nearly three quarters of a million words, often barely readable) that Thomas More poured over him. All these still exist in a number of good copies. Tyndale's first expansion of Luther on Romans, the *Compendious Introduction*, printed by Peter Schoeffer in Worms, exists now in a single copy, in the Bodleian Library, Oxford. His translation of a book much favoured by the Reformers, the brief prophecy of Jonah, to which was added his own long Prologue (several times the length of the book), also survives in a single copy, found in the late nineteenth century bound with other pamphlets, and now in the British Library. It was printed in Antwerp by Martin de Keyser. His Expositions of the Sermon on the Mount, and of John's three Epistles, were again printed in Antwerp, probably both by de Keyser.

Tyndale's revision of his New Testament was printed in November 1534 by 'Martin Emperor', that is, de Keyser. This modest little book is the most important of all de Keyser's output, indeed of the output of all the sixty and more printers in Antwerp in the 1530s. It is the true ancestor of the English Bible, and mercifully a good handful of copies have survived: one of them, printed on vellum, was the personal, and personally annotated, copy belonging to Queen Anne Boleyn; it is among several in the British Library.

This time there are two longish Prologues to the whole New Testament. The first begins with that account of his discovery, mentioned above, of the presence of Hebrew in New Testament Greek. The fonts are Bastard throughout. Every book has a Prologue, which sometimes follow Luther closely: that to Romans is exceptionally long, and a faithful translation of Luther's own Romans Prologue, with additional paragraphs by Tyndale, making a treatise almost as long as Paul's epistle. It is a densely-written statement of the centrality of the 'most pure evangelion, that is to say glad tidings and that we call gospel, and also a light and a way into the whole scripture'.[17] The emphasis is both pure Luther, and pure Tyndale. In matters of scholarship, however, Tyndale made up his own mind: unlike Luther, he avoided condemning any Scripture as he found it in the Greek. Over the matter of the Epistle to the Hebrews, where the ascription to Paul had been disputed from earliest times, Tyndale is more charitable than Luther. The only books without Prologues are Acts and Revelation, which has twenty-two three-quarter-page emblem-style woodcuts, in form close to those in Luther's second, December 1522 New Testament. Throughout the Testament there are fairly frequent marginal notes, a few in roman, all without exception brief (often even one word) and elucidatory. The revision of the 1526 New Testament is thorough: Tyndale is a professional translator, constantly revising, and he takes what new help he can, from wherever he finds it, not least now from his knowledge of Hebrew. Among much else on Tyndale, a study remains to be done of the sources of Tyndale's revisions: we can confidently watch him using Erasmus's Latin parallel to his Greek text, and Luther's New Testament, the French New Testament translation from Le Fèvre, and the Hebrew Scriptures. (It is a matter of grief that Tyndale did not live to translate the poetic books and prophecies of the Old Testament. We should then have had them in English far surpassing that of Miles Coverdale, which is what went forward: more importantly, we should have had even finer tuning of the New Testament, so much of which is directly entwined with those very books and prophecies. Instead, by a vicious, paltry, and mean villain he was tricked into arrest and certain death. It as if William Shakespeare had been murdered by a real-life jealous Iago half-way through his life, never to write the great tragedies.)

Mercifully, we do have the 1534 New Testament, which is effectively (certainly for over eighty per cent of the time) the New Testament as English speakers have known it until only a few decades ago. In Luke 2, Tyndale has:

And there were in the same region shepherds abiding in the field and watching their flock by night. And lo: the angel of the Lord stood hard by them, and the brightness of the Lord shone round about them, and they were sore afraid. But the angel said unto them: Be not afraid. For behold, I bring you tidings of great joy that shall come to all the people: for unto you is born this day in the city of David, a saviour which is Christ the Lord. ...¹⁸

Chapter fourteen of John's Gospel begins,

And he said unto his disciples: Let not your hearts be troubled. Believe in God and believe in me. In my father's house are many mansions. If it were not so, I would have told you. I go to prepare a place for you. And if I go to prepare a place for you, I will come again, and receive you even unto myself, that where I am, there may ye be also. And whither I go ye know, and the way ye know.¹⁹

Antwerp printers had for thirty years been profitably supplying English readers. A print-run of three thousand was clearly only the start, in spite of the book still being forbidden. That, however, is not by any means the whole story. The second Prologue in this little book is entitled 'W.T. yet once more unto the Christian Reader', and it is an extended protest against his former assistant George Joye.

Joye had been persuaded to proof-read pirated editions of Tyndale's 1526 Worms New Testament by an Antwerp printer, 'the Widow of Christopher van Endhoven' (her husband had been imprisoned in London in 1531 for selling Tyndale's English New Testaments; he died in prison). This he did: it makes another story. Van Endhoven successfully produced and sold three pirated editions in all, in 1527, 1530, and 1533/4. We know from later printings that they were awkward, small, fat, inhibiting, badly-set sextodecimos. But van Endhoven sold seven thousand of those three printings, which again tells us much about the market and British readers: with two more piracies, and then Tyndale's 1534 revision, we have a total of sixteen thousand copies in circulation before the end of 1534.

Joye, however, did more than proof-read – with what now seems folly he silently altered Tyndale's translation, changing, for example, 'resurrection' to 'life after this life', a very sensitive matter at the time. Tyndale's protest is powerful in that second prologue. George Joye can tinker with the text, he says – as long as he puts his name to it. Tyndale put his initials to his own edition, rebuked Joye, told readers how to tell which edition was his, and left it at that (Joye went on quarrelling, on his own).

Tyndale was now working on the next quarter of the Old Testament, the historical books from Joshua to II Chronicles. Here he needed a much wider range of Hebrew, and of English. That these stories are in Tyndale so compelling is a significance ignored until now. No one else in 1535 was using English with such range of styles, from the most ancient hymn of victory in the 'Song of Deborah' in Judges 5, and fine embedded psalms elsewhere, to the long narratives of court intrigues of Samuel and Kings, and the epic deeds of David, and then of Elijah and Elisha. Here are the ringing tones of drama in Tyndale's I Kings 18:

And Ahab went against Eliah [Elijah]. And when Ahab saw Eliah, he said unto him: Art thou he that troubleth Israel? And he said: it is not I that trouble Israel, but thou and thy father's house …

And Eliah came to all the people and said: why halt ye between two opinions? If the Lord be very God, follow him: or if Baal be he, follow him. And the people answered him not one word.[20]

That is an English quite unknown elsewhere in the 1530s, a dramatic use of the plain prose style which Tyndale gave to England for two and a half centuries, until Samuel Johnson sent our 'elevated' writers back to Latin models.

Tyndale was living in the flourishing English House in Antwerp with the English merchants. It acted as a sort of 'safe house' for him, as long as he stayed in its precincts. But in May 1535 an egregious Englishman called Henry Phillips (probably though not certainly in the pay of Tunstall's successor to the see of London, John Stokesley), having inveigled his way into the house over some months, tricked Tyndale into leaving it. As they left by a narrow alley, Tyndale was arrested. He spent sixteen months in a dungeon cell in the castle of Vilvoorde outside Brussels, apparently without books, his own warm clothes, or even a light for the evenings. A fellow member of the English House, Thomas Poyntz, with connections at the English court, devoted all his energies to getting him released, at the cost of his own business and family life, and court favour. He was on the point of getting Tyndale released, when Phillips had Poyntz arrested as a Lutheran heretic himself, and Tyndale was not released. Tried for and convicted of heresy, he was in a public ceremony degraded from the priesthood, handed over to the secular authority, strangled, and burned. His last words were said to be 'Lord, open the king of England's eyes'. The causes of his death are not clear, apart from the degenerate Phillips's desperate need for money (he had stolen and gambled away money of his father's), and the evil malice of Bishop John Stokesley, who boasted on his death-bed that he had personally been responsible for burning alive thirty-five people.

Only months after Tyndale's martyrdom in 1536, John Rogers, the Chaplain to the Antwerp English House, later the first to be burned alive under Queen Mary, collected all Tyndale's translations, including the then unpublished historical books, and printed them in a handsome folio, with money from two London printers, Grafton and Whitchurch. We do not know where this was printed (probably Antwerp), but with tragic irony the title-page declares 'Set forth with the King's most gracious licence'. Had Tyndale lived only a few months longer, he would have seen the King's eyes at least partially opened.

Rogers could not declare the 'heretic' Tyndale, so the Bible is said to have been edited by 'Thomas Matthew', the names of two disciples. It is a large, attractive volume, with some excellent woodcuts and much explanatory matter, and six very decorative initials; the one set between the prophets and the Apocrypha is 'WT' – the identity of the translator was thus no secret, except possibly to Henry VIII himself. The half of the Old Testament that Tyndale did not live to reach, the poems and prophetic books, Rogers took from Coverdale's 1535 Bible. This, the first completed printed Bible in English, is important, but though it is dependent on Tyndale, the scholarship is altogether inferior – as can be seen from the Psalms. Those printed in the Book of Common Prayer of

William Tyndale, the English Bible, and the English Language

1549, and all successive editions up to the 1960s, are from Coverdale's 1535 Bible and, though sometimes fine of phrase, are often incomprehensible, which Tyndale never is. The mark of Tyndale is always clarity.

Tyndale's work, from 'Matthew's', went into Coverdale's revision in the 1539 Great Bible, and then into the 1560 Geneva Bible and its revisions, reaching the panels of King James's revisers in 1607, and there being very largely taken straight over, so that wherever in the world, for almost four centuries, the King James Bible of 1611 has been, there has been, silently, Tyndale. His influence has been greater than any other writer in English.

It is commonly remarked that it is no wonder that the King James Bible is so magnificent, as it was written exactly at the time when the English language had risen from virtually nothing in the 1520s and 1530s to the glory which is Shakespeare, whose last plays coincided with that Bible. Schoolchildren outside Britain are sometimes taught that 'King James brought Shakespeare in to add the poetry to his version'. That is unhappy in every possible way (though Kipling made a good short story out of the notion, 'The Proofs of Holy Writ'), but it does recognize a truth about the English language. In the first third of Shakespeare's century, 1500 to 1530, English was a poorish language, easily outstripped by Latin, especially the new humanist Latin. Some parts of English life, for example wills or churchwarden's accounts, were beginning to be written in English: but nothing great. English was not a vehicle for the most serious freight. In the next third of the century, the expressiveness of the language increased. It overtook Latin in the last third. The last two decades of the sixteenth century gave us 'a nest of singing birds'. In the 1590s, English expressibility apparently became limitless. In 1611, King James's revisers could use the English language in its full fruition.

Yet though King James's 'translators' made, over the whole Bible, several thousand small changes, the New Testament they produced, and half the Old, were Tyndale's, in vocabulary, syntax, and above all cadence – and they were written when English was a poor thing, eighty years before King James, and sixty years before Shakespeare began. Tyndale gave his life, in both senses, to bring to ordinary men and women the word of God. It is still a language that speaks to the heart. Tyndale's Luke 15 ends:

And he said unto him: Son, thou wast ever with me, and all that I have, is thine: it was meet that we should make merry and be glad: for this thy brother was dead, and is alive again: and was lost, and is found.

NOTES

1 See my *William Tyndale: a Biography* (New Haven & London: Yale University Press, 1994), *passim*.

2 S. H. Steinberg, *Five Hundred Years of Printing* (Harmondsworth: Penguin Books, 3rd edn, 1974), pp. 62-3.

3 Daniell, pp. 109, 401.

4 Thomas More, 'A Dialogue Concerning Heresies', in *The Complete Works of St Thomas More*, ed. by Thomas M. C. Lawler, Germain Marc'hadour, & Richard C. Marius, vol. 6, part 1 (New Haven & London: Yale University Press, 1981), p. 341.

5 J. F. Mozley, *William Tyndale* (Westport, CN: Greenwood Press, 1937), p. 53.

6 Daniell, p. 254.

7 William Tyndale, *The First New Testament … reproduced in facsimile*, intro. by Francis Fry (Bristol, 1862), pp. 8-10, 27-8.

8 John Foxe, *Acts and Monuments*, 4th edn, ed. by J. Pratt; intro. by J. Stoughton, 8 vols (London: G. Seeley, 1870), V, p. 421.

9 Eberhard Zwink, 'Confusion about Tyndale: the Stuttgart Copy of the 1526 New Testament in English', *Reformation* 3 (1998), 28-47.

10 William Tyndale, *Old Testament*, ed. by David Daniell (New Haven & London: Yale University Press, 1992), p. 5.

11 Ibid., p. 3.

12 Ibid., p. 15.

13 Daniell, pp. 308-12.

14 William Tyndale, *Doctrinal Treatises*, ed. by H. Walter (Cambridge: University Press for the Parker Society, 1848), pp. 148-8.

15 William Tyndale, *Old Testament*, p. 17.

16 Ibid., p. 254.

17 William Tyndale, *Tyndale's New Testament*, ed. by David Daniell (New Haven & London: Yale University Press, 1989), p. 207.

18 Ibid., p. 91.

19 Ibid., p. 154.

20 William Tyndale, *Old Testament*, p. 492.

JOHN KNOX'S BIBLE

David Wright

RUNNING LIKE A REFRAIN through the writings of John Knox, the prophetic leader of the Reformation settlement in Scotland who died in 1572, is an appeal to 'the express Word of God'. 'Express' here seems to mean both explicit and specific. In his sermon of 1550 delivered at Newcastle before the Bishop of Durham, Cuthbert Tunstall, and the Council of the North, Knox set out to demonstrate the idolatrous character of the Mass. The ground of King Saul's iniquity, he declared, had been

that he wald honour God utherwayes than wes commandit by his express word. ... For no honoring knaweth God, nor will accept, without it have the express commandement of his awn Word to be done in all poyntis.[1]

Knox can sum up the first part of his argument as follows: 'That all wirschipping, honoring, or service of God inventit be the braine of man, in the religion of God, without his own express commandement, is Idolatrie.'[2] 'The plain Word of God', 'the manifest testimony of the Scripture', and other similar phrases are pressed into service to spell out that radical application of the biblical criterion which distinguishes the Scottish Reformation from the English experience, the Lutheran, and even the Genevan.

Recent standard typology of the sixteenth-century Reformations sets magisterial over against radical as rival patterns of reform, yet in the thoroughgoing exclusiveness of his resort to the Bible, Knox seems at times more like a Restorationist radical than a mainstream Reformer of the Church catholic.[3] His longest doctrinal work by far was a defence of predestination against the criticism of an unnamed English Anabaptist, probably one Robert Cooke. At one point Knox catches the English writer citing 'the ancient Doctors' in support of his interpretation of God's hardening of Pharaoh's heart (cf. Exodus 10.20):[4]

Wonder is it [Knox comments in response], that amongst the ancient Doctors ye will seke patrocinie or defense in this mater, seing it is a statute amongst you, that ye will beleve nor admit the wordes nor authoritie of no writer in any mater of controversie, but all things you will have decided by the plaine Scripture. And truly I am not contrary to your mynd in that case, so that you understand that ye will not admitt the authoritie of man against God's plaine trueth; neither yet that you will beleve man any further, then that he proveth his sentence by God's evident Scriptures.[5]

'[T]ruly I am not contrary to your mynd in that case'; it is surely rare, if not unparalleled, to find a churchman Reformer agreeing so openly with an Anabaptist or other radical opponent in the latter's strictly exclusive stance on Scripture. Knox relished wrongfooting the English anti-predestinarian's thoughtlessness in alleging 'the ancient Doctors' in his defence.

John Knox's Bible, then, was a Bible which enjoyed unqualified authority in determining matters of religious dispute and in ordering the detailed life of the Church. It comes as something of a surprise, therefore, that he seldom cited the text of Scripture with precision. This circumstance makes it difficult, if not impossible, to ascertain which English version or versions he used before the publication of the Geneva Bible in 1560, and even to be confident that thereafter he consistently used this translation. Its provenance, its appearance in the very year of the Reformation settlement, and Knox's almost certain association with the project made it the obvious choice as the Bible of the newly-reformed Kirk and of Knox himself.

Knox's pervasive tendency not to cite 'the express Word of God' with textual precision demands illustration. While at Dieppe in early 1554 Knox composed an exposition of Psalm 6 for his mother-in-law, Mrs Elizabeth Bowes. It may have been printed the same year; the edition in the standard collection of Knox's works edited by David Laing is based on a 1556 printing.[6] Verse 1 of the Psalm is displayed at the outset in wording that agrees with available versions (e.g., Coverdale, Matthew's Bible), except that it reads 'thy hote displeasure' instead of 'thy hevy displeasure'. This latter rendering, however, was apparently known to Knox as his expository phrase twice suggests: 'I have experience how intolerabill is the hevines of thy hand. ... Remitte and take awaie thy hevie displeasure.'[7]

Knox proceeds to recommend to Mrs Bowes the reading of Psalm 88, verses 3-8 of which he introduces with 'saith he' (i.e. David) but gives in a form that diverges from any printed English version in numerous respects, by abridgement, rearrangement, and in other ways.[8] Deuteronomy 7.22 is presented as 'Moses wordes to the Israelites, saienge', but is cited, perhaps from memory, as 'He [God] will not cast them out all at ons', instead of Coverdale's 'thou [Israel] canst not consume them at one time'.[9] A free summary of part of Deuteronomy 8 then follows.[10]

As the exposition moves on, the second verse of the Psalm is set out in a form identical to Coverdale, but thereafter – Knox does not get beyond verse 6 – none of it is textually close to any English version in print. Thus verse 5 reads ('in theis words he [David] declareth'): 'For thair is no rememberance of thee in death: who laudeth thee in the pitt?', where Coverdale (1535) has: 'For in death no man remembreth the: Oh who wil geve the thankes in the hell?'[11] The only other longer scriptural citation in the second part of the treatise is taken from Job 10; what is introduced by 'whair he sayeth' comes out as a loose rendering of most of verses 3, 8-9 and 11-12.[12]

This freedom in quotation is not restricted to Knox's more private or personal writings. A similar latitude is observable in his earlier vindication of the idolatrous character of the Mass (1550). The range of Scripture adduced here is more extensive, but it appears to include no single verbatim citation from published English Bibles. Not untypical is this instance: 'Paule sayith, "The Kirk is foundit upon the fundatioun of the Prophettis and Apostillis;" whilk fundatioun, no doubt, is the Law and the Evangile.'[13] Knox's interpretation is facilitated by his reversal of the order of Apostles and Prophets. 'My scheip heir my voyce, and a stranger thai will not heir, but flie frome him' is a conflation of John 10.27 and John 5.[14] Other verses or passages variously fall closer to or more distant from, say, the Great Bible, but none coincides precisely with it or with any other in print. Some divergences are not readily explicable, such as 'Why spend ye silver for that whilk is not sure' for Isaiah 55.2 ('Esay asketh of thame'),[15] while others reflect a particular exegesis, such as this presentation of part of Acts 15.20: 'Ye sall absteane ... frome thingis offerit unto idollis, from strangillit ...'.[16]

This same work nevertheless throws valuable light on Knox's use of the Bible. In several places he cites it in Latin – apparently from the Vulgate, which would accord with the apologetic occasion of the address. Furthermore, the Vulgate is quoted exactly, for example, *Ego accepi a Domino quod et tradidi vobis* (I Corinthians 11.23). Knox then renders it into English a little paraphrastically: 'I have ressavit and learnit of the Lord that whilk I have taught you.'[17] The learning/teaching gloss is without parallel in the English versions. The use of the Vulgate (or just conceivably some other Latin version), whether from memory or in the preparation or delivery of the sermon, undoubtedly explains some of Knox's English translations. 'All that is of the veritie, heir my voyce' (John 18.37) echoes the Latin *veritas*, where all the printed versions had 'truth'.[18] Similarly in the letter to the church of Thyatira in Revelation 2, 'who that hath not the doctrine' probably recalls *doctrinam* from the Vulgate; English translators from Tyndale on gave 'learning'.[19] Knox's text of Jeremiah 7.8-10 is reasonably close to Coverdale, except for the wholly different first clause, 'Ye beleif fals wordis whilk sall not profit you', which makes sense as a rendering of the Vulgate: *vos confiditis vobis in sermonibus mendacii qui non proderunt vobis.*[20]

The last sentence of this citation of Jeremiah 7 provides another clue to Knox's handling of Scripture: 'ye say, We ar delyvered or absolved, albeit we haif done all theis abominations.' In the alternatives 'delyvered or absolved', Knox advances two variant translations of (so it seems) the Vulgate's *liberati sumus*. The twofold 'ressavit and learnit' for the single Latin verb *accepi*, noted above in I Corinthians 11.23, no doubt belongs in the same category. Elsewhere in the same sermon in adducing Isaiah 28.25, Knox gives 'ye mak a band or covenant with death', where the original has only one noun (Vulgate *foedus*).[21]

Moreover, when Knox develops a case that rests four-square on textual precision, it is based on the Latin. The so-called 'words of consecration' in the Mass ('By whome haif thai that name, I desyre to know?') are as follows: *Accipite et manducate ex hoc omnes. Hoc est enim corpus meum. Similiter et calicem.* But in which of the Gospels, protests Knox, are the words *ex hoc omnes* attached to the eating of the bread? Christ spoke them of the cup, not of the bread. Knox flows into a colourfully ironic attack on the denial of the cup to the laity: 'O Papistis! ye have maid alteration, not so mekill in wordis as in deid.'[22]

Knox is not finished. As for *Hoc est enim corpus meum*, where do they get *enim* from?[23] 'Is not this thair awn inventioun, and addit of thair awn braine?' Nothing of substance hinges on this insertion, which merely furnishes Knox with a debating point of some weight. For as they have added to Christ's words, 'so steall thai frome thame', by stopping short at *corpus meum*, without the continuation *quod pro vobis datur*, or *frangitur*:

Theis last wordis, whairin standis our haill comfort, omit thai, and mak no mentioun of thame. And what can be judgeit more bold or wickit than to alter Chrystis wordis, to add unto thame, and to diminische frome thame? Had it not bene convenient, that eftir thai had introduceit Jesus Chryst speiking, that his awn wordis had bene recytit, nothing interchangeit, addit, or diminischit.[24]

The rhetoric comports well with the Knoxian insistence on 'the express Word of God' already noted in this same sermon, and with his appeal to the Deuteronomic ban on addition to and subtraction from God's Word.[25] More than once he makes play with

Jesus' reference to the jot and tittle which must be scrupulously observed in full.[26] In similar vein the sermon treats as 'precedents' incidents in the Old Testament history which saw condign punishment meted out to those who dared to determine on their own authority how God should be honoured, without the command of his own Word.[27] Such are the trademarks of Knox's biblical usage, but do they not fit somewhat ill with his generally free or loose citation of Scripture's own text? We find a couple of instances in the sermon on the idolatry of the Mass of his imprecision in adducing even the Latin Bible. *Nulla amplius restat Oblatio* has its nearest parallel in Hebrews 10.18, *iam non oblatio*, but it may be simply Knox's own retroversion into Latin from his preceding, liberal quotation of this verse: 'Remissioun of synnis anis gotten, thair resteth na mair Sacrifice.'[28] In whichever direction the translation flows, the case illustrates both Knox's lack of concern with textual exactitude and the ease with which he moved between Latin and English. The same phenomenon of Knoxian retroversion may explain his Latin of Hebrews 9.24, *Apparet nunc in conspectu Dei pro nobis*, where the Vulgate reads *appareat ... vultui Dei* but the English versions all have 'sight'.[29]

A broadly similar picture is to be gathered from a later work of Knox's, the *Appellation* of 1558, written to the nobility and estates of Scotland in reaction to the sentence of excommunication passed on him in his absence. It was written and published in Geneva. It provides some evidence of dependence on Coverdale's version; furthermore it is pertinent to recall that Miles Coverdale was for a time an elder in the Geneva congregation in which Knox served as pastor. The *Appellation* presents I Peter 2.13-14 in a form very close to Coverdale's of 1535, but distant from William Whittingham's Genevan New Testament of 1557, which was largely incorporated into the full Geneva Bible of 1560.[30] On the other hand, an earlier part-summary, part-quotation of Jeremiah 26.11-16 displays both obvious affinities with and obvious differences from Coverdale, as well as a couple of indications that the Vulgate continued to influence Knox's memory.[31] But overall the *Appellation* shows that Knox is patently not intending to reproduce any printed text of the scriptural material he adduces. His independence is evident in Acts 25.12, 'Hast thou appealed to Cesar? Thou shalt go to Cesar.'[32] All the English printings (and the Vulgate) have the order 'To/unto Caesar/the Emperor' in the second sentence. Each order achieves its own rhetorical effect.

John Knox's *Answer to a Great Number of Blasphemous Cavillations written by an Anabaptist, and Adversarie to Gods Eternal Predestination*, published in Geneva in 1560, has been credited with 'the honour of being the first work which quotes the Genevan version' of the Bible.[33] But Knox's part in such quotation is not a straight-forward matter. The claim reported immediately above is based only on the appearance of Proverbs 30.12 on the title-page of the work.[34] The completed Geneva Bible was published in that city between 10 April and mid-May 1560, probably a month or more later than Knox's elaborate apologia for predestination.[35] Knox had completed it several months before 1560, perhaps even in 1558.[36] It had been seen through the press and the licensing procedures at Geneva by, among others, William Whittingham, the chief translator and reviser of the Geneva Bible.[37] It may well be to Whittingham, and perhaps other colleagues still in Geneva during 1559 and into 1560 (Knox left in late January or early February 1559), that the dependence on the Geneva Bible evident in Knox's treatise should be ascribed.

Some such dependence is indeed identifiable, for example, in Elihu's words in Job 34.18-21 and in the same book's account of the 'Estrich', i.e. the Geneva Bible's 'ostriche', in 39.17-20.[38] But such instances, although not infrequent, are not the rule. It is certain that Whittingham, if any role be assumed for him, did not follow a consistent policy of conforming Knox's biblical citations to the Genevan revision. As often as not we encounter the same mix of variables at work here as in the earlier works examined above. Isaiah 55.8 reads: 'My cogitations are not your cogitations, neither are your waies your wayes, saieth the Eternall' (a variant on 'Lord' frequently adopted by Knox), but the next verse is the more familiar 'my thoghtes [exell] your thoghtes'.[39] The Vulgate has *cogitationes*. The wording of Romans 5.8-10 is reasonably close to Geneva – but only marginally closer than to earlier English versions – but it begins with 'God specially commendeth his love'.[40] The English translations from Tyndale on used 'setteth out' or 'setteth forth', but again the Vulgate's verb is *commendat*.

Ephesians 1 is naturally given close attention by Knox, to interesting effect. Here is his verse 5: 'Who hathe predestinat us that he should adoptat us in children by Jesus Christe.'[41] The verbs parallel Geneva 1560: 'Who hathe predestinate us, to be adopted through Jesus Christ.'[42] However, Geneva lacks Knox's 'in children', which Knox repeats three or four times in subsequently invoking the sentence.[43] Once more the Vulgate comes up with a simple explanation: *qui praedestinavit nos in adoptionem filiorum*. Knox's preferred rendering echoes the Latin's separate words for 'adopt' and 'children'. In Ephesians 1.9 Knox presents 'the secrete of his will', where all the English versions reflect the Greek with 'mystery' and the Vulgate has *sacramentum*.[44] In the next verse 'summarily to restore' may well be Knox's own brave attempt to capture the weighty Greek verb *anakephalaiosasthai*, wholly unlike any of the English translations, which mostly use the verb 'gather'.[45] The Vulgate reads *instaurare*, which is fairly near to Knox's 'restore'.

The independence of Knox's biblical usage continues to the very end of the book, where first Romans 11.33 and 36 and then Isaiah 54.17 round off the work in texts patently not taken from the Geneva Bible.[46] The *protevangelium* in Genesis 3.14-15 bears distinctive nuances in Knox: the serpent is cursed 'amongst all the beastes of the earth', and will 'break doune' the heel of the woman's seed.[47] The Vulgate may again account for the former, with *inter omnia animantia*, but less obviously for the latter (its *insidiaberis* means 'ambush, lie in wait for').

Two more examples from the volume on predestination will introduce a fresh possibility to this enquiry into Knox's treatment of the text of Scripture. He adduces Philippians 3.7-12, partly abridged, partly paraphrased, in wording neither noticeably removed from the Genevan translation nor distinctively Genevan.[48] It begins: 'That all justice which before he looked for in the Law, was become to him as domage and doung.' 'Justice' at first sight may pick up the Vulgate's *iustitia*, but when combined with 'domage' should prompt us to consider the influence of French Bible translation on Knox's usage. This is a possibility suggested also by Knox's earlier notice of a rendering given by Sebastian Castellio.[49] Knox cited Job 36.5-6 exactly according to the Geneva Bible (see further below): 'Behold the mightie God casteth away none that is mightie and valiant of courage.' The Anabaptist had quoted it more abruptly: 'The great God casteth away no man.' Knox takes delight in pointing out that 'your master Castalio' (as Knox repeatedly refers to him throughout this work):

notwithstanding that he useth to take large libertie in translation, where anything may seeme to serve his purpose, is more circumspect and more faithfull then you be, for thus he translateth that place: 'Althogh that God be excellent, yea, excellent and strong of courage, yet is not so dissolute, that either he will keepe the wicked, or denie judgement to the poore.'

Castellio's reading of the contested construction diverges sharply from the Genevan one, but it is grist to Knox's controversial mill. Knox knew an excessively loose translation when he saw one, even though his own practice did not entail dedicated precision in his citation of Scripture.[50]

However, on investigation it is clear that Knox consulted not Castellio's French translation of 1555, *La Bible nouvellement translatée*, but his Latin Bible, which was first published complete in 1551. Although close to his French, its rendering of Job 36.5-6 contains tell-tale evidence of Knox's dependence on it: '*Quum sit Deus excellens, quum sit inquam et excellens et magnanimus, non est tam dissolutus, ut vel impios conservet, vel ius inopibus non concedat.*'[51] But if Knox did not consult Castellio's French Bible of 1555 to undermine the English critic's usage, what may be said of the possibility that a more acceptable French translation influenced his English citations? The most obvious candidate would be the French Genevan version which, based on Olivetan's 1535 Neuchâtel Bible, underwent repeated revision at the hands of the pastors of Geneva. Its renderings in some places suggest an alternative explanation to that of the influence of the Latin Vulgate advanced above.[52] To limit the consideration to the texts discussed earlier in this essay, the French '*verité*' (rather than Latin *veritas*) might stand behind Knox's 'veritie' in John 18.37, and similarly the French '*doctrine*' in Revelation 2.24. Perhaps more evidently, 'domage' and 'justice' in Knox's free version of Philippians 3.7-12 reflect French originals – and here the Vulgate can account only for 'justice'. But other instances surveyed above are not amenable to this hypothesis, and there is no alternative to an examination one by one of all the cases where Knox's wording diverges notably from the available English versions.

Another factor has to be kept in view in considering what biblical version might lie behind Knox's use of words like 'veritie' and 'cogitation' in his citations. Like both the Older Scots and the Early-Modern English of his day,[53] Knox's vocabulary comprised a Latin element which on Janton's calculations averaged around 20 per cent, but in some works counted some 50 per cent or more of his substantives.[54] The question then becomes whether his common stock of vocabulary has influenced the wording of his biblical quotations, or his familiarity with the Latin (or French) Bible the frequency of Latin-derived terms in his general usage.

Knox's extended defence of predestination on three occasions, as we have seen, quotes Job in a form that requires dependence on the Geneva Bible's text: Job 34.18-21, 36.5-6 and 39.17-20. A fourth may be added: Job 1.8.[55] The only evidence to the contrary is the Reformer's version of Job 17.4, which is close neither to the Geneva Bible (1560) nor to Coverdale (1535): 'Thou hast excluded their heart from wisedom, and therfore this mater shall not be to their praise.' The Anabaptist writer had cited the first clause only, 'Thou has withholden their hearts from understanding', which agrees with Coverdale (1535), but the latter continues, 'therfore shall they not be set up an hye', and Geneva reads very similarly.[56] Despite this exception, it is clear that Knox had access to the translation of Job that later appeared in the Geneva Bible. Whether he contributed to the work of translation must remain at best highly uncertain, but his use of the English Genevan version of Job confirms his familiarity with the translation project.

One further possibility falls to be considered. If the quotation from the Geneva Bible's Proverbs on the title-page of Knox's *Answer to a Great Number of Blasphemous Cavillations written by an Anabaptist, and Adversarie to Gods Eternal Predestination* was the choice of Knox himself and not of Whittingham or the like, did Knox avail himself especially of a larger section of the Genevan translators' Old Testament, from, say, Job to Proverbs? Proverbs 17.15 is given by Knox in wording close to Geneva,[57] but the Psalms are rarely quoted as such, and never in a form suggestive of dependence on the Genevan rendering. But other Old Testament books were known to Knox (or to his editors), as several identical or almost identical quotations in the latter part of the work on predestination demonstrate.[58] Only a new critical edition of the treatise will enable a final assessment to be made of its use of the Geneva Bible.

Among Knox's last printed works was his sermon on Isaiah 26.13-21 preached in St Giles Edinburgh on August 19, 1565. This was the sermon that so infuriated Queen Mary and her new husband Lord Darnley that Knox was inhibited from preaching for a period. It was printed the following year, probably in London, with a title-page that includes: 'I Timoth. 4. The time is come that men can not abyde the Sermon of veritie nor holsome doctrine.'[59] In the Geneva Bible II Timothy 4.3 reads, 'For the time will come, when they will not suffer wholesome doctrine.' The sermon itself expounds the Genevan version (which differs markedly from, for example, Coverdale 1535), in its original 1560 form, it seems. As Knox proceeds through the passage, he occasionally paraphrases, gives an alternative translation with a reference to the Hebrew, glosses the text (so that 'the dead' of verse 14 become 'tiraunts', as in Coverdale 1535),[60] and introduces other minor variants to cope with what he patently finds a taxing sequence of verses. As he commented on verses 14-19, 'it apeareth that the prophet observeth no order; yea, that he speaketh things directly repugning one to another.'[61] In his scriptural citations other than Isaiah 26, Knox is generally not far removed from the Geneva Bible, yet again he hardly ever reproduces it with verbatim fidelity. Nevertheless the sermon warrants the affirmation that by the mid-1560s Knox's Bible is surely the Geneva Bible.

This sermon on Isaiah 26 is the sole surviving specimen of Knox's pulpit discourses. Even this one he has faithfully reconstructed from memory, so he tells the reader in his preface, which he wrote one month to the day after the delivery of the sermon.[62] The preface also contains an important autobiographical fragment:

Wonder not, Christian Reader, that of al my studye and travayle within the Scriptures of God these twentye yeares, I have set forth nothing in exponing anye portion of Scripture, except this onely rude and indigest Sermon. ... That I did not in writ communicat my judgement upon the Scriptures, I have ever thought and yet thinke my selfe to have most juste reason. For considering my selfe rather cald of my God to instruct the ignorant, comfort the sorrowfull, confirme the weake, and rebuke the proud, by tong and livelye voyce in these most corrupt dayes, than to compose bokes for the age to come, seeing that so much is written (and that by men of most singular condition), and yet so little well observed; I decreed to containe my selfe within the bondes of that vocation, wherunto I founde my selfe especially called.

Knox proceeds to speak more specifically about this vocation of his to be a 'tong and livelye voyce', particularly as a seer, 'a trumpet, to forwarne realmes and nations, yea, certaine great personages, of translations and chaunges, when no such thinges were feared, nor yet was appearing'.[63] To students of Knox this is a familiar passage. It commonly helps them to frame him in the lineaments of an Old Testament prophet. In the context of this article, Knox's self-testimony links up with his use of the Bible surveyed above and with some other strands of evidence, enabling us to characterize his handling of the Scriptures in the round. They lead to the conclusion that Knox's Bible is essentially an oral Bible, that is, the Bible of an oral communicator, whether as preacher (like other leading Reformers he preached steadily through books of the Bible, without following this pattern alone), as prophetic herald, as debater and controversialist. He did not approach Scripture first and foremost as a writer, and hence scholars have noted that oral styles mark many of his writings. Pierre Janton comments that most of his letters are written as sermons, and that his controversial works are cast in the form of oral debates. Oral techniques persist throughout his literary production.[64]

To make the point from another angle, the argument may be advanced that Knox's Bible is not a scholar's Bible. He does not for the most part handle the Bible as a scholar, which in my judgement distances him definitively from John Calvin. Such an assertion does not impugn his intellectual capacities or his learning, but suggests rather that he does not routinely treat Scripture as a text for the trained expert – the academic, if you will – to decipher. Reformation scholars from time to time consider how far we may trace the roots of later biblical criticism to the work of Erasmus, Luther, Calvin, and others. Whether one can envisage any sixteenth-century biblical writers welcoming subsequent centuries of critical study, most certainly Knox cannot for a moment be visualized doing so. For one of the first and gravest casualties of the era of biblical criticism has been the plainness of the meaning of Scripture of which he was so powerfully persuaded.

John Knox was not a humanist by formation. He displays little of his century's biblical humanists' passionate attention to the individual words of Scripture, such as we find in Martin Bucer or Wolfgang Musculus or supremely John Calvin. The six volumes and more of his writings contain no mention of Erasmus, but more importantly they reveal very little in the way of close wrestling with biblical vocabulary, in Latin or Greek or Hebrew. He came to the learning of both biblical languages late. Of Hebrew he was still ignorant in 1550, as he admits in his vindication of the idolatry of the Mass.[65] In his defence of predestination, at the end of the 1550s, he writes at a number of points as though he knew Hebrew – and faults his Anabaptist target for not knowing it – but the references betray the judicious caution of the student none too assured in his grasp of the language.[66] In Janton's judgement this makes it unlikely that he could have been of much help in the translation of the Bible into English in Geneva.[67] On the question of his participation in this enterprise sundry modern authors comment, to varying effect, but nothing seems established. John Alexander's judgement is a salutary caution:

Anyone approaching the Geneva versions with a preconceived desire to ascribe specific portions of the translations to some one or another of the Exiles known to have been in Geneva during the years 1555 to 1560 may indeed find the task difficult, if not impossible of fulfillment.[68]

He concludes that Knox played 'in all likelihood [a] negligible' part in the project, not least because, by his own testimony, he 'seems to have thought of his responsibility to the exiles in somewhat different terms from those of a translator'.[69] Knox was in

Geneva altogether for somewhat less than two years during the period the translation was undertaken.[70] Further detailed investigation of both Knox's writings and the Geneva Bible may add to the evidence of a link between Knox and the project established in this paper.

As for translation of the Bible into Scots, the question of why the Reformation in Scotland produced no vernacular version has repeatedly been raised.[71] Blame has been heaped on Knox, from contemporary critics to the present day, for his part in the anglicization of Scottish linguistic usage. Furthermore, his handling of the Bible's text evident through many of his works makes him a most unlikely candidate for the desk of Bible translator. The suggestion has been made that other urgent employments prevented him from deploying an erudition that would have been adequate to the task.[72] Whether his erudition was equal to it remains uncertain, but he certainly lacked the mental temperament of a Bible translator.

This verdict must not be taken to imply that Knox's mind was not brim-full to overflowing with the contents of the Bible. '[I]t was his practice to read himself, every day, some chapters both of the Old and New Testament, but especially the Psalms, and the gospel history.'[73] 'Knox was as much soaked in the English Bible as ever John Bunyan was. ... [H]ow constantly his writing breathes the atmosphere of the Bible. He must have known it by heart.'[74] This deep and thorough familiarity – perhaps not solely with the Bible in English – may provide another reason why he rarely cited it according to the precise text of any one translation. He must often have quoted from memory, not from the page. More than one writer has illustrated Knox's facility in crafting sentences and paragraphs which are little more than catenae of biblical phrases and images. Here is one example, from his *Godly Letter ... to the Faithfull in London, Newcastle, and Berwick* (1554):

For the Lord hes appoyntit the day of his vengeance, befoir the whilk he sendis his trompettis and messingeris, that his elect, watcheing, and praying, with all sobrietie, may, be his mercie, eschaipe the vengeance that sall cum.[75]

Janton identifies here borrowings or echoes of Matthew 24.36, Deuteronomy 32.35, Ezekiel 33.3, Luke 21.36, Romans 13.13, and Matthew 3.7. But such a mosaic of biblical allusions and expressions is, in Knox, not a textual exercise but the utterance of a biblically saturated mind.

This mind of Knox found its most natural outlet in preaching and prophesying. The *First Book of Discipline* includes the preaching of the Word among 'utterly necessarie' exercises of the kirk, but the reading of the Scriptures among the merely profitable.[76] Although the investigation conducted in this article leaves several lines of enquiry for future researchers to pursue, its results so far should remind us how limiting a perspective it can be to view the Reformation Bible as a scholarly, literary text rather than as the flaming and searing sword of the Spirit, wielded in living combat for the souls of men and women and for the heart of the church.

POSTSCRIPT

At a conference at St Andrews in the summer of 1997 on 'John Knox and the British Reformations', Professor Patrick Collinson, Emeritus Regius Professor of Modern History at Cambridge, reported being shown 'Knox's Bible' on a visit to the State

Library of Victoria in Melbourne. No mention of it had, it seems, ever surfaced in the literature on Knox. I am grateful to Mr Brian Hubber, the Rare Books Librarian, and to Professor Ian Breward of Ormond College for preliminary information on what is a 1566 copy of the Great Bible published at Rouen (see T. H. Darlow & H. F. Moule, *Historical Catalogue of Printed Editions of the English Bible 1525-1961*, ed. by A. S. Herbert (London & New York: British & Foreign Bible Society and The American Bible Society, 1968), pp. 67-8, no. 119). It bears a purported signature of 'John Knox' (which has yet to be compared with other specimens of his signature, to be seen, e.g., in *Works*, VI, pp. xxx, 74, 126, 134, and in P. Hume Brown, *John Knox*, 2 vols (London: A. & C. Black, 1895), II, p. 248). Although the list of subsequent owners at first sight reveals no link with Knox, further investigation seems called for. What appears to be a sixteenth-century hand has divided the Psalms into morning and evening readings for each day of the month, which would concur with Knox's reported practice (see n. 73 below). And there is even printed evidence in the Bible itself that this copy may have been produced specifically for presentation to Knox. I intend to compile a short study of this Bible's supposed links with Knox.

NOTES

1 *The Works of John Knox*, ed. by David Laing, 6 vols (Edinburgh: Bannatyne Club Publications, 1846-64), III, p. 35. Here the sermon is entitled 'A Vindication of the Doctrine that the Sacrifice of the Mass is Idolatry'. For its original title see Ian Hazlett, 'A Working Bibliography of Writings by John Knox', in *Calviniana. Ideas and Influence of Jean Calvin*, ed. by Robert V. Schnucker, Sixteenth Century Essays and Studies Series: 10 (Kirksville, MO: Sixteenth Century Journal Publishers, 1988), pp. 185-93 (p. 188, no. 9).

2 *Works*, III, p. 47.

3 Cf. Richard G. Kyle, *The Mind of John Knox* (Lawrence, KS: Coronado Press, 1984), p. 44: 'Knox could be called a "radical" reformer who knew no middle way even in what Calvin called "indifferentia".' Kyle is commenting on Knox's tendency to interpret Scripture as a book of precedents or literal models.

4 *Works*, V, p. 321. For the title see Hazlett, p. 190, no. 18.

5 *Works*, V, p. 331.

6 Cf. Hazlett, p. 187, nos 2, 2a.

7 *Works*, III, p. 121.

8 *Works*, III, pp. 123-4: 'But my soule was replenished with dolour: I am as a man without strength: I am lyke unto those that are gone downe into the pitt, of whom thou hast no more mynde; lyke unto those that are cut of by thy hande: Thou hast put me in a depe dongeon: All thy wraith lyeth upon me. Why leavest thou me, O Lorde? Why hydest thou thy face so fare fro me? Thou hast removed all my frends fro me; thou hast made me odyous unto them.' By comparison, Coverdale's 1535 translation (where the Psalm is 87) renders as follows: 'For my soule is full of trouble, and my life draweth nye unto hell. I am counted as one of them that go downe unto the pytte, I am even as a man that hath no strength. Fre amonge the deed, like unto them that lye in the grave, which be out of remembraunce, and are cutt awaye from thy hande', etc. The Great Bible of 1541 has minor variations from 1535: '... I have bene even as a man that hath no strength ... them that be wounded and lye in the grave ...'.

9 *Works*, III, p. 129. Knox has assimilated the subject, God, to that of the preceding part of the verse. The Coverdale Bible of 1535 is available in a facsimile edition edited by S. L. Greenslade (Folkestone: Wm. Dawson & Sons, 1975). Coverdale's rendering of the clause is typical of the English versions.

10 *Works*, III, p. 129.

11 Ibid., p. 151. The Vulgate gives *non est in morte recordatio tui*.

12 *Works*, III, p. 145, where the marginal reference is wrong.

13 Ibid., p. 41.

14 Ibid., pp. 40-1.

15 Ibid., p. 53.

16 Ibid., p. 45.

17 Ibid., p. 42. For this and other New Testament texts, see *The New Testament Octapla. Eight English Versions of the New Testament in the Tyndale-King James Version*, ed. by Luther A. Weigle (New York: T. Nelson, [1962]), is of invaluable help in comparison. For parallels to Knox's freedom in citation, see David Norton, *A History of the Bible as Literature*, 2 vols (Cambridge: University Press, 1993), I, pp. 135-8, 225-8.

18 *Works*, III, p. 41.

19 Ibid., p. 42.

20 Ibid., p. 53.

21 Ibid.

22 Ibid., p. 50; *ex hoc omnes* means *all [eat/drink] of this*.

23 In English, *enim* becomes *for* at the beginning of the clause.

24 *Works*, III, pp. 50-1. Knox may be implying that the amputation of the text after *corpus meum* paved the way for the insertion of *enim*, to provide a smoother self-contained statement. Conversely, *Hoc est corpus meum* without insertion naturally looks forward to its completion, which the formula in the Mass has curtailed.

25 Ibid., p. 37, citing Deuteromony 4.2.

26 Ibid., pp. 41, 42.

27 Ibid., pp. 40, 42.

28 Ibid., p. 55.

29 Ibid., p. 57. In the debate with Quintin Kennedy, Abbot of Crossraguel in Ayrshire, held at Maybole in 1562, Knox rejects Kennedy's claim that, in Genesis 14.18, Melchizedek as the figure of Christ 'did offer unto God bread and wine', but fails to cite the exact words of the text in any language; see *Works*, VI, pp. 200-2.

30 For the *Appellation* see Hazlett, p. 189, no. 13. The text of I Peter 2.13-14 in *Works*, IV, p. 510, differs in only one significant detail from the published English Bibles, with *praise* instead of *laude* at the end. In this, but not in other points, it agrees with the Genevan version. On the Whittingham New Testament of 1557, see John David Alexander, 'The Genevan Version of the English Bible' (unpublished doctoral thesis, University of Oxford, 1956), pp. 37 ff.

31 *Works*, IV, pp. 472-3. In verses 11 and 12 Knox (and Geneva) has *prophesy*, like the Vulgate (Coverdale, *preach*); in verse 13, Knox has *evil* (Vulgate, *mali*; Coverdale and Geneva, *plague*), and *good and righteous* (Vulgate, *bonum et rectum*; Coverdale, *expedient and good*; Geneva, *good and right*).

32 Ibid., p. 477.

33 Alexander, p. 201; *The Geneva Bible. A Facsimile of the 1560 Edition*, ed. by Lloyd E. Berry (Madison: University of Wisconsin Press, 1969), p. 19.

34 Alexander, p. 201 (omitted by Berry); *Works*, V, p. 17.

35 Alexander, p. 67; Berry, p. 12.

36 According to Laing, *Works*, V, p. 15*, it was chiefly written at Dieppe in early 1559 (and approval for its publication was granted in Geneva to William Whittingham and John Barron in November of that year). Pierre Janton, *John Knox (ca. 1513-1572). L'homme et l'oeuvre* (Paris: G. de Bussac, 1967), p. 145, reckons that it may have been composed in 1558.

37 *Works*, V, pp. 15*-16*.

38 Ibid., pp. 98, 57.

39 Ibid., p. 46.

40 Ibid., p. 52. Cf. later in the same work Knox's rendering of Deuteronomy 30.19: 'Behold, I have laid before you this day life and death, benediction and execration' (ibid., p. 411), where the Vulgate has *benedictionem et maledictionem*. Knox substitutes another Latin equivalent for the second noun.

41 Ibid., p. 43.

42 Both Tyndale and the Great Bible read 'ordeyned us before thorow Jesus Christ to be heyres'; Coverdale (1535) reads: 'ordeyned us before, to receave us as children thorow Jesus Christ'.

43 *Works*, V, pp. 44-5.

44 Ibid., p. 43.

45 Ibid.

46 Ibid., p. 468. Acts 7.51-2 is given in wording not distinctively Genevan but then 'brast for anger' (7.54) shows Geneva's mark (ibid., p. 384). But in Revelation 7.1-2 'ascending from the uprising of the sonne' recalls almost all English versions apart from the Genevan (ibid., p. 268).

47 Ibid., p. 61.

48 Ibid., p. 121.

49 Ibid., pp. 111, 110.

50 On another occasion Knox excused himself that 'I haif usit a greater libertie than sum men will approve in a translatour or interpretour' (*Works*, IV, p. 347). He had freely embellished a colleague's English translation of an apology by French Protestant prisoners in Paris. On this work see my paper on 'John Knox and the Early Church Fathers' in *John Knox and the British Reformations*, ed. by Roger Mason, St Andrews Studies in Reformation History (Aldershot: Ashgate, 1998), pp. 99-116.

51 *Biblia Sacra ex Sebastiani Castellionis interpretatione eiusque postrema recognitione* (Basel: J. Oporinus, 1551, 1556). (It is remarkable that this translation was republished more than once in London and in Glasgow in the eighteenth century.) *La Bible nouvellement translatée* (Basel: J. Hervage, 1555) has '… il n'est pas si nonchallant de sauver aux méchants la vie, et de ne faire iustice aux soufretteux'. On Castellio's Bible translations see Hans R. Guggisberg, *Sebastian Castellio 1515-1563* (Göttingen: Vandenhoeck & Ruprecht, 1997), pp. 55-79, p. 333.

52 I have consulted *La Bible* (Geneva: Jean Girard, 1540), which is Chambers no. 82, B. T. Chambers, *Bibliography of French Bibles* (Geneva: Droz, 1983), I, pp. 109-11; and *La Bible, Qui est toute la Saincte Escripture* (Geneva: Robert Estienne, 1553), Chambers, I, pp. 195-6, no. 172.

53 Cf. *The Concise Scots Dictionary*, ed. by Mairi Robinson (Aberdeen: University Press, 1985), pp. xv-xvi. *Veritie* is entered in the *Dictionary* but not *cogitation*.

54 Janton (n. 36 above), pp. 475-6.

55 *Works*, V, p. 336. The clauses follow a different order in Coverdale 1535. Knox's version of Job 39.20 (ibid., p. 333) is that first provided by his opponent (ibid., p. 321).

56 Ibid., pp. 333, 321.

57 Ibid., p. 223. Knox has *innocent* where Geneva gives *just*.

58 Ibid., p. 236 (II Samuel 12.11-12). I Kings 20.42 is near enough to Geneva (ibid., p. 224), but with the distinctive *the Eternall*. See also ibid., pp. 286-7 (Numbers 23.8, 19-21); p. 371 (II Chronicles 28.9-10); p. 374 (Isaiah 47.6-8); p. 375 (Ezekiel 21.3-5, 11); p. 379 (Isaiah 45.1-3); p. 380 (Jeremiah 51.25-6, Daniel 2.20-21).

59 See *Works*, VI, p. 227.

60 Ibid., p. 242. Rehearsing the text shortly thereafter he changes to *the proud giants*, recalling the Vulgate's *gigantes* (p. 244).

61 Ibid., p. 242, cf. p. 243.

62 Ibid., pp. 230, 231.

63 Ibid., p. 229.

64 Janton, p. 403. One might cite as a parallel the tendency for every form of public worship to take on a 'pulpit tone'; cf. Eustace Percy, *John Knox*, 2nd edn (London: Hodder & Stoughton, 1954), p. 165; David F. Wright, '"The Commoun Buke of the Kirk": The Bible in the Scottish Reformation', in *The Bible in Scottish Life and Literature*, ed. by David F. Wright (Edinburgh: St Andrew's Press, 1988), pp. 171-4. (Copies of this book are obtainable from the present writer.)

65 *Works*, III, p. 47.

66 *Works*, V, pp. 98, 241-2, 283, 295. Twice he speaks of those who have only 'a mean knowledge' of Hebrew (pp. 242, 283).

67 Janton, pp. 128-9.

68 Alexander (n. 30 above), p. 12; cf. pp. 13 ff., for a review of attempts to identify the team.

69 Ibid., pp. 32-3. Janton, p. 434, thinks it improbable that Knox collaborated in the translation of the Geneva Bible because he seemed comfortable only in translating from Latin.

70 He was in Geneva from September 1556 to September 1557, and *c.* March 1558 to early 1559.

71 See the review in Wright, pp. 155-78.

72 John Eadie, *The English Bible*, 2 vols (London: Macmillan, 1876), II, pp. 39-41.

73 From the account of Knox's last days written probably by James Lawson, *Works*, VI, p. 654. Knox's assistant and secretary in his last years, Richard Bannatyne, recorded that every day Knox read 'certaine psalmes, quhilk psalmes he passed through everie moneth once' (*Works*, VI, p. 634; see ibid., p. 524 for other printings, and *The Last Days of John Knox, by … Richard Bannatyne*, ed. by D. Hay Fleming, Knox Club Publications: 35 (Edinburgh: Knox Club, 1913), 10). Thomas McCrie's *Life of John Knox*, 5th edn (Edinburgh: W. Blackwood, 1831), II, 219, transmitted Bannatyne's report (without a precise reference) with no ambiguity ('the Psalms of David, the whole of which he perused regularly once a-month'), and more recent writers have retailed McCrie, e.g. George Johnston, 'Scripture in the Scottish Reformation', *Canadian Journal of Theology* 9 (1963), 40-9 (p. 46), and Kyle (n. 3 above), p. 42.

74 Johnston, p. 46, p. 47.

75 *Works*, III, p. 168, cited by Janton, pp. 482-3.

76 *The First Book of Discipline*, ed. by James K. Cameron (Edinburgh: St. Andrew Press, 1972), p. 180.

THE VULGATE AS REFORMATION BIBLE
THE SONNET SEQUENCE OF ANNE LOCK

Susan M. Felch

> Have mercy, God, for thy great mercies sake.
> O God: my God, unto my shame I say,
> Beynge fled from thee, so as I dred to take
> Thy name in wretched mouth, and feare to pray
> Or aske the mercy that I have abusde.
> But, God of mercy, let me come to thee:
> Not for justice, that justly am accusde:
> Which selfe word Justice so amaseth me,
> That scarce I dare thy mercy sound againe.
> But mercie, Lord, yet suffer me to crave.
> Mercie is thine: Let me not crye in vaine,
> Thy great mercie for my great fault to have.
> Have mercie, God, pitie my penitence
> With greater mercie than my great offence.

THESE are the opening lines of a twenty-one sonnet paraphrase of Psalm 51, *A Meditation of a penitent sinner ... upon the 51. Psalme*, published in 1560 by the English Reformation printer John Day.[1] The poems are significant in a number of ways: together with five prefatory sonnets they constitute the earliest known sonnet sequence in English; they probably were written by Anne Vaughan Lock (who lived from *c.* 1534 to *c.* 1590), a merchant-class woman with impeccable Protestant credentials;[2] and they are based on the Vulgate translation of the Psalms. Of these three statements, the last may be the most startling. We are accustomed to thinking of the English Reformers as people dedicated to the vernacular Bible and opposed to the Latin Vulgate as an inherently corrupt and 'papist' text. Indeed, if asked to find a synonym for 'The Reformation Bible', the immediate response might well be 'The Vernacular Bible'.

Yet Anne Lock, a true woman of the Reformation by birth and by choice, favoured the Vulgate rather than one of the many English translations that were readily available. Her preference for the traditional Latin text gives us cause to rethink the role of the Vulgate in the life of the sixteenth-century English church. There are three claims, then, that this essay will attempt to substantiate: first, Anne Lock is a writer with impeccable Protestant credentials; second, this thoroughly Reformed writer appears to have favoured the Latin Bible; and third, her positive regard for the Vulgate is not unique among the English Reformers.

Lock was born into a family of first-generation Protestants.[3] Her father, Stephen Vaughan, a crown financial agent for Henry VIII on the Continent, wrote letters in support of a number of prominent Reformers who were later executed for their faith, including William Tyndale, Robert Barnes, and Hugh Latimer.[4] Her mother, Margaret Gwynnethe, served as silkwoman to both Anne Boleyn and Catherine Parr, queens known for their reforming sympathies. Margaret Gwynnethe may well have known such Reformation luminaries as Anne Askew and Katherine Brandon Bertie, themselves intimates of Queen Catherine.

Lock's education, following the death of her mother in 1544, was entrusted to a Mr Cob who was brought up on charges by the Privy Council for translating 'a certeyne postilla [commentary] upon the Gospelles' filled with erroneous opinions.[5] Although Stephen Vaughan thought highly of his children's tutor, he reluctantly dismissed him after Cob was summoned again to appear before the authorities. Lock and her siblings then came under the care of their new stepmother, Margery Brinkelow, a family friend and the widow of Henry Brinkelow who had written a pair of polemical Protestant pamphlets comparing Londoners with the ungodly citizens of Jerusalem and inciting the godly remnant to disobey unrighteous laws.[6]

It is clear that Lock spent her childhood surrounded by adults who were committed to the Protestant cause, and she established her own household along similar lines. In her late teens, she married Henry Lock, whose family closely mirrored her own – financially, religiously, and politically. According to the recollections of Henry's sister, Rose Lock Hickman Throckmorton, the Lock family bought and read Protestant books during the 1530s when they were being smuggled illicitly into England from the Continent.[7]

Shortly after their marriage, Anne and Henry Lock, along with Rose Hickman, hosted the Scottish Reformer John Knox while he was in London as a court preacher to Edward VI. The next year, they sheltered him from Mary Tudor's wrath when he became *persona non grata*. After his escape to the Continent, Knox began a correspondence with Anne Lock that extended over six years.[8] At his urging, she left London in 1557 and travelled to Geneva where she remained for nearly two years. When she returned to London, John Day published her English translation of four sermons by John Calvin, dedicated to Katherine Brandon Bertie the dowager Duchess of Suffolk, to which were appended her poetic paraphrase of Psalm 51 with an accompanying prose translation (1560).[9]

In England, Lock continued her activities on behalf of reformed Protestantism. She served as an intermediary for Knox and pressed the cause of the Scottish Reformation in the English court. Her friends among the increasingly nonconformist Protestants included the well-connected Cooke sisters. The eldest sister, Mildred, was married to William Cecil, later Lord Burghley and Queen Elizabeth's Lord Treasurer. Like Lock, Mildred Cecil supported the Scottish Reformation and carried on an extensive correspondence with several of its leaders.[10] Lock's son, Henry, probably received part of his education at the Cecil home along with Peregrine Bertie, son of the Duchess to whom Lock had dedicated her 1560 book. The youngest surviving Cooke sister, Katherine, married to the Marian exile and diplomat Sir Henry Killigrew, was a close friend of Lock's second husband, the Puritan preacher and Greek scholar Edward Dering, whom Anne married a year after Henry Lock's death.

The Vulgate as Reformation Bible

After Dering himself died in 1576, Lock married Richard Prowse of Exeter, a man of considerable prominence and a dedicated Puritan partisan who served his city at various times as bailiff, sheriff, alderman, Member of Parliament, and mayor.[11] In 1590, when she was nearly sixty years old, Anne Lock Prowse published a second book, dedicated to Anne Russell Dudley, the Countess of Warwick. The entire volume, a translation of Jean Taffin's *Of the Markes of the Children of God*, introduced by a dedicatory epistle and concluded by a poem on the benefits of suffering, was intended to comfort the afflicted Puritan nonconformists in their ongoing struggle against the established Elizabethan church.[12]

Although this brief account of her life omits much of real interest, the point has been made: Anne Vaughan Lock was a woman who by birthright and by choice whole-heartedly embraced the cause of reforming the English nation and church. However, despite this lifelong commitment to Protestantism, it appears that Lock preferred the Vulgate to any of the available English translations. Thus the second claim of this essay is that, in Lock, we have an example of a thoroughly Protestant writer who chose to use the Latin Bible rather than a vernacular version.

Lock certainly knew Latin well, although only one small sample survives to demonstrate her competence in the language: a four-line Latin poem, written in elegiac metre, included in a 1572 manuscript dedicated to the Earl of Leicester, Robert Dudley, and presented to Queen Elizabeth.[13] The centre-piece of the manuscript, an encyclopedia entitled *Giardino cosmografico coltivato*, was written in Italian by Doctor Bartholo Sylva, an émigré from Turin. Lock's dedicatory poem elegantly puns on Sylva's name, comparing the doctor's cultivated mind to a sylvan grove.

Not only was Lock competent in Latin, but she actually preferred the Vulgate to the available English translations. Although she does not state this preference directly, an analysis of the lexical and grammatical choices in her own works shows her dependence on the Latin text.

A particularly striking example of Lock's reliance on the Vulgate can be seen in the dedicatory epistle to the Duchess of Suffolk, with which her 1560 volume begins. The epistle describes the sorry state of a diseased soul and contrasts the true medicine of God's word, preached by the Protestants, with the false medicine of the Roman Catholic church. In the course of her argument, Lock alludes to the parable of the rich man and Lazarus, recorded in Luke 16.19-31, and accuses Catholic priests of sending their converts to Hell: 'they which taught him to trust of salvation by mans devises have set his burnyng hert in that place of flames, where th'everlasting Chaos suffreth no droppe of Godes mercye to descende' (fol. A5[r]).

The key word here is *Chaos*. In the Vulgate, the unbridgeable breach between heaven and hell that prevents the righteous Lazarus from offering a drop of water to the tormented rich man is translated *chaos magnum* from the Greek *mega chasma*. Lock transliterates the Latin *chaos*, substituting 'everlasting' for 'great'. Lock's dependence on the Latin text is highlighted by the fact that none of the vernacular Bible translations follow the Vulgate's rendition of *mega chasma*. Wyclif translates the term 'derke place', Tyndale (and following him Coverdale and the Great Bible) 'greate space', and the Genevan scholars 'great gulfe', adding 'swallowing pit' as a marginal reading. Only by reference to the Vulgate would Lock know to use *chaos* to describe the gulf between Heaven and Hell. Furthermore, Lock uses the term *chaos* again in her poetic paraphrase of Psalm 51, which concludes the 1560 volume. In the fourth psalm sonnet, the *chaos* that separates Heaven from Hell is extended beyond its context in the Lazarus parable, and is personalized to the narrator. The persona of the sonnet cries out to God: 'My Chaos and my heape of sinne doth lie, / Betwene me and thy mercies shining light' (Psalm Sonnet 4, lines 11-12, fol. Aa4ᵛ).

Lock's use of the Vulgate in the dedicatory epistle is particularly significant because, as a whole, the letter is so determinedly anti-Catholic. Throughout, Lock derides Roman Catholic doctrines and equates the 'papists' with infidels and philosophers. It is Roman Catholic teachers who are the false doctors, promising to heal spiritual diseases while consigning their patients to further distress and even death. Yet it is apparent that Lock feels no disjunction between her own use of the Latin Bible and her polemic against the Roman church.

This nod toward the Vulgate in the dedicatory epistle is thoroughly confirmed in the sonnet sequence on Psalm 51 that concludes the 1560 volume. Following the five prefatory sonnets, the psalm itself is paraphrased in twenty-one sonnets that roughly correspond to the nineteen verse divisions in the text (two sonnets each are devoted to verses one and four). Accompanying each of the psalm paraphrase sonnets is a prose translation of the corresponding verse printed in the margin. This prose version is clearly a unique translation of the Vulgate, a translation that is not dependent on the previous English versions. In the following analysis, I have compared Lock's marginal prose translation with four Latin and ten English versions that antedate her work. A collation of Psalm 51, including all fifteen renditions, is printed as appendix A to this article. References to the various translations are keyed to this parallel version. Each verse, or partial verse, accompanies a single poem from the sonnet sequence.

There are two versions of the Vulgate Psalter, both originating with St Jerome.[14] Jerome's translation from the Hebrew text, the 'Hebrew' Psalter [designated 'b' in the parallel version], predominates in manuscripts up to the ninth century. In the eighth century, however, the liturgical reformer Alcuin replaced the Hebrew Psalter with the text commonly used in Gaul, the so-called 'Gallican' Psalter. This Gallican Psalter [a], St Jerome's earlier revision of the Old Latin Psalter on the basis of the Hexapla, became the accepted text in the manuscripts after the ninth century and was the Vulgate version with which the English Church was most familiar. It is this Gallican version of the Vulgate Psalter from which Lock translates Psalm 51. In addition to these Vulgate Psalters, two sixteenth-century Latin translations, both of which followed the Masoretic Hebrew text of the Old Testament, were particularly important for the English church: Sante Pagnini's 1528 version [c], which Coverdale consulted for his 1535 Bible; and Sebastian Münster's 1534-5 parallel Hebrew-Latin translation [d], to which Coverdale had recourse in his preparation of the Great Bible. As a well-educated woman and a Protestant partisan, Lock may have had access not only to the Gallican Psalter which she used, but to these other Latin translations as well.

She certainly would have had access to several English versions of the Psalms. The most important sixteenth-century English prose translations of the Psalms came from four hands: George Joye, William Marshall, Miles Coverdale, and the Genevan translators. To Joye goes the honour of the earliest translation of psalm selections in his 1529 Primer, no longer extant. This was followed by his translation of Martin Bucer's Latin Psalter, *The psalter of David in Englishe tr. aftir the texte of ffeline* [2] (1530).[15] In 1534

Joye published *Davids psalter, diligently and faithfully tr. by G. Joye with breif arguments* [3], a new translation based on Ulrich Zwingli's *Enchiridion Psalmorum* of 1532.[16]

The same year that Joye completed his translation of the Zwingli Psalter, William Marshall translated Girolamo Savonarola's exposition of Psalm 51: *An exposition after the maner of a contemplacyon upon the .li. psalme, called Miserere mei Deus* [4]. This proved to be an enormously popular work; it was reprinted at least a dozen times in the next eight years, was often bound with primers and other devotional works, and formed the basis for the translation used in the first authorized Primer of 1545 [9].

Miles Coverdale translated four separate prose versions of the Psalter: a 1535 translation of Johannes Campensis's Latin Psalter, *A paraphrasis, upon all the psalmes of David* [5]; the 1535 Coverdale Bible [6];[17] the Great Bible of 1539 [7]; and the 1540 *The psalter or boke of psalmes both in Latyn and Englyshe, with a kalendar, and a table* [8].[18]

Two Genevan Psalters are of particular interest for a study of Lock's sources, given her personal involvement with the English exile community in that city: *The psalmes of David tr. accordyng to th'Ebrue, wyth annotacions moste profitable* [10], the first Genevan Psalter published in 1557, which retains much of the language of the Great Bible with some revisions from the Hebrew that are carried over into the 1560 Geneva Bible; and the complete Geneva Bible itself, published in 1560. Although the latter was printed after Lock had returned to London, the translation of the Psalter was issued in 1559 [11] and may have been available to Lock even earlier in manuscript form.[19]

These ten English translations, from Joye's 1530 version of Bucer's Psalter to the 1560 Geneva Bible, were all available to sixteenth-century readers; they were reprinted in various editions or served as sources for subsequent translations. Lock, however, chose not to utilize any of these versions for her prose translation of Psalm 51 which accompanies the sonnet paraphrase; instead she turned to the Vulgate, creating a new translation from the Gallican Psalter.

Lock's rendition of the opening statement from Psalm 51 demonstrates her reliance on the Vulgate:

> [1] Have mercie upon me (o God) after thy great merci
> [a] *Miserere mei Deus secundum magnam: misericordiam tuam*
> [b] *Miserere mei Deus secundum misericordiam tuam*
> [c] *Miserere mei deus secundum pietatem tuam,*
> [d] *Miserere mei deus secundum pietatem tuam:*
> [2] Have mercy upon me (god) for thy jentlenes sake:
> [3] Have mercy upon me oh god / accordinge unto thy goodnes:
> [4] Have mercy upon me (oh god) accordynge to thy greate mercye.
> [5] Have mercye upon me o God for thy naturall kyndnesse sake,
> [6] Have mercy upon me (o God) after thy goodnes,
> [7] Have mercy upon me (O God) after thy (greate) goodnes:
> [8] Have mercy on me o god, accordyng to thy great mercy
> [9] Have mercy upon me, O God, according to thy great mercy.
> [10] Have mercie upon me (O God) after thy great goodnesse:
> [11] Have mercie upon me, ô God, according to thy loving kindenes:

As can be seen from this example, while Lock's version echoes various English translations, it is not identical to any single version; on the other hand, its indebtedness to the Gallican Psalter is patently demonstrable. Lock's 'Have mercie upon me (o God) after thy great merci' matches the repetition of 'mercy' in the Gallican text: *Miserere* and *misericordiam*. Furthermore, she picks up the adjective 'great' (*magnam*) from the Gallican Psalter which is omitted in the Hebrew, Pagnini, and Münster Psalters. The closest English parallels – the translations found in Marshall [4], Coverdale's diglot Psalter [8], and the King's Primer [9] – also begin with 'mercy' and conclude with 'great mercy' but translate *secundum* as 'according' while Lock renders it 'after'. Thus Lock's translation remains unique among the English translations that predate 1560.[20]

Lock's careful attention to the Latin, which results in a singular translation, can be demonstrated in numerous other verses. In verse 2 the Latin *amplius* is rendered carefully as 'yet more', a translation also used in Coverdale's diglot Psalter [8]; Lock, however, does not replicate Coverdale, again suggesting her own translation from the Latin. Similarly in verse 3, Lock chooses a unique word, 'wickednes' to translate *iniquitatem*, the closest parallel being Coverdale's paraphrase [5] 'wyckednesses'. In that same verse she renders *contra me* as 'before me' rather than using the preferred earlier translation 'before mine eyes'. Although 'before me' also appears in the Coverdale [6], Great [7], and Geneva [11] Bibles as well as the Geneva Psalter [10], the choice of 'wickednes' rather than 'fautes', 'rebellions', or 'iniquities', distinguishes Lock's translation from these predecessors.

In verse 4a Lock does not repeat the *tibi* ('Against thee, against thee') favoured by many translators but not included in the Gallican Psalter. The second part of verse 4 also illustrates Lock's independence from her English predecessors. The final three words, *vincas cum iudicaris*, pose a difficulty for translators, some of whom make God the subject who judges and others the object who is judged. Lock opts for the latter, translating the Latin closely as 'maiest over come when thou art judged'. This choice echoes the translations found in Coverdale's Bible [6] and diglot Psalter [8], as well as the King's Primer [9]; but her translation of the earlier part of the verse, 'That thou mightest be founde just in thy sayinges', finds no exact parallel in any existing translation.

In verse 5, *shapen* may echo the translation choice of the Great Bible [7], but Lock subtly alters the lexical and grammatical contour of the verse: 'For loe, I was shapen in wickednes, and in sinne my mother conceived me' in contrast to the Great Bible's 'Beholde, I was shapen in wickednesse, and in synne hath my mother conceaved me'. Similarly, in verse 16 Lock's three most significant lexical choices – 'desired' (*voluisses*), 'delytest' (*delectaberis*), and 'burnt offringes' (*holocaustis*) – also appear in the Great Bible [7], the King's Primer [9], and the Genevan translations [10 and 11], but the grammatical shape of her sentence is unique: 'If thou haddest desired sacrifice, I wold have geven thou delytest not in burnt offringes.'

This first set of examples, as noted above, shows that Lock's renderings consistently employ a unique combination of lexical choices and grammatical structures that are closely dependent on the Gallican Psalter.

In the second set of examples that follow, this same pattern holds true, but in addition the vocabulary of the prose version is reinforced in the accompanying sonnets. While it is impossible to say which came first – the prose translation or the poetic paraphrase – the generous semantic repetition suggests that poetic diction may have influenced Lock's particular lexical choices. But that poetic diction is in turn influenced by the Vulgate's translation of Psalm 51. In other words, the reflection of the Vulgate in the sonnets suggests Lock's deep familiarity with, and even love for, the cadences of the Gallican Psalter; it was, we might say, bred in her bones and in her poetic imagination.

Verse 6 provides a paradigmatic case of the Vulgate's influence on the sonnets as well as the prose translation. The accompanying sonnet reads as follows:

> Thou lovest simple sooth, not hidden face
> With trutheles visour of deceiving showe.
> Lo simplie, Lord, I do confesse my case,
> And simplie crave thy mercy in my woe.
> This secrete wisedom hast thou graunted me,
> To se my sinnes, and whence my sinnes do growe:
> This hidden knowledge have I learnd of thee,
> To fele my sinnes, and howe my sinnes do flowe
> With such excesse, that with unfained hert,
> Dreding to drowne, my Lorde, lo howe I flee,
> Simply with teares bewailyng my desert,
> Releved simply by thy hand to be.
> Thou lovest truth, thou taughtest me the same.
> Helpe, Lord of truth, for glory of thy name.   (Psalm Sonnet 8, fol. Aa5^r)

In this sonnet the 'hidden knowledge' and 'secrete wisedom' of God (lines 7, 5) reveal to the narrator her own overwhelming sins. These words reflect Lock's unique translation of the Gallican Psalter's *incerta et occulta sapientiae*, 'the hidden and secrete thinges of thy wisedome'. In the imagery of the sonnet, the true 'hidden knowledge' of God contrasts sharply with the false 'hidden face' whose 'trutheles visour of deceiving showe' masks the sinner who is attempting to hide from the all-seeing eye of a sovereign Lord (lines 1, 2). Furthermore, the 'trutheles visour' of the hypocritical sinner stands in absolute contrast to the God who not only 'lovest truth' but is indeed the 'Lord of truth' (lines 13, 14). The relatively straightforward prose translation of the Vulgate is thus refracted into the expanded poetic imagery of the sonnets.

In verse 6, Lock's dependence on the Gallican Psalter is also shown in the way she divides 'truth' from 'hidden and secrete things': 'But lo, thou haste loved trueth' (*ecce enim veritatem dilexisti*) is delineated from 'the hidden and secrete thinges of thy wisedome thou haste opened unto me' (*incerta et occulta tuae sapientiae manifestasti mihi*). The Great Bible [7], and the two Geneva translations [10 and 11], follow Pagnini [c], Münster [d], and the Hebrew text in translating 'hidden' as 'inward' and linking it with the first clause, 'But lo, thou requirest treuth in the inward partes', while associating 'secret' with wisdom: 'and shalt make me to understonde wisdome secretly'. Lock, however, prefers the Vulgate reading.

Lock's reliance on the Gallican Psalter can also be seen in the subsequent sonnets. In verse 7, Lock retains the Vulgate's *asparges* as 'sprinkle' rather than following Münster's *expiabis* [d] or the later English versions, which translate the word as 'purge'. Lock's lexical choice is reinforced in the accompanying sonnet where 'besprinkle' or 'sprinkle' is used three times:

> With swete Hysope besprinkle thou my sprite:
> Not such hysope, nor so besprinkle me,
> As law unperfect shade of perfect lyght
> Did use as an apointed signe to be
> Foreshewing figure of thy grace behight.
> With death and bloodshed of thine only sonne,
> The swete hysope, cleanse me defyled wyght.
> Sprinkle my soule.   (Psalm Sonnet 9.1, fols Aa5ʳ-ᵛ)

In verse 9, Lock parallels her translations of *averte* and *dele*: 'Turne *away* thy face from my sinnes, and do *away* all my misdedes', a unique and poetic rendering. While these particular locutions are not repeated in the accompanying sonnet, the poem does reflect on the consequences of God's turning away from a sinner. In a sequence of puns on the poet's name, the narrator pleads with God not to turn away his face from her, even as she acknowledges that he cannot look on her sin: 'Loke on me, Lord'; 'thou canst not loke on me'; 'Loke on me, Lord: but loke not on my sinne'; 'Looke not how I / Am foule by sinne' (Psalm Sonnet 11. 1, 4, 6, 11-12, fols Aa5ᵛ-Aa6ʳ). Similarly, Lock's decision to translate *vitulos* in verse 19 as 'young bullocks', may be a pun on her own name.[21]

One of Lock's most 'deviant' translations occurs in verse 10, where she retains the physical impact of the Latin *visceribus*: 'Create a cleane hart within me, O God: and renew a stedfast spirit within my *bowels*'.[22] She echoes this translation in the parallel sonnet as well:

> Renew, O Lord, in me a constant sprite,
> That stayde with mercy may my soule susteine,
> A sprite so setled and so firmely pight
> Within my bowells, that it never move,
> But still uphold thassurance of thy love.   (Psalm Sonnet 12.10, fol. Aa6ʳ)

Although she does not repeat 'stedfast' in the sonnet, her synonyms – 'constant', 'setled', 'firmely pight' – echo this choice of vocabulary more closely than do the alternative English translations 'upright', 'right', or 'perfect'.

In verse 11, she again retains a close tie to the Vulgate, translating *ne proicias me a facie tua* as 'Cast me not away from thy face'. In the accompanying sonnet she uses 'face' six times, four times within as many lines:

> Dryve me not from thy face in my distresse,
> Thy face of mercie and of swete relefe,
> The face that fedes angels with onely sight,
> The face of comfort in extremest grefe.   (Psalm Sonnet 13.4, fol. Aa6ʳ)

In verse 13, against every other English translation and the likeliest transliteration of the Latin text, Lock translates *convertentur* as 'turned' rather than 'converted', possibly to highlight the word 'return' in the sonnet: 'The wicked I wyll teache thyne only way [...] To rue theyr errour and returne to thee' (Psalm Sonnet 15.5, 8, fol. Aa6ᵛ). Likewise, the final clause of verse 14 is unique to Lock; while the other English translations use 'righteousness' or a similar word, Lock retains a transliteration of the Latin *iustitiam*: 'my tong shall joyfullye talke of thy *justice*'. As with the choice of 'return' in verse 13, the word 'justice' resounds in the accompanying sonnet: 'My voice shall sounde thy justice, and thy waies, / Thy waies to justifie thy sinfull wight' (Psalm Sonnet 16.11, fol. Aa7ʳ).[23]

In verse 15 Lock's 'Lord, open thou my lippes', her translation of *Domine labia mea aperies*, is replicated in the seventh line of the accompanying sonnet: 'Lord open thou my lippes to shewe my case' (Psalm Sonnet 17, fol. Aa7ʳ). In verse 17, Lock's decision to translate *spiritus contribulatus* as 'trobled spirit', a lexical choice first found in Coverdale's Bible [6], is amply echoed in the accompanying sonnet: 'To God a trobled sprite is pleasing hoste. / My trobled sprite doth drede like him to be'; and 'I offre up my trobled sprite: alas, / My trobled sprite refuse not in thy wrathe' (Psalm Sonnet 19.3-4, 11-12, fol. Aa7ᵛ). In the same verse, Lock's translation of *contritum et humiliatum* as 'broken and humbled' is unusual but not unique, appearing also in Joye's translation of Zwingli's Psalter [3]; it too is repeated in the sonnet: 'Such offring likes thee, ne wilt thou despise / The broken humbled hart in angry wise' (Psalm Sonnet 19.13, fol. Aa7ᵛ). The final word of verse 17, *spernet* is translated by Lock and every other English translator as 'despise'; while this might seem counter-intuitive to Lock's predilection for close adherence to the Vulgate, the sixteenth-century Gallican Psalters substituted *despicies* for *spernet*; thus, while it might appear that Lock was imitating her fellow translators, she was also simply transliterating the Latin text.

Finally, to conclude this second section of examples, Lock's close translation of the Gallican Psalter's prepositional phrase in verse 18 is echoed in the second line of the accompanying sonnet. *In bona voluntate tua* is translated 'in thy good will' in the prose version and then becomes in the sonnet this prayer for grace:

> Shew mercie, Lord, not unto me alone:
> But stretch thy favor and thy pleased will,
> To sprede thy bountie and thy grace upon
> Sion, for Sion is thy holly hyll: (Psalm Sonnet 20.1, fol. Aa7ᵛ)

Only the Coverdale diglot Psalter [8] also includes the phrase 'in thy good wyll'.

As is demonstrated by the textual analysis above, Lock's prose translation of Psalm 51 closely adheres to the Vulgate text and is also unique among the English translations that preceded it. Furthermore, the influence of the Gallican Psalter is extended into the sonnets, which pick up the lexical and grammatical patterns of the prose translation.

There are only two instances where Lock appears to depart from her close dependence on the Gallican Psalter. In each case, it may be possible that echoes of familiar English phrases affect Lock's choice of vocabulary. In verse 8, where the Gallican *ossa humiliata* suggests a translation similar to that used in Coverdale's diglot Psalter [8] 'the bones which are brought lowe', Lock prefers the stronger sense of the Hebrew Psalter's [b] *confregisti* translating the clause 'the bones which thou hast broken', in keeping with a number of previous English translations. In this case, the prose translation of broken bones is not picked up by the sonnet, which uses instead the expression 'broosed bones', a locution favored by Marshall [4] and the King's Primer [9] (Psalm Sonnet 10.12, fol. Aa5ᵛ).

The translations of verse 12 vary widely. Lock rejects the earlier 'saving health' for 'saving help' to translate *salutaris*; but, more interestingly, she departs from the Latin text *spiritu principali* in choosing the simple 'free spirit' favored by the Coverdale [6], Great [7], and Genevan [10 and 11] translations rather than the more literal 'principal spirit' or the earlier 'chief governing free spirit' or 'free benign spirit'. This decision suggests that, while Lock primarily was making her own translation from the Latin, her ear may occasionally have been influenced by the cadences of earlier English translations.

To summarize, it is clear from this textual study of Lock's translation not only that it is unique among the English versions, but also that it is based on the Gallican Psalter. Verbal echoes of earlier English translations indicate not promiscuous borrowing from various sources but rather multiple translations from a common source. What is particularly striking, given Lock's involvement in the Genevan exile community, is that she does not follow the translations of either the 1557 Geneva Psalter or the 1560 Geneva Bible, both of which depend on the Hebrew text, when these deviate from the Vulgate.[24]

Lock's preference for the Latin text, while it may strike some modern scholars as disjunctive with her Protestant beliefs, apparently went unremarked in the sixteenth century. Thus the third claim of this essay is that Lock's positive regard for the Vulgate was not unique among the English Reformers, nor should it be considered paradoxical, heterodox, or ironic. It was not Latin in general, or even the Vulgate in particular, to which the English Reformers objected, but rather the inaccessibility of the Latin Bible to the common people. Vernacular translations were seen not as an end in themselves, but as a means to attaining the goal of biblical literacy.

Coverdale himself consulted the Vulgate in the translation of the 1535 Bible and again in the revision of the Great Bible, where he printed the material found in the Latin, but not in the Hebrew or Greek texts, in smaller type and within brackets. J. F. Mozley dismissively comments that 'This was of course done to placate the conservatives, who resented any omission from the familiar text, but it meant a certain decline in the scholarship of the book, since the interpolations of the Vulgate are usually of small authority'.[25] Such a view, and it is commonly held, draws too sharp a line between the Vulgate and Coverdale's other sources, even as it anachronistically applies a twentieth-century reverence for 'scholarship' to the sixteenth-century Reformers.

In his diglot New Testament of 1538, Coverdale used the 'common texte' for the Latin version partly to counter the charges that his English translation perverted the Scripture and condemned the Vulgate but also because, as he argued in the dedication, he believed God's word to have authority in any language: 'The scripture and worde of God is truly to every Christen man of lyke worthynesse and authorite, in what language so ever the holy goost speaketh it.'[26] While political realities may have influenced Coverdale, as Mozley implies, Lock's use of the Vulgate warns against a purely accommodationist interpretation. There seems to be no compelling reason for her to use the Gallican Psalter other than personal choice.

That the Vulgate could be used honourably by Protestants, at least during the first half of the century, is also suggested by the prefaces to the English Bibles and Primers themselves. These dedicatory letters, prologues, and epistles to the readers make clear that the purpose of vernacular translations is to ensure that the common people who do not know Latin, and the uneducated clergy who know it poorly, have access to the Word of God; at the same time, these prefaces do not claim authority for any particular translation. In other words, the vernaculars are a means to an end, not the end itself. The goal is the universal reading (and obeying) of the Scriptures; the means are a variety of translations in many different languages. Coverdale's epistle to the reader in the 1535 Bible explicitly pays tribute to other versions, including the Vulgate:

I toke the more upon me to set forth this speciall translacyon, not as a checker, not as a reprover, or despyser of other mens translacyons (for among many as yet I have founde none without occasyon of great thankesgevynge unto god) but lowly and faythfully have I folowed myne interpreters, and that under correccyon.[27]

Even more pointedly, the King's Primer (1545) notes that vernacular translations are necessary for the 'youthe of our realmes' because if they are taught 'al in latin and not in englysshe' they will not be 'brought up in the knowlege of their faith, duti and obedience wher in no christen person ought to be ignoraunt'.[28] Yet having authorized instruction in English, primarily as an elementary exercise preliminary to achieving competence in Latin, the injunction concludes by stating that students 'at their libertie' may use the Primer either in Latin or in English, the emphasis falling on its use rather than its use in a particular language.

When the translators criticize the use of Latin, they usually take aim against those who prefer the scholastic commentaries to the actual reading of the Scriptures themselves.[29] For instance, Tyndale is dismissively contemptuous of those whose knowledge of the Bible is limited to what they find in their 'duns' (i.e. the works of Duns Scotus).[30] Similarly, Coverdale, defending the use of various translations, notes that

there commeth more knowlege and understondinge of the scripture by theyr sondrie translacyons, then by all the gloses of oure sophisticall doctours. For that one interpreteth somthynge obscurely in one place, the same translateth another (or els he him selfe) more manifestly by a more playne vocable of the same meanyng in another place.[31]

The very profusion of translations also points to the use of the vernaculars as a means rather than an end. Coverdale answers the objection that many translations may cause division in the church by citing the examples of Greek and Latin Fathers who did not limit themselves to a single translation:

Amonge the Grekes had not Origen a specyall translacyon? Had not Vulgarius one peculyar, and lykewyse Chrysostom? Besyde the seventye interpreters, is there not the translacyon of Aquila, of Theodotio, of Symachus, and of sondrye other? Agayne amonge the Latyn men, thou findest that every one allmost used a specyall and sondrye translacyon: for in so moch as every bysshoppe had the knowlege of the tongues, he gave his diligence to have the Byble of his awne translacion. The doctours, as Hireneus, Cyprianus, Tertullian, S. Jherome, S. Augustine, Hylarius and S. Ambrose upon dyverse places of the scripture, reade not the texte all alyke.[32]

Similarly, the Genevan translators defended the propriety and benefit of multiple translations, noting in their own use of marginal variants that 'some translations read after one sort, and some after another, whereas all may serve to good purpose and edification'.[33]

The impulse to create new translations, to enhance the 'edification' of the reader, is illustrated in Butterworth's collation of Psalm 51. His compilation of variants, taken from English prose translations between 1530 and 1545, requires the citation of sixteen different works.[34] One of those editions, the Redman Primer of 1535, includes four versions of Psalm 51: Marshall's translation of Savonarola [4] in the Matins setting; the same translation in the Seven Psalms and the Dirge, but with a variant first verse; and Joye's translation of Bucer's Psalter [2] in the so-called 'St Jerome Psalter'.[35] As Butterworth comments, 'in the four places where the 51st Psalm occurs in the Redman Primer the opening verse appears in three different forms. [...] Thus we can realize how fluid and unfixed was the state of Bible translation during these formative years'.[36] As exemplified in Lock's translation, this fluidity extended well into the middle of the century.

Not only were multiple English translations used, but the Latin Bible itself continued to be promoted by the Reformers. In 1559, a year before Lock's psalm version was published, a set of guidelines was drawn up for parish visits to insure that Protestantism was being promulgated in the churches. It included the following question to be asked of priests:

Item, whether they do discourage any person from readynge of any parte of the Byble, eyther in latyn or englyshe, and do not rather comforte, and exhort every person to read the same at convenient times, as the very lively word of god and the speciall fode of mans soule.[37]

Although the 56 items included in these articles forbid such Roman Catholic practices as the saying of mass, the accumulation of images, the promotion of pilgrimages, and the use of Latin in the public worship services, reading the Bible in Latin was not only not forbidden, but positively encouraged. Whether Latin or English it was 'the very lively word of god'. This emphasis on the substance of God's word, regardless of its linguistic garb, and its daily use was more important to the Reformers than the question of whether it was read in English or in Latin.

As vital as the vernacular Bible was to the promotion of the Reformation in England, the Vulgate continued to hold an honoured place among well-educated Protestants. Lock herself understood the value of vernacular translations; she devoted most of her creative energies to composing poems in English and translating spiritual works from French into English. In her dedicatory epistle to the Duchess of Suffolk, she describes herself as an apothecary's assistant who packages God's medicinal word in an 'Englishe boxe'. Yet while she forwarded the cause of the Reformation in England through her own English words, she herself continued to read, and use, the Bible of her youth – St Jerome's Vulgate.

NOTES

1 The paraphrase (STC 4450) was published with a translation of four sermons by Calvin.

2 For a defence of Lock's authorship, see Susan M. Felch, *The Collected Works of Anne Vaughan Lock*, Medieval & Renaissance Texts & Studies Series, vol. 185, Renaissance English Text Society, vol. 21 (Tempe, AZ: Arizona Center for Medieval and Renaissance Studies, 1999), pp. liii-liv.

3 For Lock's biography see Patrick Collinson, 'The Role of Women in the English Reformation Illustrated by the Life and Friendships of Anne Locke', in *Godly People: Essays on English Protestantism and Puritanism* (London: Hambledon Press, 1983), pp. 273-87; first published in *Studies in Church History*, 2 (1965), 258-72; W. C. Richardson's monograph on her father, *Stephen Vaughan, Financial Agent of Henry VIII: A Study of Financial Relations with the Low Countries* (Baton Rouge: Louisiana State University Studies, 1953), pp. 1-80; and Felch, *Collected Works*, pp. xvi-xxxvi.

4 For these letters, see *Letters and Papers, Foreign and Domestic, of the Reign of Henry VIII, 1509-1547*, ed. by J. S. Brewer, James Gairdner, & R. H. Brodie, 21 vols (London: Longman, 1862-1910), V, 303, 533, 957; X, 633.

5 *Acts of the Privy Council of England*, ed. by John Roche Dasent, n.s. 1 (London: Eyre & Spottiswoode, 1890), 115; Brewer, XVIII.1, 431.

6 Henry Brinkelow, *The complaynt of Roderyck Mors for the redresse of certen wicked lawes* ([Strassburg: W. Köpfel, 1542?]), STC 3759.5; Henry Brinkelow, *The lamentacion of a christian against the citie of London, made by R. Mors* ([Bonn]: L. Mylius, 1542), STC 3764.

7 'Certaine old stories recorded by an aged gentlewoman a time before her death, to be perused by her children and posterity' (London, British Library, Add. MS 43827), fols 3ᵛ-4ᵛ. Transcribed in Maria Dowling & Joy Shakespeare, 'Religion and Politics in mid Tudor England through the eyes of an English Protestant Woman: the Recollections of Rose Hickman', *Bulletin of the Institute of Historical Research* 55 (1982), 94-102.

8 For a discussion of this correspondence see Susan M. Felch, '"Deir Sister": The Letters of John Knox to Anne Vaughan Lok', *Renaissance and Reformation/Renaissance et Reforme* 19, no. 4 (1995), 47-68.

9 John Calvin, *Sermons of John Calvin, upon the songe that Ezechias made after he had bene sicke, and afflicted by the hand of God, conteyned in the 38. Chapiter of Esay*, trans. by 'A.L.' (London: John Day, 1560), STC 4450.

10 Pearl Hogrefe, 'Mildred Cooke Cecil, Lady Burghley 1526-1589', in *Women of Action in Tudor England*, ed. by Pearl Hogrefe (Ames, IO: Iowa State University Press, 1977), pp. 3-36. See pp. 22-8 regarding the issue of Scottish correspondence.

11 *The History of Parliament: The House of Commons 1558-1603*, ed. by P. W. Hasler, vol. 3 (London: The History of Parliament Trust, 1981), p. 256.

12 Jean Taffin, *Of the markes of the children of God, and of their comforts in afflictions* (London: T. Orwin for T. Man, 1590), STC 23652.

13 The manuscript is now at the Cambridge University Library (MS Ii.5.37); it was first located and transcribed by Louise Schleiner in *Tudor and Stuart Women Writers* (Bloomington: Indiana University Press, 1994), pp. 39-45, p. 256, notes 10-11; for a facsimile, transcription, and translation of the poem, see Felch, *Collected Works*, pp. 72-3.

14 Citations from both Psalters are taken from *Biblia Sacra* (Stuttgart: Württembergische Bibelanstalt, 1975).

15 This version was reprinted with a few variations in *A Prymer in Englyshe, with certeyn prayers and godly meditations, very necessary for all people that understonde not the Latyne tongue* (London: J. Byddell for W. Marshall, 1534), STC 15986.

16 For Joye's life and works, see Charles C. Butterworth and Allan G. Chester, *George Joye, 1495?-1553: A Chapter in the History of the English Bible and the English Reformation* (Philadelphia: University of Pennsylvania Press, 1962); and Butterworth, *The English Primers (1529-1545): Their Publication and Connection with the English Bible and the Reformation in England* (Philadelphia: University of Pennsylvania Press, 1953).

17 The Coverdale Bible, the Matthew's Bible of 1537 (STC 2066), and the Taverner Bible of 1539 (STC 2067) have virtually identical translations of Psalm 51. The one exception occurs in verse 7 where Matthew and Taverner follow Münster, rather than the Vulgate, translating *expiabis* as *purge*.

18 For a fuller discussion of Coverdale's translations, see J. F. Mozley, *Coverdale and His Bibles* (London: Lutterworth Press, 1953).

19 *The boke of psalmes, where in are contened praiers* (Geneva: R. Hall, 1559), STC 2384.

20 The nearest duplicate of an existing translation is found in verse 1b where, except for the initial 'and', Lock's translation matches the versions in the Great Bible [7] and Geneva Psalter [10].

21 For a discussion of Lock's puns, see Linda Dove, 'Women at Variance: Sonnet Sequences and Social Commentary in Early Modern England' (unpublished doctoral thesis, University of Maryland at College Park, 1997), pp. 42-3, 48.

22 Among the English translations, only the Rouen English-Latin Primer in its 'St Jerome's

Psalter' also retains *bowells*; *Thys prymer in Englyshe and in Laten is newly translatyd after the Laten texte* (Rowen: N. le Roux?, 1536), STC 15993, fol. X2ᵛ.

23 The word *justice* is used seven times in the sonnet sequence as a whole.

24 Margaret Hannay's suggestion that Lock was influenced in her translation by the Genevan Psalter appears to be based on the differences between that Psalter and the complete Bible published in 1560. These differences, however, are themselves due to the Psalter's reliance on the Great Bible, which, in turn, was influenced by the Vulgate. Margaret P. Hannay, '"Unlock my lipps": the *Miserere mei Deus* of Anne Vaughan Lok and Mary Sidney Herbert, Countess of Pembroke', in *Privileging Gender in Early Modern England*, ed. by Jean R. Brink, Sixteenth Century Essays and Studies 23 (Kirksville, MO: Sixteenth Century Journal Publishers, 1993), pp. 19-36 (p. 22).

25 Mozley, p. 221.

26 *The newe testamen [sic] both in Latin and English after the vulgare texte* (London: F. Regnault for R. Grafton & E. Whitchurch, 1538), STC 2817; cited in *Records of the English Bible*, ed. by Alfred W. Pollard (Folkestone: Dawsons, 1974), p. 209.

27 Miles Coverdale, *Biblia The bible, that is, the holy scripture* ([Cologne?] E. Cervicornus & J. Soter?, 1535), STC 2063, fol. *5ʳ.

28 *The primer, set foorth by the kynges maiestie and his clergie* (London: E. Whitchurch, 1545), STC 16038, fols *1ᵛ-*2ʳ.

29 Coverdale, in the dedication of the diglot New Testament, does complain of corrupt readings in the Vulgate but suggests they can be corrected through comparison with other versions.

30 In the preface to the reader in the Tyndale Pentateuch; *The fyrste boke of Moses called Genesis* ([Antwerp: J. Hoochstraten], 1530), STC 2350.

31 Coverdale, *Biblia*, fol. *6ᵛ.

32 Coverdale, *Biblia*, fol. *4ᵛ.

33 *The bible and holy scriptures conteyned in the olde and newe testament* (Geneva: R. Hall, 1560), STC 2093, fol. ⁂4ʳ.

34 Butterworth, *The English Primers* (n. 16 above), pp. 291-300.

35 *This prymer of Salysbery use bothe in Englyshe and in Laten* (London: R. Redman, 1535), STC 15986.3.

36 Butterworth, *The English Primers*, p. 98.

37 *Articles to be enquyred in the visitation, in the fyrste yeare of the raygne of our moost drad soveraygne Lady, Elizabeth* (London: R. Jugge & A. Cawood, 1559), STC 10118, fol. A2ᵛ.

APPENDIX A
THE COLLATION OF PSALM 51

In the following texts, the original spelling and punctuation remain intact, except for the following changes: I have followed modern orthographic conventions for *i, j, u, v, w,* and the long *s,* expanded abbreviations, altered the tilde over a vowel to *m* or *n* as needed, and corrected obvious printing errors, such as turned letters. Individual copies of a single edition may vary slightly; therefore, except for complete Bibles, I have indicated the specific copy from which each transcription is taken.

[1] Anne Lock, *A Meditation of a Penitent Sinner: written in maner of a Paraphrase upon the 51. Psalme of David* (London: John Day, 1560), fols Aa3ᵛ-Aa8ʳ; STC 4450, BL 696.a.40.

[a] The Gallican (Vulgate) Psalter of St Jerome; the Coverdale diglot variants [8] are noted in square brackets.

[b] The 'Hebrew' (Vulgate) Psalter of St Jerome.

[c] Sante Pagnini, *Biblia Sacra* (1528; the 1542 version revised and edited by Michael Servetus is used here).

[d] Sebastian Münster, *Hebraica Biblia* (1534-35).

[2] George Joye, *The Psalter of David in Englishe purely and faithfully translated aftir the texte of ffeline* ([Antwerp: M. de Keyser], 1530), fols L2ᵛ-L4ʳ; STC 2370, BL C.17.a.2.

[3] George Joye, *Davids Psalter, diligently and faithfully translated by George Joye with breif Arguments before every Psalme declaringe the effecte therof* ([Antwerp]: M. Emperowr, 1534), fols K3ᵛ-K5ʳ; STC 2372, Cambridge University Library Syn. 8.53.89.

[4] William Marshall, *An exposition after the maner of a contemplacyon upon the .li. psalme, called Miserere mei Deus* (London: J. Byddell for W. Marshall, 1534), fols A1ᵛ-D5ʳ; STC 21789.3, Cambridge University Library Syn. 8.53.41.

[5] Miles Coverdale, *A Paraphrasis upon all the Psalmes of David* (London: Gybson, 1539), fols G4ʳ-G5ᵛ; STC 2372.6, BL 3090.a.8. The first edition of this translation ([Antwerp], 1535), STC 2372.4, is incomplete.

[6] Miles Coverdale, *Biblia The bible, that is, the holy scripture* ([Cologne?], 1535), STC 2063; the variants in the Matthew's (1537), STC 2066, and Taverner (1539), STC 2067, Bibles are noted in square brackets.

[7] *The byble in Englyshe* ([Paris & London, 1539), STC 2068.

[8] Miles Coverdale, *The psalter or boke of psalmes both in Latyn and Englyshe, with a kalender, and a table* (London: R. Grafton, 1540), fols F2ᵛ-F3ʳ; STC 2368, BL C.111.aa.30.

[9] *The primer, set foorth by the kynges majestie and his Clergie* (London: Grafton, 1545), fols J4ʳ-K1ʳ; STC 16034, BL C.35.c.15.

[10] *The psalmes of David tr. accordyng to th'Ebrue, wyth annotacions moste profitable* (Geneva: M. Blanchier, 1557), fols K7ʳ-K8ᵛ; STC 2383.6, Cambridge University Library Pet. D.1.50².

[11] *The boke of psalms, where in are contened praiers* (Geneva: R. Hall, 1559), fols H7ᵛ-H8ᵛ; STC 2384, HN 96522.

Verse 1a

[1] Have mercie upon me (o God) after thy great merci

[a] *Miserere mei Deus secundum magnam: misericordiam tuam*

[b] *Miserere mei Deus secundum misericordiam tuam*

[c] *Miserere mei deus secundum pietatem tuam,*

[d] *Miserere mei deus secundum pietatem tuam:*

[2] Have mercy upon me (god) for thy jentlenes sake:

[3] Have mercy upon me oh god/ accordinge unto thy goodnes,

[4] Have mercy upon me (oh god) accordynge to thy greate mercye.

[5] Have mercye upon me o God for thy naturall kyndnesse sake,

[6] Have mercy upon me (o God) after thy goodnes,

[7] Have mercy upon me (O God) after thy (greate) goodnes:

[8] Have mercy on me o god, accordyng to thy great mercy

[9] Have mercy upon me, O God, according to thy great mercy.

[10] Have mercie upon me (O God) after thy great goodnesse:

[11] Have mercie upon me, ô God, according to thy loving kindenes:

Verse 1b

[1] And according unto the multitude of thy mercies do away myne offences.

[a] *et: secundum multitudinem miserationum tuarum dele iniquitatem meam*

[b] *iuxta multitudinem miserationum tuarum dele iniquitates meas*

[c] *secundum multitudinem miserationum tuarum, dele praevaricationes meas.*

[d] *secundum multitudinem miserationum tuarum dele scelera mea.*
[2] for thy grete mercyes sake wype awaye my sinnes
[3] for thy grete infinite mercyes do awaye my transgressions.
[4] And accordinge to the multitude of thy compassions wype awaye myne iniquite.
[5] put out my synnes. for thy greate goodnesses sake.
[6] and acordinge unto thy greate mercies, do awaye myne offences.
[7] according unto the multitude of thy mercyes, do awaye mine offences.
[8] And accordynge to the multitude of thy lovynge kyndnesses do awaye myne iniquyte.
[9] And according to the multitude of thy compassions, wipe away myne iniquitie.
[10] according unto the multitude of thy mercies do awaie mine offenses.
[11] according to the multitude of thy compassions put awaie mine iniquities.

Verse 2
[1] Wash me yet more from my wickednes, and clense me from my sinne.
[a] *amplius lava me ab iniquitate mea et a peccato meo munda me*
[b] *multum lava me ab iniquitate mea et a peccato meo munda me*
[c] *Plurimum lava me ab iniquitate mea, et à peccato meo munda me.*
[d] *Lava me plurimum ab iniquitate mea, et à peccato meo munda me.*
[2] And yet ageine washe me more/ fro my wikednes and make me cleane fro my ungodlines.
[3] Nowe and yet agene washe me from my wikednes/ and pourge me fro my sinne.
[4] Yet washe me more from myne iniquite and clense me from my synne.
[5] Put out my iniquyte by washynge it awaye more and more, and make me clene fro my synne.
[6] Wash me well fro my wickednesse, and clense me fro my synne.
[7] Wash me thorowly fro my wickednesse, and clense me fro my sinne.
[8] Wash me yet more fro myne iniquyte, and clense me fro my synne.
[9] More and more washe me from myne iniquitie, and clense me from my sinne.
[10] Washe me thrughly from my wickednesse: and clense me from my sinne.
[11] Wash me throughly from mine iniquitie: and clense me from my sinne.

Verse 3
[1] For I knowledge my wickednes, and my sinne is ever before me.
[a] *quoniam iniquitatem meam ego cognosco et peccatum meum contra me est semper*
[b] *quoniam iniquitates meas ego novi et peccatum meum contra me est semper*
[c] *Quoniam praevaricationes meas ego agnosco, et peccatum meum coram meest semper.*
[d] *Quoniam scelera mea ego agnosco, et peccatum meum coram me (versat) iugiter.*
[2] For my grevous sinnes do I knowledge: and my ungodlynes is ever before myn eyes.
[3] For my transgressions do I knowlege/ and my sinne never gothe out of my mynde.
[4] For I knowlege myne inyquyte, and my synne is ever before myne iyes.
[5] For now that I am come to my selfe agayne, I knowe my wyckednesses, and my synne is ever before myne eyes.
[6] For I knowlege my fautes, and my synne is ever before me.
[7] For I knowleg my fautes, and my synne is ever before me.
[8] For myne iniquite do I knowe, and my synne is alwaye in my syght.
[9] For I knowledge myne iniquitie and my sinne is ever before myne eyes.
[10] For I knowlege my rebellions: and my sinne is ever before me.
[11] For I know mine iniquities: and my sinnes *is* ever before me.

Verse 4a
[1] Againste thee onelye have I sinned, and don evill in thy sight.
[a] *tibi soli peccavi et malum coram te feci*

[b] *tibi soli peccavi et malum coram te feci*
[c] *Tibi, soli tibi peccavi, et malum in oculis tuis feci:*
[d] *Contra te solum peccavi, et malum hoc in oculis tuis feci,*
[2] Ageinste the/ ageinste thee/only have I sinned/ and that at sore offendeth the have I done:
[3] Agenst the onely to have so sinned it beruweth me and it repenteth me to have had done this grevouse sinne in thy sight:
[4] Agaynst the only have I synned: and have done that which is evyll in thy sight:
[5] Agaynst the, agaynst the only have I synned and made thys grevous faulte, not fearynge thy presence:
[6] Agaynst the only, agaynst the have I synned, and done evell in thy sight:
[7] Agaynst the onely have I sinned, and done this evell in thy syght:
[8] Agaynst the onely have I synned, and done evell before the:
[9] To the alone have I sinned, and have done evill in thy sight,
[10] Against the, against the onely have I sinned and done this evill in thy sight:
[11] Against thee, against thee onely have I sinned, and done evil in thy sight:

Verse 4b
[1] That thou mightest be founde just in thy sayinges, and maiest over come when thou art judged.
[a] *ut iustificeris in sermonibus tuis et vincas cum iudicaris*
[b] *ut iustificeris in sermonibus tuis et vincas cum iudicaveris*
[c] *ut iustifices te, quum locutus fueris, purifices te cum iudicaveris.*
[d] *ut iustus sis in sermone tuo, et purus cum iudicaveris.*
[2] wherfore very juste shalt thou be knowne in thy wordis and pure/when it shalbe juged of the.
[3] wherfore justifie me acording to thy promise and make me clene according to thy equite.
[4] that thou maist be justified in thy words: and mayst have the victorie when thou art judged.
[5] wherfore yf thou wylt forgyve me this offence, and kepe thy promyses with me that have broken myne, thou shalt (as reason is) be counted most indifferent, but most faythfull in kepynge thy promyses and most ryghtuous in damnyng them that wyll not amende.
[6] that thou mightest be justified in thy saynges, and shuldest overcome when thou art judged.
[7] that thou myghtest be justifyed in thy sayinge, and cleare when thou art judged.
[8] so that thou mayest be founde true in thy sayenges, and over come whan thou art judged.
[9] that thou maist be justifyed in thy wordes, and maist overcome when thou art judged[.]
[10] that thou may be knowne juste whan thou speakest and pure when thou judgest.
[11] that thou maiest be juste when thou speakest, *and* pure when thou judgest.

Verse 5
[1] For loe, I was shapen in wickednes, and in sinne my mother conceived me.
[a] *ecce enim in iniquitatibus conceptus sum et in peccatis concepit me mater mea*
[b] *ecce in iniquitate conceptus sum et in peccato peperit me mater mea*
[c] *Ecce cum iniquitate genitus sum, et cum peccato calefacta est de me mater mea.*
[d] *Ecce in iniquitate formatus sum, et in peccato calefecit me mater mea.*
[2] Lo I was fashoned in wikednes: and my mother conceyved me polluted with sinne.
[3] Beholde/ with sorowe and payne was I borne: and with sinne my mother conceived me.
[4] Lo I was fasshoned in wyckednes and my mother conceyved me poluted with synne.
[5] Verely it is not unknowen to the that (as for me) synne is myne by nature, and that my mother was subdued unto synne in the very heate of my concepcion
[6] Beholde, I was borne in wickednesse, and in synne hath my mother conceaved me.
[7] Beholde, I was shapen in wickednesse, and in synne hath my mother conceaved me.
[8] For beholde, I am conceaved in iniquyties, and in synnes dyd my mother conceave me.

81

[9] Beholde I was begotten in wickednes, and my mother conceyved me in sinne.

[10] Beholde, I was shapen in wickednesse: and in sinne hath my mother conceived me.

[11] Beholde, I was borne in iniquitie: and in sinne hathe my mother conceived me.

Verse 6

[1] But lo, thou haste loved trueth, the hidden and secrete thinges of thy wisedome thou haste opened unto me.

[a] *ecce enim veritatem dilexisti incerta et occulta sapientiae tuae manifestasti mihi*

[b] *ecce enim veritatem diligis absconditum et arcanum sapientiae manifestasti mihi*

[c] *Ecce veritatem voluisti in renibus, et in occulto sapientiam scire fecisti me.*

[d] *Ecce veritatem exigis in interioribus, et in occulto sapientiam me scire facies.*

[2] But lo/thou woldst trowith to occupye and rule in my inwarde partes: thou shewedste me wysdome which thou woldst to sitte in the secrets of my harte.

[3] [omitted from the text]

[4] Lo thou hast, loved truth/ the unknowne and secrete thyngs of thy wysdome, haste thou uttered unto me.

[5] Then, though I have gotten a foule fall thorow the mocyon of my corrupte flesh, yet wast thou wont to love fayth and innocencye that lyeth wythin the harte, from the whych I am not swarved all together, for I have not done thys wyckednesse so greately of malyce, as overcome with concupyscence: wherfore thou shalt yet voutsafe to teach me thy perfecte wysdome, as thou was wont to do by secrete inspyrcyons.

[6] But lo, thou hast a pleasure in the treuth, and hast shewed me secrete wysedome.

[7] But lo, thou requirest treuth in the inward partes, and shalt make me to understonde wisdome secretly.

[8] For lo, thou hast loved treuth: the secretes and pryvities of thy wysdome hast thou declared unto me.

[9] Lo, thou hast loved truth, the unknowen and secret thinges of thy wisdome thou hast reveled unto me.

[10] But lo, thou requirest truth in th'inwarde affections: and haste made me to understand wysedome secretly.

[11] Beholde, thou lovest treuth in the inwarde affections: therfor hast thou taught me wisedome in the secret *of mine heart.*

Verse 7

[1] Sprinkle me, Lorde, with hisope and I shalbe cleane: washe me and I shalbe whiter then snow.

[a] *asparges me hysopo et mundabor lavabis me et super nivem dealbabor*

[b] *asparges me hysopo et mundabor lavabis me et super nivem dealbabor*

[c] *Purificabis me hyssopo, et mundabor, lavabis me, et prae nive dealbabor.*

[d] *Expiabis me hyssopo et mundabor, lavabis me et nive candidior ero.*

[2] Sprinkle me with hyssope and so shall I be clene: thou shalt wasshe me/ and then shall I be whighter then snowe.

[3] Bespreigne me with ysope and I shalbe clene: washe me/ and so shal I be whyter than snowe:

[4] Sprynkle me Lorde with ysope and so shall I be clene/ thou shalt washe me/ and then shall I be whytter then snowe.

[5] If thou therfore wylt wasshe awaye this wyckednesse of myne wyth ysope, I shalbe clene even as thorowe the most parfecte purgacyon: And yf thou wasshest out thys spot of myne, I shall be whyter agayne then the very snowe.

[6] O reconcile me with Isope, and I shal be clene: wash thou me, and I shalbe whyter then snowe. [Matthew's: O purge me with Isope; Taverner: Purge me with Isope]

[7] Thou shalt pourge me with Isope, and I shal be cleane: thou shalt wash me, and I shalbe whiter then snowe:

[8] Thou shalt sprynkle me wyth ysope O Lorde, and I shalbe clensed: thou shalt wash me, and I shall be whyter then snowe.

[9] Sprynckle me lorde with Hysop, and I shalbe clensed. Thou shalt washe me, and I shal be made whighter than snowe.

[10] Purge me with Isop, and I shal be cleane: washe me, and I shall be whiter than snow.

[11] Purge me with hyssope, and I shal be cleane: wash me and I shal be whiter then snowe.

Verse 8

[1] Thou shalt make me heare joye and gladnesse, a[n]d the bones which thou hast broken shal rejoyse

[a] *auditui meo dabis gaudium et laetitiam* [Coverdale diglot: *et*] *exultabunt ossa humiliata*

[b] *auditum mihi facies gaudium et laetitiam ut exultent ossa quae confregisti*

[c] *Audire facies me gaudium, et laetitiam: exultabunt ossa, quae contrivisti.*

[d] *Facies me audire laetitiam et gaudium, ut exultent ossa (quae) contrivisti.*

[2] Powre uppon me joye and gladnes: make my bones to rejoyse which thou hast smyten.

[3] Shewe me joye and gladnes/ and my bones shal rejoyse/ which thou hast broken.

[4] Unto my hearynge shalte thou geve joye and gladnes and my brosed bones shall be refreshed.

[5] When thou makest me rejoyse wyth the myrth and gladnesse that I was wont to have, then shall my bones be mery, whych thou haddest wounded

[6] Oh let me heare of joye and gladnesse, that the bones which thou hast broken maye rejoyse.

[7] Thou shalt make me heare of joye and gladnesse, that the bones which thou hast broken, maye rejoyse.

[8] To my hearyng thou shalt geve joye and gladnesse, and the bones which are brought lowe, shall rejoyse.

[9] Unto my hearing shalt thou geve joy and gladnes, and the brused bones shal rejoyse.

[10] Make me to heare joie and gladnesse: that the bones whiche thou hast broken, maie rejoise.

[11] Make me to heare joye and gladnes, *that* the bones, *which* thou hast broken, maie rejoyce.

Verse 9

[1] Turne away thy face from my sinnes, and do away all my misdedes.

[a] *averte faciem tuam a peccatis meis et omnes iniquitates meas dele*

[b] *absconde faciem tuam a peccatis meis et omnes iniquitates meas dele*

[c] *Absconde faciem tuam à peccatis meis, et omnes iniquitates meas dele.*

[d] *Absconde faciem tuam à peccatis meis, et omnes iniquitates meas dele.*

[2] Turne thy face fro my sinnes: and wype awaye all my wikednes.

[3] Averte thy face fro my sinnes/ and do awaye al my iniquites.

[4] Turne thy face from of my synnes and wype awaye all my wyckednes.

[5] I beseke the turne thy face awaye fro my synnes, and put out all my iniquyties

[6] Turne thy face fro my synnes, and put out all my mysededes.

[7] Turne thy face from my synnes, and put out all my misdedes.

[8] Turne awaye thy face from my synnes, and put out al myne iniquyties.

[9] Turne thy face from my sinnes, and wipe away al my wickednes.

[10] Hide thy face from my sinnes: and put out all my misdedes.

[11] Hide thy face from my sinnes: and put awaie all mine iniquities.

Verse 10

[1] Create a cleane hart within me, O God: and renew a stedfast spirit within my bowels.

[a] *cor mundum crea in me Deus et spiritum rectum innova in visceribus meis*

[b] *cor mundum crea mihi Deus et spiritum stabilem renova in visceribus meis*

[c] *Cor mundum crea mihi deus, et spiritum rectum innova in visceribus meis:*

[d] *Cor mundum crea in me deus, et spiritum rectum innova in intimo meo.*

[2] A pure harte create in me (Oh lorde): and a stedfaste right spyrit make a newe withyn me.

[3] Create a clene herte in me oh god and a stable spirit renewe with in me.

[4] A pure herte create in me oh god and an upryghte spiryte make a newe within me.

[5] Cause myne hart to be pure within me (o god) and renew in myne hart that stedfast spirit of thyne.

[6] Make me a clene hert (o God) and renue a right sprete within me.

[7] Make me a cleane hert (O God) and renue a ryght sprete within me.

[8] Make a new hert within me o god, and renew a right sprete in my body.

[9] A pure harte create in me, o God, and a perfit spirit renue within me.

[10] Make me a cleane heart (O God) and renue a right spirite within me.

[11] Create in me a cleane heart, ô God, and renue a right spirit within me.

Verse 11

[1] Cast me not away from thy face, and take not thy holy spirit from me.

[a] *ne proicias me a facie tua et spiritum sanctum tuum ne auferas a me*

[b] *ne proicias me a facie tua et spiritum sanctum tuum ne auferas a me*

[c] *Ne projicias me à facie tua, et spiritum sanctitatis tuae ne capias à me.*

[d] *Ne projicias me à facie tua, et spiritum sanctum tuum ne tollas à me.*

[2] Caste me not awaye: and thy holy ghoste take not fro me.

[3] Cast me not out of thy sight: and thy holy spirit take not fro me

[4] Caste me not away from thy face/ and thy holy ghost take not from me.

[5] Put me not from thyne olde favoure, and take not fro me that most holy spyrite of thyne.

[6] Cast me not awaie from thy presence, and take not thy holy sprete fro me.

[7] Cast me not awaye from thy presence, and take not thy holy sprete from me.

[8] Cast me not out of thy syght, and take not thy holy ghoost awaye fro me.

[9] Cast me not away from thy face, and thy holy spirit take not from me.

[10] Caste me not awaie from thy presence: and take not thy holy spirit from me.

[11] Cast me not awaie from thy presence: and take not thine holie Spirit from me.

Verse 12

[1] Restore to me the comforte of thy saving helpe, and stablishe me with thy free spirit.

[a] *redde mihi laetitiam salutaris tui et spiritu principali confirma me*

[b] *redde mihi laetitiam Iesu tui et spiritu potenti confirma me*

[c] *Redde mihi gaudium salutis tuae, et spiritu voluntario confirma me.*

[d] *Restitue mihi laetitiam salutis tuae, et spiritu munifico suffulci me.*

[2] Make me ageine to rejoyse whyls thou bryngest me thy savynge helthe: and let thy chefe governynge fre spyrit strengthen and lede me.

[3] Restore me the gladnes of thy savinge helth: and sustayne me with thy fre benigne spirit.

[4] Make me agayne to rejoyse in thy savynge healthe/ and strengthen me with a pryncypall spirite.

[5] But rather fede me the gladnesse againe which I had gotten because of the health that thou shuldest gyve me, and kepe thou me wyth thy principal spyryte.

[6] O geve me the comforte of thy helpe agayne, and stablish me with thy fre sprete.

[7] O geve me the comforte of thy helpe agayne, and stablish me with thy fre sprete.

[8] Graunt me the gladnesse of thy salvacyon agayne, and stablishe me wyth thy princypall sprete.

[9] Restore to me the gladnes of thy salvation, and strengthen me with the principal spirit.

[10] O geve me againe the joye of thy salvation, and stablishe me with thy free spirit.

[11] Restore to me the joye of thy salvation, and stablish me with *thy* fre Spirit.

The Vulgate as Reformation Bible

Verse 13

[1] I shal teach thy waies unto the wicked, and sinne[r]s shall be tourned unto thee.

[a] *docebo iniquos vias tuas et impii ad te convertentur*

[b] *docebo iniquos vias tuas et peccatores ad te revertentur*

[c] *Docebo praevaricatores vias tuas, et peccatores ad te convertentur.*

[d] *Docebo iniquos vias tuas, et peccato res ad te convertentur.*

[2] I shall instructe cursed and shrewed men in thy waie: and ungodly men shalbe converted unto the.

[3] And I shal directe transgressors into thy waye: and sinners shalbe converted unto the.

[4] I wil instructe the wycked that they may knowe thy wayes: and the ungodly shall be converted unto the.

[5] When thou hast done thys for me I shal teach synners by whyche wayes they maye come unto the, and they that are greved wyth synnes shall (by my example) be converted unto the.

[6] Then shal I teach thy wayes unto the wicked, that synners maye be converted unto the.

[7] Then shall I teach thy wayes unto the wicked, and synners shall be converted unto the.

[8] I wyll teache the wycked thy wayes, and the ungodly shalbe converted unto the.

[9] I wyll instruct the wicked in thy wayes, and the ungodly shalbe converted unto the.

[10] Then shall I teache thy waies unto the wicked: and sinners shall be converted unto the.

[11] *Then* shal I teache thy waies unto the wicked: and sinners shal be converted unto thee.

Verse 14

[1] Deliver me from bloud o God, God of my helth and my tong shall joyfullye talke of thy justice.

[a] *libera me de sanguinibus Deus Deus salutis meae* [Coverdale diglot: *et*] *exultabit lingua mea iustitiam tuam*

[b] *libera me de sanguinibus Deus Deus salutis meae laudabit lingua mea iustitiam tuam*

[c] *Erue me de sanguinibus deus, deus salutis mea: laudabit lingua mea iustitiam tuam.*

[d] *Libera me de sanguinibus deus, deus salutis meae, et cantabit lingua mea iustitiam tuam.*

[2] Delyvre me from the synne of murther (oh god) oh god my savioure: and my tonge shall triumphe upon thy mercy wherwith thou makest me rightwise.

[3] Delyver me from that blody synne oh god/ oh god my saviour/ that my tongue might/ magnify the forme of thy rightwysmakinge.

[4] Delyver me frome bloudes (oh god) the god of my helthe/ and my tongue shal tryumphe upon thy ryghtwysnes.

[5] O God/O God the authoure of my health, delyver me from the murther that I have commytted, that my tongue maye wyth gladnesse prayse that greate ryghtuousnesse of thyne.

[6] Delyver me from bloudegyltynesse o God, thou that art the God of my health, that my tonge maye prayse thy righteousnesse.

[7] Delyver me from bloud giltynesse (O God) thou that are the God of my health, and my tonge shall syng of thy righteousnesse.

[8] Delyver me from bloude O God thou God of my salvacyon, and my tonge shall tryumphe of thy ryghteousnesse.

[9] Deliver me from bludshed, o God, the God of my helth, and my tong shal exalt thy righteousnes.

[10] Deliver me from blood giltinesse, O God thou that art the God of my health: and my tonge shall sing forth thy rightuousnesse.

[11] Deliver me from blood, ô God, *which art* the God of my salvation: *and* my tongue shal sing joyfully of thy righteousnes.

Verse 15

[1] Lord, open thou my lippes, and my mouth shal shewe thy praise.

[a] *Domine labia mea aperies et os meum adnuntiabit laudem tuam*

[b] *Domine labia mea aperies et os meum adnuntiabit laudem tuam*

[c] *Domine labia mea aperies, et os meum annunciabit laudem tuam.*

[d] *Domine, labia mea aperies, et os meum annunciabit laudem tuam.*

[2] Lorde opene thou my lyppes: and then my mouthe shall shewe forthe thy prayse.

[3] Open my lippes/ Oh Lorde/ that my mouth mought shewe forthe thy prayse.

[4] Lorde open thou my lippes: and then my mouth shal shewe forthe thy prayse.

[5] Open my lyppes (o Lorde) that my mouth maye speake of thy prayses.

[6] Open my lippes (O LORDE) that my mouth maye shewe thy prayse.

[7] Thou shalt open my lyppes (O Lord) my mouth shall shew thy prayse.

[8] Lorde thou shalt open my lyppes, and my mouth shall shew forth thy prayse.

[9] Thou shalt open my lippes, and my mouth shal shewe thy prayse.

[10] Thou shalt open my lippes, O lord: my mouthe shall shew thy praise.

[11] Open thou my lippes, ô Lord: and my mouth shal shew forthe thy praise.

Verse 16

[1] If thou haddest desired sacrifice, I wold have geven thou delytest not in burnt offringes.

[a] *quoniam si voluisses sacrificium dedissem utique holocaustis non delectaberis*

[b] *non enim vis ut victimam feriam nec holocaustum tibi placet*

[c] *Quoniam non vis sacrificium, alioqui darem: et holocaustum non vis:*

[d] *Nam non desideras sacrificium, alioquin darem, neque holocaustum gratum habes.*

[2] For as for sacryfyces thou delyghtest not in them: orels I had offred them/ and as for brente sacrifices thou regardest them not.

[3] For if thou lovedst any slayne sacrifice/ I wolde paye it unto the: but brent sacrifices delyght not the.

[4] Yf thou hadst desyred sacrifices I had surely offered them but thou delyghtedst not in brente sacryfices.

[5] Thou wylt not be pacifyed wyth outwarde sacrifyces (thoughe I wolde offre never so many) nether wylt thou have pleasure in the offerynge that is layed upon the aultare.

[6] For yf thou haddest pleasure in sacrifice, I wolde geve it the: but thou delytest not in burntofferynges.

[7] For thou desyrest no sacrifice, els wolde I geve it thee: but thou delytest not in burntofferynge.

[8] For yf it had bene thy pleasure, I wolde have gevyn the sacrifyce: in burntofferinges verely wilt thou have no delyte.

[9] For if thou haddest desired sacrifice, I had suerly geven it, but thou delitest not in whole burntofferinges.

[10] For thou desirest no sacrifice, elles wolde I geve it the: but thou delitest not in burnt offeringes.

[11] For thou desirest no sacrifice, thogh I wolde give it: thou delitest not in burnt offring.

Verse 17

[1] The sacrifice to God is a trobled spirit: a broken and an humbled hart, o god, thou wilt not despise.

[a] *sacrificium Deo spiritus contribulatus cor contritum et humiliatum Deus non spernet* [Coverdale diglot: *deus non despicies*]

[b] *sacrificium Dei spiritus contribulatus cor contritum et humiliatum Deus non dispicies*

[c] *sacrificia dei, spiritus contritus, cor contritum, et confractum: haec deus non despicies.*

[d] *Sacrificia dei sunt, spiritus confractus, cor contritum et concussum: (haec) deus non despicies.*

[2] Acceptable sacrifyces to god/is a broken spirit: a contrite and a dejected harte thou shalt not despyse (Oh God).

[3] The sacrifice that god desierth/ is a contrite spirit/ a broken and hombled herte/ these thinges (oh god) thou despiseth not.

[4] A sacryfyce to god is a broken spyryte: a contrite and humble herte thou shalte not despyse (oh god)

[5] But the oblacyons that God is reconcylied wythall, are these: a stomack broken wyth repentaunce, and an harte smyten and wounded wyth sorowe: These thynges who so ever offre unto the (o GOD) thou canst never despyse them.

[6] The sacrifice of God is a troubled sprete, a broken and a contrite hert (o God) shalt thou not despise.

[7] The sacrifice of God is a troubled sprete, a broken and a contrite hert (O God) shalt thou not despise.

[8] A sacryfyce unto God is a troubled sprete: a contryte and humbled hert, O God, wylt thou not despyse.

[9] The sacrifyce to God is a lowely spirit, o God, thou wylt not dispise a contrite and an humble harte.

[10] The sacrifice of God is a troubled spirite: a broken and a contrite hearte O God thou wilt not despise.

[11] The sacrifices of God *are* a contrite spirit: a contrite and a broken heart, ô God, thou wilt not despise.

Verse 18

[1] Shew favour, o lord in thy good will unto Sion, that th[e] walles of Hierusalem may be bylded.

[a] *benigne fac Domine in bona voluntate tua Sion et aedificentur muri Hierusalem*

[b] *benefac Domine in voluntate tua Sion et aedificentur muri Hierusalem*

[c] *Benefac in voluntate tua ipsi Siion, aedifica muros Ierusalaim.*

[d] *Benefac ex benevolentia tua Zion, et aedificamuros Ierusalem.*

[2] Deale jently of thy favourable benevolence with Zyon: let the walles of Hierusalem be edyfied.

[3] Be thou good and merciful therfore unto zion/ that the wallis off Jerusalem mought be edified and preserved.

[4] Deale gentlye of thy favourable benevolence with syon, Let the walles of Hierusalem be bylte agayne.

[5] Shewe thy kyndnesse unto Syon as thou wast wont (I beseke the) that thou mayst buylde the walles of Hierusalem.

[6] O be favorable and gracious unto Sion, that the walles of Jerusalem maye be buylded.

[7] O be favorable and gracious unto Sion, buylde thou the walles of Jerusalem.

[8] Deale graciously unto Sion O Lorde, in thy good wyll, that the walles of Hierusalem maye be buylded.

[9] Deale gently of thy favorable benevolence with Sion, that the walles of Jerusalem may be builded up.

[10] O be favourable and gracious unto Syon: builde thou the walles of Jerusalem.

[11] Be favourable unto Zión for thy good pleasure: builde the walles of Jerusalem.

Verse 19

[1] Then shalt thou accept the sacrifice of righteousnesse, burnt offringes and oblations. Then shall they offre yonge bullockes upon thine altare.

[a] *tunc acceptabis sacrificium iustitiae oblationes et holocausta tunc inponent super altare tuum vitulos*

[b] *tunc suscipies sacrificium iustitiae oblationes et holocausta tunc inponent super altare tuum vitulos*

[c] *Tunc voles sacrificia iustitiae, holocaustum et oblationem, tunc offerent super altare tuum vitulos.*

[d] *Tunc acceptabis sacrificia iustitiae, holocaustum et integram (oblationem:) tunc offerent super altare tuum iuvencos.*

[2] Then shalt thou delyght in very sacryfyces in the right brent sacryfice and in the oblacion of rightwisnes: then shall they laye uppon thy altare the very oxen.

[3] For thus wilt thou be pleased with the slayne sacrifices of rightwisnes/ with offraunce and brent sacrifice/ thus shal the very bullocks be put upon thy autare.

[4] Than shalte thou accepte the sacryfyce of ryghtwysnes/ oblacyons and brente offerynges: than shall they laye upon thyne altare wanton calves.

[5] Then shalt thou be pleased wyth sacrifyces (whyche are tokens of the inwarde ryghtuous-nesse) namely every oblacyon and burnt offerynge: Then they that offre as they shulde do, wyll laye theyr calves upen thyne aultare.

[6] For then shalt thou be pleased with the sacrifice of rightuousnesse, with the burntofferynges and oblacions: then shal they laye bullockes upon thine aulter.

[7] Then shalt thou be pleased with the sacrifice of ryghteousnesse, with the burntofferynges and oblacions: then shall they offre yonge bullockes upon thyne aulter.

[8] Then shalt thou accepte the sacryfce, oblacyons and burntofferynges of ryghteousnesse: then shall they laye calves upon thyne altare.

[9] Then shalt thou accept the sacrifice of righteousnes, oblations and whole burntoffringes, then shal they ley calves upon thyne alter.

[10] Than shalt thou be pleased with the sacrifice of rightuousnes, with the burnt offerings and oblations, then shall thei offer calves upon thine altar.

[11] Then shalt thou accept the sacrifices of righteousnes, *even* the burnt offring and oblation: then shal thei offer calves upon thine altar.

THE 1535 COVERDALE BIBLE AND ITS ANTWERP ORIGINS[1]

Guido Latré

MILES COVERDALE, 'CORRECTOR' FOR MERTEN DE KEYSER

Miles Coverdale's 1535 edition, the first complete Bible to be printed in English, is generally regarded as the *editio princeps* of the English Bible. Answering the vexed question of where it was printed becomes, therefore, more than a matter of bibliographical correctness. In the sixteenth century printers were much more than technicians. Many among them had a profound intellectual background, and understood very well the contents of the books that authors were writing for them. They had a strong influence on the intellectual and religious climate in which the translators of the early printed Bibles were working. In his preliminary matter, the Low Countries printer Willem Vorsterman, who published the second complete Dutch Bible in print (Antwerp, 1528, NK 392),[2] shows his knowledge not only of the dangers of pirate editions but also of the reasons why his own edition is superior. He has, so it is claimed in the court order that protects his exclusive right to print and spread his Bible, chosen the best experts in the field to be his translators. Here is a part of the Antwerp magistrate's text, which Vorsterman includes after the title-page, and which obviously renders his own view:

Extract wten Registere vanden Vonnissen/ der wethouderen der Stadt Antwerpen.

Alsoe Willem Vorsterman printer/poirtere ende ingesetene der Stadt van Antwerpen/ den Eerweerdigen zeere wisen ende voorsienighen heeren Borghermeesteren ende Scepenen der voorseyder stadt geremonstreert ende verthoont heeft/ dat hoewel hi met groote arbeyde/ coste ende ernstiger diligentie heeft doen drucken/ den Bible/ inhoudende Doude ende Tnieuwe testament/ in nederlantscher duytscher talen/ ende tselve alsoe tzijnen grooten swaren coste ende laste/ wtghestelt ende overgheset is geweest/ by gheleerde ende getrouwe oversetters ende interpretatuers inder Hebreuscher/ Griecscher ende Latijnscher talen/ geleert ende expert zijnde/ ende de selve translatien met diverse ongecorrumpeerde Biblen/ niet suspect wesende van eenigen merckelijcken erruere/ ghetrouwelijc doen collationeren/ oversien/ ende corrigeren/ Desen nochtans niet tegenstaende vanteren ende vermeten hen eenighe printers inder voorseyder stadt den voorseiden Willeme/ den selven Bible nae te willen drucken/ tzijnder verderffelijcker ende onverdrachghelijcker schaden ende verliese.

[As Willem Vorsterman, printer/citizen and inhabitant of the Town of Antwerp has demonstrated and shown to the Honourable, wise and considerate Lord Mayor and aldermen of the aforesaid town that although with much labour, expense, and diligence he has had the Bible printed containing the Old and New Testament in the 'German' of the Low Countries [i.e. Dutch] and [although] the same [Bible] has also been made available and translated at his own expense by learned and faithful translators and interpreters who are skilled experts in the Hebrew, Greek, and Latin tongues, and although he [Vorsterman] has had the same translation collated, compared, and corrected with divers uncorrupted Bibles not suspect of any significant error, nevertheless, in spite of all this, some printers in the aforesaid town are proud and bold enough to make printed copies of the Bible from the aforesaid Willem to his most wicked and unbearable damage and loss.]

The phrase 'met diversche ongecorrumpeerde Biblen/ … corrigeren' (to 'correct' using divers uncorrupted Bibles) is interesting. In the jargon of the Dutch-speaking printer and his colleagues, the translators are called 'correctuers' ('correcteurs' or 'correctors'), and are seen to be doing 'correction work' on the best originals and earlier translations. Printers of pirate editions employ inferior 'correctors'.

Having first addressed his readers himself indirectly via the text of the court order, Vorsterman yields the floor to his own excellent correctors, who in a bowl-shaped paragraph at the beginning of their prologue ('Die prologhe'), identify their job as follows:

Die Prologhe

Die Correctuers deser translatien wensche[n]/allen den ghene[n]
die desen onsen arbeyt sien en[de] lesen sullen/warachtige ken-
nisse des vaders/ door Jesum Christum den sone/ en[de]
die gratie des heylighen gheests/ ende die hey-
lighe schrift/ alsoo te lesen datmen daer
door verbetert mach worden/ en-
de alle sonden te laten.

(The Prologue. The correctors of this translation wish all those that will see and read this our labour true knowledge of the Father through Jesus Christ the Son and the grace of the Holy Ghost, that they may read the Holy Scripture in such a manner that they may stand corrected by it and avoid all sins.)

In this English translation of the Dutch, the phrase 'that they may stand corrected by it' is an attempt to render the subtlety of the Dutch 'datmen daerdoor verbetert mach worden', with its veiled allusion to the corrector as someone who improves or corrects (Dutch infinitive: 'verbeteren') his readers by doing his translation work diligently. In a sense, both text and reader are corrected.

The idea that solid philology should lead to moral improvement is a well-known Erasmian one. It is also at the basis of the following extract from the last page of the prologue addressed by Coverdale 'Onto the Reader' in his 1538 New Testament:[3]

As for so moche as the Concordaunces of the new Testament haue ben sore corrupte/ bothe concernynge the Alphabete/ the nombre of the Chapters/ and the places alledged in the margent/ therfor so haue we set a newe Alphabete with a diligent Concordance in this newe Testament: Which we haue so poynted & marked with starres * and crosses + that thou mayest easely perceaue/ wherfore euery scripture is alledged/ how swetely and welfauoredly Gods worde hangeth together/ and how clearly one place expoundeth another. Which thynge yf thou diligently obserue/ submytynge thyne understandyng in mekenesse unto the holy goost/ it shall greatly increace thy knowledg in the scripture, And for so moche as ther be many now in oure dayes/ that peruersly and frowardly expounde the manyfest word of God (to the great delusyon of the symple) the same is the cause that I haue humbly under correccyon compared certayne textes of the newe Testame(n(t together/ and poynted them by the cyffres 1 2 3 4 5 unto soch gloses & annotacyons/ as I trust shalbe to thyne edifienge.

Glosses and annotations are seen as essential parts of the corrector's task. Classical and mediaeval rhetoric already emphasized the balance between what was useful (*utilis*) and what was agreeable (*dulcis*); Coverdale's use of the adverb 'swetely', in a text that also emphasized the 'edifying' aspects of the Scripture, shows his awareness of this long tradition. In his earlier 1535 Bible, however, the Bible translator humbly admits his limitations as a corrector; he does so on the second page of the Prologue 'unto the Christen Reader':[4]

For the which cause (acordyng as I]was desyred) I toke the more upon me to set forth this special tranlacyon, not as a checker, not as a reprouer, or despyser of other mens translacyons (for amonge many as yet I haue founde none without occasyon of greate thankesgeuynge unto god) but lowly + faythfully haue I folowed myne interpreters, + that under correccyon.

Here the wheel comes full circle; Coverdale himself stands corrected by his models. Who these models are has been well established by J. F. Mozley,[5] who directs us to Tyndale, Luther, the Zurich version, the Vulgate, and Pagninus. There are no Antwerp translators among these, but that does not exclude the influence Coverdale may have undergone, through the Antwerp printers and translators, regarding his attitude towards his job as a corrector. It is in this town that the first complete Dutch, French, and English Bibles in print all saw the light of day within one and the same decade: the Jacob van Liesveldt Bible of 1526 (Dutch NK 386), the Jacques Lefèvre d'Étaples Bible of 1530 (French – Chambers 51),[6] and Coverdale's own English Bible of 1535. Coverdale himself must have arrived there in the early 1530s to work together with Tyndale.[7] Hitherto, however, no one has been able to establish with certainty where he had his 1535 Bible printed. Catalogues and bibliographies are generally confused as to whether the place of printing is Cologne or Marburg; they usually add question marks to these places of printing, and some still stick to the suggestion of Zurich.[8] A. L. Sheppard's 1935-6 scholarly article for *The Library* first gives evidence in favour of Cologne but then suggests Marburg.[9] Mozley follows him only as far as Cologne; Sheppard's move to Marburg he 'cannot but call an aberration'.[10] Sheppard bases his arguments about Coverdale's place of printing mainly on initials, but these 'travelled' because they were often sold or borrowed; as a consequence, the place of printing might be neither Cologne nor Marburg, which makes the confusion complete.

In a slightly adapted form (the Great Bible, 1539) the great work of Coverdale, and through him the work of Tyndale, was mounted on lecterns the length and breadth of England from 1538 onwards, in accordance with Henry VIII's famous injunction.[11] For the first time all Englishmen could hear the same English (to a large extent Tyndale's) read to them. This Bible played a crucial role in the building of a common English language, helping to unify the nation. Together with its successors it is thus in no small part responsible for the English that has today become one of the primary languages of global communication. The fact that we remain in the dark regarding the place of printing of the first complete Bible in English is all the more astounding when placed beside the importance of this work and the knowledge that we have amassed concerning all other aspects of the English Bible.

We do have reliable evidence, however, that at around the time of this publication, Coverdale was working as a corrector for Merten de Keyser, one of the most significant printers of the Low Countries town of Antwerp. For evidence, Mozley refers to J. P.

Gelbert's *Magister Johann Bader's Leben und Schriften Nicolaus Thomae und Seine Briefe* (1808). Mozley had no access to Gelbert's sources but we can safely share his faith in the exactness of this author's statements.[12] Mozley does not quote the German, but because of its importance the evidence is perhaps better quoted here in the original language; Gelbert refers to Coverdale's journey to 'Niederdeutschland' (Low Germany, including the Low Countries), where Coverdale travelled to 'Antwerpen, wo er früher Corrector bei dem Buchdrucker Causar war' ('Antwerp, where earlier he had been corrector to the printer Causar').[13] The name 'Causar' refers to the same person as the Latin 'Caesar', the French 'Lempereur', or the Dutch 'de Keyser'. In view of the current use of the term 'corrector' (Dutch 'correctuer'/'correcteur', see above), Mozley's reference to Coverdale's job with de Keyser as 'proof-corrector'[14] is surely too limiting. It is probable that Coverdale translated and edited for de Keyser rather than simply proof-reading his texts.

We know a good deal about de Keyser. In her dictionary of 'Belgian' printers Anne Rouzet[15] refers to his house in the Lombaerdevest, which is just around the corner from Cammerstraat, where one house after another had been occupied by printers.[16] From the English House north of the Cathedral of Our Lady, both Coverdale and Tyndale could have reached de Keyser's printing house in about fifteen minutes, walking towards the south. Rouzet mentions that de Keyser came from France, and follows Monceaux in assuming that he established himself in Antwerp following the advice of the French Humanist and Bible translator Lefèvre ('sur les conseils de Le Fèvre d'Etaples').[17] As a punch-cutter, he continued to use the French bâtarde typefaces he had no doubt become familiar with in his father-in-law's printing house.[18] Thanks to a meticulously written article by the Dutch bibliographer Paul Valkema-Blouw in 1996, we now have a much better idea of de Keyser's contribution to the Reformation. Rouzet has counted more than two hundred works originating from his printing house,[19] but apparently even more have now to be attributed to him. Under the title 'Early Protestant Publications in Antwerp, 1526-30: The Pseudonyms Adam Anonymus in Basel and Hans Luft in Marlborow',[20] Valkema-Blouw argues that both the pseudonyms referred to here in fact stand not for Johannes Hoochstraten, as Miss Kronenberg of the celebrated NK (Nijhoff-Kronenberg bibliography) assumed, but to Merten de Keyser. For our understanding of the origins of the early English Bibles in print and other Protestant works, this has spectacular consequences. It implies that Tyndale's *The Practyse of Prelates*, his *Parable of the Wicked Mammon*, and his *The Obedience of a Christen Man*, all printed under the pseudonym 'Hans Luft' of 'Marburg', were printed by de Keyser. Under the same name was printed Tyndale's Pentateuch, two books of which – volumes I (Genesis) and IV (Numbers) – were exclusively by de Keyser, whereas volumes II (Exodus), III (Leviticus) and V (Deuteronomy) appeared in close cooperation with Joannes Grapheus.[21] Valkema-Blouw also mentions how George Joye's Psalms and *Ortulus anime* were likewise published by de Keyser under the false address 'Emprinted at Argentine ... by me Francis Foxe'.[22] And these are by no means the only 'new' titles to be added to the more or less two hundred we already knew were from de Keyser's printing house.

Apart from his efforts on behalf of the English Protestant writers and their polemical works and Bible translations, de Keyser also published widely in Latin, Dutch, and French. A count based on B. T. Chambers reveals that before the appearance of the

The 1535 Coverdale Bible and its Antwerp Origins

Coverdale Bible of 1535, his printing house is associated with no less than seven Bibles (complete or in part) for the aforementioned French Bible translator Jacques Lefèvre d'Étaples (one in 1528, two in 1529, one in 1530, one in 1531 and two in 1534). Rouzet mentions five works he printed jointly with Willem Vorsterman, who printed his several editions of the Vorsterman Bibles.[23] Among the five works is the 1529 French New Testament by Lefèvre d'Étaples. The latter's first complete French Bible mentions directly (i.e. without pseudonym) its de Keyser provenance: 'Imprime [sic] en Anvers par Martin Lempereur'.[24]

Admittedly Vorsterman was by no means exclusively in the Protestant camp. In his 1528 Bible he follows van Liesveldt (1526) in his Protestant choice of *oudste en ghemeinte* for respectively *presbyteroi* (Tyndale's *elders*) and *ekklesia* (Tyndale's *congregation*), but the 1532 Vorsterman Bible replaces these words by the Catholic 'priesters' and 'kerc'. Moreover, Lefèvre d'Étaples based his French Bible translations primarily on the Vulgate (but also on Humanist revisions, especially that of Pagninus). But then, in general, both the French and Dutch early Bibles in print show much more hesitation and compromise than Luther or Tyndale.

And so, in fact, does de Keyser himself. This, at least, is the general tendency perceived in the printer by Benoît Senden in his unpublished dissertation.[25] De Keyser's basic conviction must have been more Protestant than Catholic, as appears from the mottoes on several of his publications: 'Sola fides sufficit', a clear echo of Luther's 'Sola fide', and 'Spes mea Jesus', with its explicit emphasis on the Gospel and an implicit questioning of mediation through saints and the Church. Moreover, one can speculate that the de Keyser publications with a more Catholic stamp may have been a mere smoke-screen to deceive the Inquisition. It is difficult to assess to what extent he was committed to the Catholic views implicit in many of the works he printed. However, Senden's hypothesis makes a lot of sense in the Antwerp context of compromising Bible translations and other reconciliatory texts.

On some occasions one perceives a similar tendency towards compromise in Tyndale. In his letter dated 18 April 1531 the king's emissary Stephen Vaughan, whose task it was to persuade Tyndale to return to England, allows us to meet a Tyndale who does not insist at all on principles of doctrine. After his second meeting with him in Antwerp, Vaughan finds Tyndale very much affected by the open invitation, communicated via Cromwell, to go back to England:

'What gracious words are these! I assure you,' said he, 'if it would stand with the king's most gracious pleasure to grant only a bare text of the scripture to be put forth among his people, like as is put forth among the subjects of the emperor in these parts, and of other Christian princes, be it of the translation of what person soever shall please his majesty, I shall immediately make faithful promise never to write more, nor abide two days in these parts after the same: but immediately to repair unto his realm, and there most humbly submit myself at the feet of his royal majesty, offering my body to suffer what pain or torture, yea, what death his grace will, so this be obtained. And till that time, I will abide the asperity of all chances, whatsoever shall come, and endure my life as it is able to bear and suffer.'[26]

'These parts', which Tyndale refers to twice here, are obviously Antwerp and its Brabant surroundings in the Low Countries. His reference to 'the translation of what person soever shall please his majesty' does not limit the choice to Protestant translations only; any Bible will do as long as it is in English. Tyndale seems very much to be working in the spirit of Antwerp here, where especially the Vorsterman translations were less concerned about doctrinal consistency. Tyndale's main concern is indeed the spreading of the word of God in the vernacular: 'Is there more danger in the king's subjects than in the subjects of all other princes, which in every of their tongues have the same, under privilege of their sovereigns?'[27] The same concern is reiterated on the first page of Coverdale's Prologue 'Unto the Christen Reader', which precedes his 1535 Bible:

It grieved me [that] other nacyo[n]s shulde be more plenteously prouyded for with [the] scripture in theyr mother tongue, then we: therfore whan I was instantly requyred, though I coulde not do so well as I wolde, I thought it yet my dewtye to do my best, and that with a good wyll.[28]

The 'other princes' and 'other nations' in these quotes were not far off. They were in the very printing shops of Antwerp where not only Greek and Latin, but also a large amount of vernacular Bible translations were produced. When we include incomplete Bibles, one counts three Danish, twelve French, and no less than forty-three Dutch-language Bibles[29] between 1526 and 1535. It is this multilingual and multinational context, the overwhelming impact of the many editions of especially the Dutch Bibles, as well as the Antwerp readiness to be expedient rather than doctrinal, that both Tyndale and Coverdale seem strongly aware of. Van Liesveldt's 1526 Dutch Bible had been available some while when Tyndale arrived in Antwerp, probably at around the time of the appearance of Vorsterman's first translation (1528), and Coverdale must have found himself in the midst of a flood of Dutch Bibles as well as the eight French ones when he published his 1535 translation. As a corrector to Merten de Keyser, whose name is so strongly connected with Bible translations in each of the languages, he found himself amidst huge stacks of loose leaves, the eloquent witnesses of hectic translation activities which both corrected and corrupted texts. All around him was the fierce competition between reliable printers or correctors and their pirate rivals. Although William Tyndale himself may have been more sheltered thanks to the protection of the Poyntz family,[30] he was likewise at work in this shape-shifting context. The extent to which he remained consistent and preserved his integrity while being accommodating is remarkable.

Given this context, which situates the two English exiles in far less isolated a position than has often been assumed, it becomes all the more urgent to define the place of origin of the first complete English Bible in print. Coverdale's association with Antwerp on the basis of his modest partnership with Tyndale in that town as well as his task as a corrector for de Keyser is strong already. It would become much stronger still if we could find evidence of the printing of his Bible in Antwerp rather than a German town. Such evidence actually exists, notably, so far, in the shape of a woodcut in the Exodus part of Coverdale's 1535 Bible.

THE 'POSTILLA' WOODCUT OF THE TABERNACLE

In the international context in which English traders and translators were working before the days of the Empire, they must have had a perception of their own language quite different from that experienced by a modern English man or woman. English was by no means a common language between traders from different parts of Europe. London ranked way below Antwerp as an international port.[31] In a French or Dutch

Bible one could reasonably expect the words in illustrations to be in the language of the Bible text itself. Preparing the woodcuts was an expensive business, but it was worth it given the prestige of Dutch and French and given the much nearer and/or much larger market.[32] In the case of English Bibles there was more hesitation. In a 1560 Geneva Bible one finds below the English text on 'The ordre of the tentes' and under the heading 'THE FIGURE OF THE TABERNACLE ERECTED, AND OF THE TENTES PITCHED ROVNDE ABOUT IT' an illustration of the tabernacle of witness.[33] The Ark is surrounded by the tents of Israel, and at each of the four edges of this illustration in what is otherwise a completely English Bible one finds the four points of the compass unashamedly named in French: OCCIDENT, SEPTENTRION, ORIENT and MIDI.

A similar phenomenon occurs in Coverdale 1535 in Exodus 40.1-5 (see Pl. 1). Here we find an illustration of the Tabernacle that is repeated in Numbers ch. 2, besides a narrow strip of text (now verses 9-13).[34] The words indicating the four points of the compass are again in a language that is decidedly not English: WEST is the only word that might belong to English, Dutch, or German. NORD is common in German and less usual but by no means uncommon in the Dutch of the period.[35] 'SVIID', with the spelling of the diphthong turned upside down because of the miscalculation of the mirror effect in reproducing the woodblock, is certainly Dutch. Evidence as to whether this spelling also exists in German is not easy to find: the dictionary of the Grimm brothers has neither 'suid' nor 'suiid',[36] but the word might still be 'Ripuarisches Deutsch',[37] the German spoken along the river Rhine in the West of Germany (Aachen-Cologne area); the spelling 'suiid' could therefore theoretically leave intact the chances that Cologne was the place of printing of the Coverdale Bible.

It is ultimately OOST that gives the strongest evidence for the Low Countries origin of the illustration. The spelling is the usual Dutch one,[38] and does not occur at all in the German dictionaries.[39] The double 'oo' definitely indicates a long vowel. Johannes Franck's *Altfränkische Grammatik* (*Old Franconian Grammar*) is very decided on the issue of the long 'o': 'Das ahd.-fr. beruht in der Regel auf germ. *au* (§ 32). Ausserdem ist es vorhanden in einigen Fremdwörtern, in denen o nicht zu *uo* geworden ist, wie *Roma, rosa, chor, corona*.'[40] In Müller's dictionary of the Rhineland the pronunciation with the long vowel for 'ost' makes it not a 'point of the compass', but the 'time for harvesting', as derived from the name of the month of 'August', 'Erntezeit s. August'[41] (a case of 'au' becoming 'o') or an 'oast' (German 'Aststelle'). This phonological distinction is an unambiguous indicator that 'oost' with a long vowel, indicating a point of the compass, is Dutch. Moreover, the diphthongization of the long 'i' in the proper name IJSACHAR likewise points in the same direction. Diphthongization in what in the old Flemish texts are long vowels occurs generally at this time in the Antwerp area, whose dialects still make a very conspicuous use of diphthongs today.

All the names on the tents in the illustration are consistent with Antwerp spellings of the first half of the sixteenth century: the names of 10 sons of Jacob, RUBEN, [S]IMEON, GAD, BENAMIN, DAN, A[S]ER, NAPHTALI, IVDA[S], IJSACHAR, and SEBVLON; the three of Levi, GERSON, KAHAT, and MERARI; and those of Joseph, EPHRAIM and MANA[SS]E (see Genesis 46). Interestingly enough, the spelling for 'A[s]er' is to be found in the Vorsterman Bible of 1528 and not in Luther (who has 'Asser'). The closest parallel one finds to the 'Ijsachar' spelling is likewise in this Vorsterman ('Isachar', whereas Luther has 'Isaschar').[42]

So far it has not been possible to find a Dutch Bible with an identical illustrations of the Tabernacle; but nor has it been possible to find the identical illustration in any German Bible. Similar illustrations of the Tabernacle, complete with tents, altar of the burnt-offering, and utensils occur in countless other sources in Germany and the Low Countries. B. A. Rosier points out that they are typical examples of the so-called *Postilla*-print:

In almost all illustrated sixteenth-century Netherlandish Bible editions, prints appear that are based on the representations in the printed versions of the Postilla by the French theologian Nicholas of Lyra (c. 1270-1349). The Postilla is a very comprehensive and in-depth Bible commentary that had been distributed over Europe in numerous manuscripts from the second quarter of the fourteenth century onward. ... The first printed editions of the Postilla illustrated with woodcuts appeared in 1481 by Anton Koberger at Nuremburg. This edition contained some forty prints.[43]

Rosier's study of Low Countries Bible illustrations makes it abundantly clear that the craftsmanship in Dutch Bibles is on the whole inferior to that found in German Bibles or editions; it is only in the latter half of the sixteenth century, especially after the arrival of Plantin in Antwerp (1550), that the Low Countries illustrations begin to rival and at times excel their German models. It is not very likely, therefore, that a German printer should have felt the need to acquire a Low Countries illustration of the Tabernacle.

The other, smaller illustrations in Coverdale's Bible look identical to some in Matthew's Bible (1537). Of the latter, we know that it was produced by the Antwerp printer Matthias Crom. An electronic scanning of both sets of illustrations, concentrating on the pictures of the slaughter of Abel, Noah's ark, Noah's drunkenness, and others, has yielded some results that point to a very strong connection, but the sets are not identical. The very detailed electronic scans, provided by Cambridge University Library, were compared in Adobe Photoshop by Professors Pamela King (University College of St Martin, Lancaster) and Meg Twycross (Lancaster University), who suggest that the prints were a second run of the same pictures, probably recut when the first woodcuts wore out. So there is a connection, if tenuous: someone would have had to have had the originals (either in the form of the woodcuts or very good prints) in order to make such close copies. Proving that none of the illustrations in Matthew's uses exactly the same woodcut as was used by Coverdale, we are deprived of an easy proof that Coverdale's Bible is very likely to have been prepared in an Antwerp printing house.[44]

However, there are other arguments in favour of Antwerp. More external historical evidence of the Low Countries' origin of Coverdale 1535 is to be found in Emanuel van Meteren's *Historie des Neder-landscher ende haerder Na-buren oorlogen ende geschiedenissen* (*History of the Wars in the Low Countries and Their Neighbours*), 1614. At the end of the book one Simeon Ruytinck gives a biographical account of the historiographer Emanuel van Meteren, who was born in the year of the Coverdale Bible translation (1535) and died in 1612. It is the description of Emanuel's father that interests us most:

Sijn Vader in sijn Ieucht hadde gheleert die edele Conste van 't Letter setten, hy was begaeft met de kenisse van veelderley talen ende andere goede wetenschappen, wist van in die tijden t' licht t' onderscheyden van duysternisse, ende bethoonde sijnen bysonderen yver in 't becostighen vande oversettinghe ende Druck vande Engelschen Bijbel binnen Antwerpen, daer toe ghebruyckende den dienst van een gheleert Student met namen Miles Couerdal, tot groote bevoorderinghe van het Rijcke Iesu Christi in Enghelandt.[45]

(His father had learnt the noble art of typesetting in his youth. He was gifted with the knowledge of several languages and other good skills. He knew at this early stage how to distinguish the light from the darkness [i.e. by adhering to the Protestant faith], and showed his special zeal in bearing the cost of the translation and printing of the English Bible inside Antwerp, using to this purpose the services of a learned student named Miles Coverdale, to the great advancement of the Kingdom of Jesus Christ in England.)[46]

Bearing the cost of the enterprise was no small matter. The clandestine transport of loose sheets from the port of Antwerp to London involved risks and no doubt increased the expenses. Even for printers of Dutch Bibles the investment involved was a worry, as appears from the extract of the Antwerp Court Register in the Vorsterman Bible quoted at the beginning of this article. Whoever the printer was, he would have been pleased with Jacob van Meteren's willingness to invest his money in the hazardous initiative to print a first complete English Bible.

Just like Jacob and Emanuel van Meteren, Ruytinck would have been sympathetic to the Protestant cause, and there is no reason to suspect that he would have tampered with the indication of the place of printing ('inside Antwerp', where the bulk of Dutch Bibles appeared).

A later English source confirming the Low Countries (though not necessarily Antwerp) for the printing is perhaps less reliable, but still very interesting. It is to be found in the writings of Samuel Clarke (1599-1683, curate of St Bennet Fink, London, 1642-62), under the lengthy title:

A Generall Martyrologie, containing a collection Of all the greatest persecutions which have befallen the Church of Christ From the Creation to our present Times, Lives of English and Christ. (1660).[47]

After 301 pages of the *Martyrologie* follows *The Lives of Two and Twenty English Divines*. Pages 4-6 of the latter are on '*The Life of* Miles Coverdale *sometimes Bishop of* Exester, *who died* Anno Christi 1568'. It is here that we find the following extract:

Miles Coverdale was born in the North of *England*, and from his childhood was much given to learning, and by his diligence and industry profited exceedingly therein; so that in the reign of King *Henry* the eighth, he was one of the first that professed the Gospel in *England*. He was very well skilled in the *Hebrew*, and translated the Bible into *English*, and wrote sundry Books upon the Scriptures, which Doctrine being new and strange in those daies, he was much hated and persecuted for it, especially by the Bishops; whereupon he was forced to fly into the *Low Countries*. There he printed the Bibles of his Translation, and by sending them over, and selling them in *England* he maintaned himself. But *John Stokesly* Bishop of *London*, hearing therof, and minding to prevent their dispersing in *England*, enquired diligently where they were to be sold, and bought them all up, supposing that by this means no Bibles would be had; but contrary to his expection it fell out otherwise; for the same money which the Bishop gave for these Books, the Merchant sent over to *Miles Coverdale*, by which means he was enabled to Print as many more, which he also sent into *England*.[48]

A similar tale about the clever selling of bibles to the Bishop of London (Stokesley) for the recuperation money (with profits) is told about Tyndale. In his *Book of Martyrs* (second edition, 1570), Foxe takes it over from Halle's *Chronicle*. Mozley wisely comments that 'this is a delightful tale, but it has lost nothing in the telling; it bears all the marks of embellishment'.[49] However, tall tales gain in the telling by using reliable details in an otherwise apocryphal narrative. The reference to the Low Countries, where Antwerp is the obvious place to look for Bible translations, may well be trustworthy as an indication of the place of printing for Coverdale's Bible.

We now have internal (words in an illustration) and external evidence (based on historical accounts by van Meteren/Ruytinck and Clarke) pointing towards Antwerp as the place of printing for Coverdale's work. What remains to be done is to find out who the printer was. Much more typographical research needs to be done on typefaces, woodcuts, title borders, and other typographical data. As Valkema-Blouw argues in several of his publications, this kind of research is often much more reliable than external evidence by contemporary historians:

> Occasionally, as we shall see, an anonymous printer of such a clandestine output can be discovered with the help of no more than a single initial. Typefaces can also play a key role, but we must keep in mind the reservation that in the course of the sixteenth century, and certainly after 1550, they were usually being employed by too many printers for them to serve as an effective indication.[50]

These comments on the reliability of typefaces to indicate a printer may yet prove to be crucial to the discovery of the printer of the Coverdale Bible. There were not many printers in Antwerp who were using a Schwabacher in 1535. In fact, it is unlikely that there was more than one. His name, unsurprisingly, is Merten de Keyser. It is the invaluable detective work of Paul Valkema-Blouw again that allows us to follow the de Keyser trace for the identification of the place of printing of the Coverdale translation in the Low Countries. The key to the answer is the Coverdale Bible's use of the Schwabacher letter type, which has made so many bibliographers take a German place of origin for granted. De Keyser, however, also used it for several of the works by the English Protestant writers in Antwerp; among these are Tyndale's Pentateuch and Joye's Psalter.[51] It is after the latter publication in 1530 that 'De Keyser abandoned the use of the Schwabacher as a principal type and thus followed the example of Adriaen van Berghen who had done away with it some time earlier'.[52] But even though it was no longer his principal type, he was still using it in 1535, before his death at the end of that year or the beginning of the next year, in *An confortable exhortation of our mooste holy Christen faith*, with, as a fake imprint, "Peter Congeth at Parishe"'.[53]

Merten de Keyser had a sense of humour, and played a highly skillful cat-and-mouse game with the Inquisition, alternatively hiding himself under the name of Balthasar Bekenth ('you know who'), Adam Anonymus ('you don't know who'), and Hans Luft of Marburg (i.e. 'I have evaporated into thin air or German "Luft" and now please confuse me with Luther's printer Hans Luft of Wittenburg'). His typefaces and the other historical evidence, both internal and external, may now give away one of his long-kept secrets at last: we can safely assume that in Antwerp, his workshop provided the English with their first complete Bible ever to have been printed.

The 1535 Coverdale Bible and its Antwerp Origins

CONCLUSION

Those who have seen *God's Outlaw*,[54] the only film made so far on Tyndale, will be familiar with the bleak picture of utter isolation Tyndale experienced as an exile in a poverty-stricken Antwerp. It is clear that this gloomy image of the Protestant martyr stands in serious need of correction. Both Tyndale and Coverdale were at work in what one could call a pool of translators whose task as so-called 'correctors' extended far beyond proof-reading. The English translators shared with the better of their Dutch- and French-speaking colleagues a genuine concern for the 'correctness' of the text – for them a moral and theological issue of the greatest importance. The number of editions prepared by the Antwerp translators working in French or Dutch was much larger, and on the whole figures like Vorsterman and de Keyser (and to a lesser extent van Liesveldt) felt much more than the English translators the need to compromise on matters of religious doctrine. However, even Tyndale may have been influenced by the general attitude of compromise prevailing in Antwerp when he expressed his willingness to accept any translation, Protestant or Catholic, for the England he had left behind. Coverdale's decision to turn especially to the Vulgate where he could not follow Tyndale (the latter being in Vilvoorde prison, unable to complete his translation task) fits perfectly within the policies of Antwerp translators in general.

The Tabernacle illustration in Coverdale's 1535 Bible, as well as the Schwabacher letter-form used for this publication, are part of the the internal evidence pointing to Antwerp and more specifically de Keyser's workshop as its place of printing. The 'moderation' that has been pointed out in this prolific printer adds a new dimension to the mild attitude found in Tyndale and Coverdale by their biographers (Mozley, Daniell). Antwerp emerges as a town of tolerance and expedience, of religious zeal and commercial interest, all mixed in a sometimes delicate, sometimes somewhat distorted balance, which in the end may have enabled both Tyndale and Coverdale to survive as intellectual, human, and humane beings. Antwerp did far more for them than simply pack and clandestinely ship the loose leaves of their Bibles. It determined the general climate, more mild than acerbic, in which the first English Bible translations, complete or incomplete, could originate.

NOTES

1 The research for this article has been done in the context of two projects in which K.U. Leuven is one of two partners. The first has the support of British Council and FWO (Flemish Research Fund); it allows the author to cooperate with Professor Meg Twycross (Lancaster University) and Professor Pamela King (University College of St Martin, Lancaster) for research on literary and iconographic relationships between England and the Low Countries in the late Middle Ages and Renaissance. The second project concentrates on the same period in history, and studies the relationships between the two above-mentioned geographical areas more generally. It is coordinated by Professor Yoko Wada of Kansai University, Japan. My sincere thanks are also due to K.U. Leuven researchers Delphine Piraprez, Susan Reed (KULAK), and Liesbeth Vercammen; to Tyndale Society members Professor David Daniell, Mr Andrew Hope, Professor David Norton, Dr Deborah Pollard, and Prof. Barry Ryan; to my colleagues in the Theology Libraries at K. U. Leuven and UCL, especially Mr Frans Gistelinck and Prof. J.-F. Gilmont; and to Dr Elly Cockx-Indestege and Dr Marcus De Schepper of the Royal Library in Brussels.

2 The first complete Bible in print in the Dutch language is Jacob van Liesveldt's (1526) (NK 386). All NK-references are to M. E. Kronenberg, *Nijhoff-Kronenberg Nederlandsche bibliografie van 1500 tot 1540*, vols 1-3 ('s Gravenhage: Martinus Nijhoff, 1923-71).

3 The copy used here is Cambridge, Univ. Libr., Shelfmark Young 157 (Herbert 18; STC 2836, NK 2498).

4 All references to the Coverdale 1535 translation are to its facsimile edition, edited from the Folkham copy in the British Library, with an introduction by S. L. Greenslade (Folkestone, Kent: Dawson, 1975).

5 See J. F. Mozley, *Coverdale and His Bibles* (London: Lutterworth Press, 1953), pp. 78-100 on Coverdale's sources.

6 See B. T. Chambers, *Bibliography of French Bibles: Fifteenth- and Sixteenth- Century French-Language Editions of the Scriptures* (Geneva: Droz, 1983), pp. 70-2, item 51.

7 Mozley, *Coverdale*, pp. 5-6.

8 The Bodleian suggests Cologne, the British Library Marburg, Cambridge University Library Cologne or Marburg, and the Huntington still sticks to Zurich. A. W. Pollard & G. R. Redgrave, *Short Title Catalogue of Books printed in England, and of English Books printed abroad, 1475-1640*, 2nd edn, 3 vols (London: Bibliographical Society, 1976-91), suggest Marburg, with a question mark, as place of printing, and 'E. Cervicornus & J. Soter?' as printers. A. S. Herbert, in *Historical Catalogue of Printed Editions of the English Bible 1525-1961* (London: The British and Foreign Bible Society, New York: The American Bible Society, 1968), keeps both options open: 'Cologne or Marburg'.

9 A. L. Sheppard, 'The Printers of the Coverdale Bible, 1535', *The Library*, 2nd series, 16 (1936), 280-9.

10 Mozley, *Coverdale*, p. 76.

11 'Before the printing [of the Great Bible] was finished, the famous injunction of 1538 was put out in the royal name ordering that a copy be set up in every church' (Mozley, *Coverdale*, p. 114).

12 Mozley, *Coverdale*, p. 6.

13 J. P. Gelbert, *Magister Johann Bader's Leben und Schriften Nicolaus Thomae und seine Briefe: Ein Beitrag zur Reformationsgeschichte der Städte Landau, Bergzabern und der links-rheinischen Pfalz, zur Feier des fünfzigjährigen Jubiläums der kirchlichen Union* (Neustadt a.d.R.: Gottschick-Witter's Buchhandlung, 1868), pp. 275-6.

14 Mozley, *Coverdale*, p. 53.

15 Anne Rouzet, *Dictionnaire des imprimeurs, libraires et éditeurs des XVe et XVIe siècles dans les limites géographiques de la Belgique actuelle* (Nieuwkoop: De Graaf, 1975), pp. 112-13.

16 The unpublished material collected by Lode Van den Branden and now residing in the Royal Library (Albertina) in Brussels is most revealing in this respect. Van den Branden has worked on maps of the Antwerp streets and traced the ownership or renting of houses by printers. Both sides of the Cammerstraat show an amazing concentration of printing houses.

17 Rouzet, p. 112. See also H. Monceaux, *Les Le Rouge de Chablis, calligraphes et minia-turistes, graveurs et imprimeurs, part II* (Paris: A. Claudin, 1896), pp. 36-8.

18 He had married Françoise Le Rouge, daughter to the French printer Guillaume Le Rouge. See Rouzet, p. 112.

19 Rouzet, p. 112.

20 Paul Valkema-Blouw, 'Early Protestant Publications in Antwerp, 1526-30: The Pseudonyms Adam Anonymus in Basel and Hans Luft in Marlborow', *Quaerendo*, 26-2 (Spring 1996), 94-110.

21 Ibid., 105-6.

22 Ibid., 108.

23 Rouzet, p. 112.

24 Chambers, pp. 70-2, item 51.

25 Benoît Senden, unpublished graduate dissertation supervised by J.-F. Gilmont at the Université catholique de Louvain (Louvain-la-Neuve), entitled 'Martin Lempereur, un imprimeur de la Réforme' (1989).

26 Quoted in David Daniell, *William Tyndale: A Biography* (New Haven & London: Yale University Press, 1994), p. 216. In his turn, Daniell quotes from J. F. Mozley, *William Tyndale* (Westport, CN: Greenwood Press, 1937), p. 198.

27 Daniell, p. 214; Mozley, *William Tyndale*, p. 194. The references here are to Vaughan's first meeting with Tyndale and his subsequent letter dated 18 April 1531.

28 Coverdale's 1535 Bible translation, Greenslade facsimile, p. 38.

29 This (hitherto unpublished) count was done by Frans Gistelinck of the Theology Library in Leuven, Belgium.

30 Daniell, pp. 361-84 *passim*.

31 See among other publications Jan Van der Stock, *Antwerp: Story of a Metropolis* (Antwerp: Hessenhuis, 1993).

32 The southern Low Countries were very densely populated, and the Reformation had made much more progress there than in England, which meant more literate readers eager to get hold of Bible translations.

33 (STC 2093) Geneva Bible 1560, Herbert 61, item 107; STC 2093. The illustration is on page 51.

34 For my earlier conjectures on this illustration, see Guido Latré, 'The Place of Printing of the Coverdale Bible', *The Tyndale Society Journal*, 8 (November 1997), 5-18.

35 The form with a short vowel, indicated by the single 'o', is even at the basis of the main entry of the word for a slightly older stage of the language. See Verwijs & Verdam, *Middelnederlands woordenboek* ('s Gravenhage: Martinus Nijhoff, 1899), Part IV.

36 Jacob & Wilhelm Grimm, *Deutsches Wörterbuch* (Leipzig: S. Hirzel, 1889), Part XIV.

37 I owe this linguistic judgement to a specialist in the field of the border dialects, Jan Goossens, emeritus professor of linguistics at Leuven (Dutch-speaking Belgium) and Münster (Germany). Also my assessment of the language area for *oost* is to a large extent based on his advice. My thanks are also due to Prof. Joop van der Horst and Professor Luc Draye, linguists at K.U. Leuven.

38 See, among others, W. L. De Vreese & G. J. Boekenoogen, *Woordenboek der Nederlandsche Taal* ('s Gravenhage & Leiden: Martinus Nijhoff, A. W. Sijthoff, 1910), Part 11, for the entry *Oost*.

39 Grimm has *ost*, not *oost*. Josef Müller's *Rheinisches Wörterbuch* (Berlin: Erika Klopp, 1944), Part VI (N-Q), p. 402, has only one entry with a double 'o'in the spelling: *Ool*, which is a proper name.

40 Johannes Franck, *Altfränkische Grammatik*, 2nd edn, ed. by Rudolf Schützeichel (Göttingen: Vandenhoeck & Ruprecht, 1971), p. 38; it does not, however, include all alternative spellings.

41 Müller, p. 427.

42 These parallel spellings have been checked by Eveline De Vuyst for her K.U. Leuven dissertation (under preparation) on de Keyser.

43 Bart A. Rosier, *The Bible in Print: Netherlandish Bible Illustration in the Sixteenth Century*, 2 vols (Leiden: Foleor Publishers, 1997), p. 69.

44 For more details about the similarities between Coverdale 1535 and Matthew's, see Latré (n. 35 above), pp. 11-12.

45 Emanuel van Meteren, *Historie des Neder-landscher ende haerder Na-buren oorlogen ende geschiedenissen* ('s Graven-Haghe: Hillebrant Iacobsz, 1614), fol. 672ʳ. For further information on van Meteren and his publications, see E. O. G. Haitsma Mulier & G. A. C.

Van der Lem, *Repertorium van geschiedschrijvers in Nederland* (Den Haag: Nederlands Historisch Genootschap, 1990), pp. 284-7 (item 333).

46 Most of this extract is also quoted, in an English translation only, by Mozley, *Coverdale*, p. 73.

47 A Generall Martyrologie, CONTAINING A COLLECTION Of all the greatest PERSECUTIONS which have befallen the CHURCH OF CHRIST From the Creation to our present Times, Both in England and all other Nations. Whereunto are added two and twenty LIVES OF ENGLISH Modern Divines, Famous in their Generations for Learning and Piety, and most of the great Sufferers in the Cause of CHRIST. The title-page mentions: London. The second edition, Corrected and Enlarged; having the two late Persecutions inserted: the one in Piemont: the other in Poland. LONDON. Printed by Tho. Ratcliffe, for Thomas Underhill and John Rothwell in Saint Pauls Church-yard, near the little North-door. MDCLX. For the bibliographical data, see Donald Wing, *Short-Title Catalogue of Books Printed in England, Scotland, Ireland, Wales, and British America and of English Books Printed in Other Countries, 1641-1700* (New York: The Modern Language Association of America, 1998), Part I, p. 577, item 4514.

48 Mr Jonathan D. Moore of Emmanuel College Cambridge has pointed out this passage to me – for which my sincere thanks. He has found that Clarke has unique information, but that where it is not unique there is sometimes conflict, with Clarke sometimes inaccurate.

49 Mozley, *William Tyndale*, p. 149. See also Daniell, pp. 196-8.

50 Paul Valkema-Blouw, 'The Van Oldenborch and Vanden Merberghe Synonyms, or Why Frans Fraet Had to Die', Part One, *Quaerendo*, 22/3 (Summer 1992), 183.

51 Valkema-Blouw, 'Protestant Publications' (n. 21 above), 104-8.

52 Ibid., 108.

53 Ibid., 109.

54 *God's Outlaw: The Story of William Tyndale*, directed by Tony Tew (a Grenville Film Production in association with Channel Four, undated).

MARTIN LUTHER AND PAUL'S EPISTLE TO THE ROMANS

William S. Campbell

INTRODUCTION

IT IS ASTONISHING that Martin Luther's lectures on Romans, now regarded as so significant for a proper understanding of the Reformer's theological development, were published for the first time only in 1908 by Johannes Ficker. At the time Ficker regarded this edition as merely provisional; however, it was not until 1938 that he managed to bring out his definitive version, published as volume 56 of the Weimar edition of Luther's works.[1]

As a young instructor Luther had already taught the basic course in Aristotle as well as the introductory course in theology, based on Peter Lombard's *Four Books of Sentences*. When he became a full member of the theological faculty he was free to choose for himself which areas of the Bible he would teach. For two years (from Easter 1513 to the end of the winter semester 1515) Martin Luther lectured on the Psalms. To aid in his teaching, he created a novel arrangement of the text with the assistance of the printer Johann Grunenberg. The text was set out with wide margins, and extra interlinear space was left to allow for the insertion of glosses alongside the relevant part of the text. Then, for two years and throughout three semesters (from Easter 1515 to September 1516), Luther went on to lecture on Romans, following the same pattern. His text of Paul's letter extended to some twenty-eight printed pages of fourteen lines each, a copy of which was given to each student. In careful handwriting on the text, Luther wrote grammatical, philological, and marginal comments. He delivered the essence of these comments to his students, who would add them above or beside their own printed texts.

However, in addition to these there existed Luther's own extended commentary, amounting to some twenty-three sheets, much of which related to contemporary controversies. Of this only a small portion was delivered to the students. The result was that although several copies of students' notes were later recovered, Luther's own longer accumulated text, extending to over five hundred pages, escaped notice altogether. It was unknown until 1908, when it was brought to public attention through two copies, one of which was held in the Vatican Library, and the other in the Royal Library of Berlin.[2]

LUTHER AND EARLIER INTERPRETIVE TRADITIONS

Every scholarly innovation links in some way with earlier interpretative traditions. Of course, this connection may not take the form of a straightforward sequential history.

William S. Campbell

This may be illustrated by taking an example from approaches to the interpretation of the New Testament. Some interest was evoked in the social and economic background of the New Testament as early as the 1880s, when Edwin Hatch gave his Bampton lectures entitled 'On the Organization of the Early Christian Church'. This interest continued to develop into the early part of this century, even up to the early 1930s, particularly through the influence of the Chicago School and scholars such as Shirley Jackson Case.[3] But in 1918 Karl Barth's commentary on Romans fell like a bombshell on the playground of the theologians, who were, he felt, too concerned with their scholarly pursuits into philology and archaeology to be able to hear what the Word of God was saying.[4] The Biblical Theology movement had been born, the outcome of which was that it was not until the 1960s that scholars again took up the search for the social, economic, and contextual background of the New Testament documents. The continuity in the study of the social context of the New Testament was not entirely lost, but had been interrupted by other, more pressing concerns.

So too with Luther in relation to the history of biblical interpretation and previous biblical commentators. He did have his predecessors, and certainly his interpretations were not all entirely novel, but neither did they always relate directly to his teachers and contemporaries. Despite this, as Peter Gorday has noted, 'the Reformation interpretation of Paul continued in the Reformation and post-Reformation periods much like that practised by the medieval exegetes'.[5] The ongoing pattern was as follows: having taken up his own particular stance, a scholar would illustrate the range of options, substantiating his own approach by supportive and accumulative citations from the authoritative Fathers. Gorday continues:

> Each interpreter tended to have his favourite patristic authority, whose nature – as he construed it – was most congenial to his own: for Luther it was Augustine; for Calvin and the Swiss Reformers it tended to be the practical and plain Chrysostom; for Erasmus, it was the spiritual and optimistic Origen. Luther liked Augustine's ability to point to the theological heart of Paul's argument; Calvin liked Chrysostom's capacity to stay close to the text and to wring homilitical value from every point; and Erasmus liked Origen's sense for symbolic levels and spiritual inwardness.[6]

To one extent or another, these sixteenth-century exegetes were also influenced by philological considerations, preferring one Father's opinion over that of another, on linguistic or grammatical grounds. However, dogmatic affinity to a particular patristic writer played an equally strong role. For Luther, Augustine was always his preferred source and authority. In his lectures on Romans Augustine is cited most frequently (more than one hundred times), in contrast to Jerome (some twelve times) and Chrysostom (only a few times). Origen is not quoted at all.[7]

The reason for this obvious partisanship is to be found in Luther's preferences, which were in exact opposition to those of Erasmus at this point. From chapter 9 onwards in his lectures on Romans, Luther introduces references to Erasmus' views, but he never shows himself dependent on the Dutch scholar for theological ideas. For Erasmus, Origen was first and Augustine last in preference; for Luther this order was reversed: 'In the exposition of Scripture, I put Jerome as far behind Augustine as Erasmus puts Augustine behind Jerome.'[8]

It was Augustine's anti-Pelagian writings that Luther found most useful. When he began his lectures on Romans, he had just become acquainted with Augustine's *On the*

Spirit and the Letter,[9] and had found it most illuminating. Luther judged that Augustine was a true Paulinist, in that Augustine enabled him to understand the message of the Apostle in a way that no one else could. Thus he regarded Augustine as his main ally in the fight against the Pelagian tendencies of Scholasticism. Luther did not offer unconditional support, however: he opposed Augustine's teaching on love, in which self-love became the model for divine love. Also (although he was better than most in the Reformer's opinion), Augustine did not reach the profundity of Paul's understanding of man's situation before God. Luther was, nonetheless, essentially in agreement with his predecessor in regarding sin not as single isolated acts, but as the basic proneness towards evil, in which every individual sin is perceived as the manifestation of a sinful nature.

Obviously, the use of Augustine's theology could not be the sole prerogative of Martin Luther; Augustine was still regarded as the foremost exegete of Paul, both in the Reformed as well as the Catholic interpretation of Romans.[10] For the Reformed, he was recognized for his stress on justification by faith through grace; the latter dubbed him the 'doctor of grace'. In both cases the heart of Paul's thought was construed in terms of the affirmation of gratuitous salvation in Christ, over and against the Jewish (i.e. Pelagian) religion of legalistic works righteousness.[11]

Luther's alienation from the Scholastics did not, therefore, simply derive from the choice of authoritative Church Fathers in lines of interpretation, since both sides acknowledged the wisdom of Augustine. It was as much, or more, the philosophical traditions and framework in which biblical interpretation took place. It appears the young Luther never found philosophy all that attractive; from the first he would gladly have changed it for theology. Paul, above all, was Luther's model for understanding, and his thought-pattern was exceedingly different from all contemporary schools of thought:

The apostle philosophises and thinks about the things of the world in another way than do the philosophers and metaphysicians. ... He does not speak of the 'essence' of the creature and of the way it 'operates', but using a strange and new theological word he speaks of 'the expectation of the creature' (Rom.8:19). ... But alas how deeply we are caught in quiddities, and how many foolish opinions befog us in metaphysics. When shall we learn to see that we are wasting much precious time with such useless studies. ... Indeed, I believe that I owe this duty to the Lord of crying out against philosophy and turning men to Holy Scripture. ... It is high time that we transferred from these other studies and learn Jesus Christ and Him crucified.[12]

It was this that caused Luther to turn against his own teachers at Erfurt University: Jodocus Trutvetter and Bartholomew of Usingen, John von Paltz and John Nathin. He saw them all as representatives of Scholasticism, which interpreted the Christian Gospel through the philosophy of Aristotle, a man whose metaphysics he regarded as fallacious (*fallax*) and whose ethics he believed to be 'the worst enemy of grace'.[13] Contrasting modern teachers and their ancient counterparts, Luther claims that the modern speak with little authority, because they are not supported by the testimony of Scripture. The ancients, on the other hand, 'say the same thing much more plainly and in line with the apostles' whereas the modern teachers teach nothing but futile and harmful imagination because 'they teach by way of interpreting Aristotle'.[14] It is probably true that Luther to some extent did remain an Occamist, in method and manner of theological argument, for the rest of his life; at the very least he was negatively influenced by it.

However, on the subject of anthropology he made a complete break with his teachers and, in opposition to what he perceived to be their too-optimistic view of the perfectibility of human nature, he embraced an Augustinianism more severe and thoroughgoing than Augustine himself.[15]

LUTHER'S THEOLOGICAL INTERPRETATION OF SCRIPTURE

In his preface to the lectures on Romans, Luther describes this letter as the key to understanding the Old Testament. In fact, Luther's Christological emphasis is total: 'every word in the Bible points to Jesus'. This underlines something which is fundamental to understanding the great Reformer: his approach is primarily theological. This is further demonstrated in Luther's habit of finding major themes expressed in various biblical passages. He was so thoroughly immersed in the Bible that, to a great extent, biblical words formed his thoughts and he expressed his own thoughts in biblical concepts. Such total immersion in Scripture puts Luther alongside the leading early Fathers, such as Tertullian and Origen.[16]

In his exegesis of Romans we find the central themes to which Luther returns again and again, and which were to occupy him throughout his life. These were concerned with: the human condition; God's dealing with man in righteousness and mercy; and man's standing before God, knowing himself as sinner or as one forgiven. Thus Luther tends to read Romans through the piety of the Psalms, and the Psalms through the eyes of Paul. In this use, of course, he was guilty of taking biblical texts out of context, but as he considered them illustrative of significant theological themes, Luther was not totally arbitrary in his use of them, and would probably have argued that they were still, in a sense, within their larger context.

It should be noted, however, that this theological, thematic interpretation of Scripture, so central to Luther and so significant for his generation, distances him from much modern criticism. Many modern critical interpreters insist on taking into account the *Sitz im Leben* of each document, and also assert the importance of interpreting a biblical text – even each individual letter of Paul – first of all as a unique document, to be investigated primarily and particularly in its own right. Although Luther, in keeping with traditional approaches, shows little interest in the first of these emphases, he does recognize the latter, explaining individual parts of Romans by illuminating them through reference to the letter's other parts.

Luther's interpretation of Scripture is also, in a strange sense, traditional. He frequently depends on the work of Augustine, often dismissing opponents by classifying them as 'Pelagians'. Thus an earlier period in the history of interpretation continues to play an important role, for the fifth-century Pelagian dispute was concerned with the nature of the human condition, and the significance of the individual's response in salvation. Luther's formulation of the Gospel was consciously designed to eliminate (what he considered to be) the great errors of Jerome and Pelagius; to this extent he is certainly (negatively at least) influenced by Pelagius.

Scholastic exegesis regarded the *sensus literalis* or *historicus* as the basis for all interpretation. This served as a norm of the *sensus spiritualis*, since (according to Thomas Aquinas) it was not permissible to give a passage a spiritual meaning that was not clearly indicated in or by another part of Scripture. The converted Jew, Nicholas of

Lyra (d. 1340), avoided 'spiritual interpretation' altogether, preferring the literal or historical readings over the allegorical.[17] Thanks to his knowledge of Hebrew, Nicholas had been able to consult Jewish commentaries, such as the work of Solomon Rashi (d. 1105).

Nicholas of Lyra's method came under attack from the French humanist, Faber Stapulensis (d. 1536). Faber identified two literal senses or meanings of Scripture: the historical-literal meaning, and the prophetic-literal. He interpreted the Bible in a literal-grammatical way, but did so on the assumption that it must have a prophetic-spiritual meaning in agreement with the Holy Spirit, or to which the Holy Spirit leads the exegete. Faber concluded that the interpretation of Scripture according to the *sensus literalis propheticus* superceded the Scholastics' exegesis of the four-fold meaning of the Bible, and he therefore abandoned the traditional approach.

Luther at first criticized Nicholas of Lyra, following Faber's arguments (the influence of Faber is visible in Luther's work on both the Psalms and Romans). He, himself, adopted a more syncretic approach, that he believed avoided the historicism of Lyra and the fancifulness of the allegorists. This *via media* is illustrated in his comments on a correct reading of Scripture: 'indeed in reading the Scripture aright, the Christian comes to know that God is and remains the same in everything that he does – yesterday (*literaliter*), today (*tropologice*), and forever (*anagogice*)'.[18] Luther did follow Nicholas of Lyra to the extent that he sought to establish an accurate grammatical understanding of the Hebrew and Greek texts of the Bible. He also took seriously Faber's contention that the interpreter of the Bible should seek for the literal sense that its author, the Holy Spirit, intended it to have.

The outcome of Luther's engagement with both traditional and contemporary interpreters was that he established the literal-prophetic (i.e. Christocentric) meaning as the basis of the four-fold meaning. Thus, what became most characteristic of Luther's approach was that the literal-prophetic understanding of Scripture was intertwined and combined with a reading of the text in terms of the tropological or moral sense.[19] This constituted the background to Luther's Christocentric interpretation: referring to Romans 1.1-2, '*The gospel of God which He had promised beforehand in the Holy Scriptures*', Luther said in a marginal gloss: 'There is opened up here a broad approach to the understanding of Holy Scripture – we must understand it in its entirety with respect to Christ, especially where it is prophetic.'[20] A good example of Luther's use of this form of exegesis is also found in his exposition of Romans 10.6, '*Say not in your heart: Who shall ascend into heaven?(That is to bring Christ down)*: Moses writes these words in Deut. 30:12, and he does not have in mind *the meaning they have here*, but his abundant spiritual insight enables the apostle to bring out their inner significance.'[21] It is significant that Luther distinguishes the two meanings here, recognizing the difference between the earlier meaning of the text in the Old Testament, and its new Christological significance.

As already noted, and despite what has just been asserted, Luther's approach was generally syncretic. At times in his lectures on Romans he appears to conform to the standards of medieval exegesis, both with respect to method of arrangement and sources used. Yet at the same time he also uses the most modern exegetical tools of his own era (for example, Reuchlin's Hebrew Dictionary, *De Rudimentis hebraicis*, and Faber's *Epistolae Pauli Apostoli*), and later, when it became available in 1516, especially also Erasmus' edition of the Greek New Testament, with its annotations.[22]

In essence, Luther followed a comparatively simple rule: the Bible must be understood to speak *literaliter spiritualiter* (in terms of its spiritual-literal meaning) only of Christ, and at the same time *tropologice* (in terms of the moral sense) of the believer in Christ. Therefore, whatever is true of Christ is true also of his disciples: 'as God is and acts in Christ, so he is and acts also in those who believe in Christ'. He appears to have developed this in his work on the Psalms and shows himself already master of it in his lectures on Romans.[23]

LUTHER ON RIGHTEOUSNESS AND GOOD WORKS

Luther's modernity was demonstrated in his biblical understanding of God's word – 'God's words are His acts. … His doing is identical with his speaking.'[24] This insight came from Luther's understanding of Hebrew and the Hebrew Bible, from which he derived this 'causative interpretation' of the biblical statements concerning God . It was a significant exegetical insight. Thus Luther construed 'God's way' to mean the way in which God causes us to walk, and 'God's holiness' to mean that He sanctifies men, causing them to become holy. Christ Himself is the righteousness of God, but this means that for human beings it is faith in Christ which *comprises* this righteousness.[25]

The prevailing pre-Reformation interpretation of the righteousness of God – *dikaiosyne theou* – spoke of distributive justice: God is the judge who judges not haphazardly but righteously, according to the norm of His own holiness and perfection. Luther opened up new interpretive possibilities by taking the construction *dikaiosyne theou*, 'righteousness of God', as an objective genitive throughout, translating it as 'the righteousness which counts before God', i.e. the righteousness which man possesses as a gift from God. Essentially 'righteousness of God' comes to mean God's gracious creative and redemptive activity on behalf of man.

The righteousness of God becomes a central theme in Romans: 'God alone is righteous; before him man is a sinner and nothing but a sinner, especially so if in view of his attainments, including the moral and righteous ones, he regards himself as righteous.'[26] This proud, presumptuous self-righteousness makes man a liar before his own true self and before God, for it prevents him not only from recognizing himself as he actually is, but from giving God the glory due to Him. The path to righteousness is not (as Aristotle taught) by doing righteous acts, but may only be found only through faith, because 'the righteousness of God is that righteousness by which he makes us righteous, just as the wisdom of God is that by which he makes us wise'.[27]

In explaining Romans 1.17 Luther is adamant that the righteousness of God, which alone is the cause of salvation, must be clearly distinguished from the righteousness of men, which comes from works.[28] In this he follows Augustine yet again; however, Luther does differ from Augustine on the weight of human sin (although Luther was slow to acknowledge this disagreement with his exemplar, probably because he realized he needed some support from the Fathers).[29] Luther claims that the sinner is both sinful and righteous at the same time, because he has the righteousness of Christ, and Christ's righteousness covers him and is imputed to him, as Paul argues (from the Psalms) in Romans 4. The sinner is forgiven because of Christ, and thus he has a foreign righteousness that comes to him from without. Man is dependent on 'resources that no one can ever call his own'.[30] We can see here that in relation to justification Luther is once again theological rather than anthropological.

In these lectures on Romans the modernist orientation of Luther's mind is most apparent in his general view of God and the world, in his psychological conceptions, and especially in his interest in the proper understanding of terms and words, and in the interpretation of them according to their etymological meaning. For example, he criticizes the translation of Romans 11.20-1 at some length. The word *phronesis* means something else than what is commonly called 'wisdom' (*sapientia*, in Greek *sophia*) and 'prudence' (*prudentia*). Its correct significance is 'to be mindful of something with a certain self-complacency. ... It has reference to an inward disposition rather than to the intellect'.[31]

He also criticizes what he sees as the foolishness of Jews (whom the heretics and spiritually proud imitate), being always inclined to make God a respector of persons – which Luther notes is specifically denied in Romans 2.11. Part of Luther's perceived goal is therefore to diminish and lay low the spiritually proud. According to Luther the Jews extolled themselves because it was they who had received the Law; they boasted of being its bearers and disciples, and resented Gentiles being put on the same level as them, 'as if all descendants of Abraham were *ipso facto* equal to Abraham in all their merits'.[32]

At this stage in his career it seems that, for Luther, the Jews are not a distinctive or unique people, but instead constitute part of a category, belonging with the proud and the heretics.[33] This demonstrates again that Luther is thinking more theologically than historically and thus, to some extent, he seeks to obscure historical peculiarity and diversity. It is interesting to note in passing that Origen differed greatly from Luther in this respect, pointing out that the Epistle to the Romans seems at some points to have a Jewish audience in mind, and at others a Gentile audience, rather than simply an un-differentiated humanity, theologically conceived. The closest Luther gets to discussing the particular audience addressed in Romans is when he opposes Nicholas of Lyra's view that the letter was written to correct an error of faith among the Romans. Luther thinks that the Roman Christians knew their faith and that Paul made available to them his apostolic witness to their faith as they struggled with unbelieving Jews and Gentiles in Rome.[34]

Luther, paradoxically, seems at one and the same time to be close to, and yet far removed from, modern scholarship. He appears to represent simultaneously both continuity and discontinuity. But despite the apparent continuity, the seeds of radical reform are already both obvious and implicit in his understanding of the text of Scripture. David Steinmetz identifies the closest links between Luther and modern scholars as lying in their theological observations on the text. The greatest distance between them arises less from their understanding of the literal sense, than in Luther's very free use of narrative imagination, which he frequently draws upon to elucidate the text.[35]

LUTHER AND LUTHERANISM

It has been argued by Krister Stendahl that we in the West have inherited an introspective conscience from Augustine, mediated via Luther, and that we need to re-read Paul afresh, but not through 'Reformation-tinted spectacles'. Stendahl argues that

Paul's theology cannot be interpreted as abstract theorizing, but must be viewed only in the context of relations between Jews and Gentiles. Stendahl shows how, in an alien context, Paul's argument that Gentiles must not come to Christ via the Law (i.e. via circumcision, etc.) has been turned into a statement according to which all men must come to Christ with their consciences convicted by the Law and its insatiable requirements for righteousness. This drastic consequence arises because 'the original framework of Jews and Gentiles is lost and the Western problems of conscience become its unchallenged and self-evident substitute'.[36]

A debate has arisen, therefore, as to whether we should de-Lutheranize Paul. Other more perceptive scholars such as Stowers argue that there is no point in just going behind Luther; we need also to re-interpret the Bible by going behind Augustine as well.[37] There is much truth in this. The history of ideas often demonstrates a development not only in the good ideas that men offer; often simultaneously there arises an exaggeration of implicit tendencies in directions the original authors either did not anticipate, or would not have recognized. So too with Luther and his writings. We not only have to deal with possible exaggerations in modern Lutheranism, we have also to address the parts of Luther's writings that were in themselves exaggerations of the work of others. Recent criticism of Lutheran interpretation of Paul has focused on two areas: justification by faith and Luther's attitude to Judaism.

Taking the first area, scholars argue that there has been too much emphasis on faith as passive, whereas human beings in the New Testament are called to respond, to act, to do something – in fact, to obey. In a gloss on Romans 4.17 Luther's own early emphasis on the response of faith is clearly evident:

If God gives his promise, and there is none who believes him as he gives it, then certainly God's promise will not amount to anything, and it cannot be fulfilled, for inasmuch as there is none to receive it, it cannot be a promise to anyone. Therefore, faith must be there to ratify the promise, and the promise needs the faith on the part of him to whom it is given.[38]

Francis Watson, however, criticizes some aspects of contemporary Lutheran interpretation of Paul as not maintaining the same emphases as the apostle in relation to the human response in faith. Watson correctly notes that although Paul in some passages does stress the idea of a miraculous divine gift, in others he stresses the human activity through which the gift is appropriated.[39] For Watson 'Faith is the abandonment of old norms and the adoption of new ones'; it is not simply that these things (i.e. good works), inevitably follow from faith, so that one could theoretically distinguish them from faith. Watson concludes that faith for Paul is thus essentially active; there is no question of an antithesis between a passive reception of the gift of salvation, followed by secondary, active consequences.[40] This leads us back to Luther's dependence on Augustine; it is probably fair to admit that some aspects of the Pauline understanding of faith as response have been underplayed because of past history – because of the understanding of grace in Augustine.

The second issue, that of Luther's attitude to Judaism, has several strands. In the first place, it appears that sometimes – in this century in particular – Lutheranism has not always followed Luther in his positive appreciation of the Old Testament. At times it stresses Gospel and Law in such a way that the Gospel appears to stand in antithesis to the Old Testament; some would interpret these as Marcionite tendencies.

If we look at Luther's actual comments in relation to Romans 3.1-9, we find a different opinion of Law and Gospel: in asking 'What advantage has the Jew and what is the value of circumcision?', Luther is careful to stress 'What Judaism did positively represent'. 'The circumcision, then, has been wonderfully useful, for through it the promise of God was begun and established.'[41] Again, Luther cannot understand why some want to understand Paul's willingness in Romans 9.1-3 to be 'anathema' for the sake of his kinsmen's salvation as a pre-conversion attitude. Luther devotes a good deal of time and attention to demonstrating the many reasons why this interpretation is untenable.[42]

The second aspect of Luther's teaching that has developed in ways that some scholars deplore and condemn, is concerned with the image of Jews and of Judaism. In particular it is argued that Luther's form of presentation of the issue 'by faith or by works' has led to an identification of first-century Judaism with sixteenth-century Scholastic Christianity. In his famous book *Paul and Palestinian Judaism* E. P. Sanders argues that post-Reformation Pauline scholarship has been guilty of a complete misinterpretation of first-century Palestinian Judaism.[43] In a subsequent book he argues that the phrase in Romans 10.3, in which the Jews reject the righteousness of Christ in favour of a righteousness of their own, should be taken not as a reference to good works by Jews, but rather as 'a righteousness ethnically limited to Jews only'. Therefore he maintains that the real issue was not righteousness by legalistic good works, but was in fact whether the righteousness of the covenant is available also to non-Jews.[44] Moreover, he argues that first-century Jews 'never sought to save themselves by legalistic law-keeping because they believed they were already within the covenant – they were born into it'.[45]

Sanders' research provoked a huge debate about the Reformation understanding of 'the righteousness of God'. However, even if Sanders is correct, Martin Luther's view of 'a foreign righteousness – a righteousness not of their own' is still very close to Sanders' modern interpretation, as a righteousness not limited or determined by purely ethnic considerations.

We have noted already that Luther categorized the Jews in that group of people who were spiritually proud, and therefore unwilling to receive the Gospel. The result is that there is an incipient anti-Judaism in much post-Reformation Lutheran theology. In fairness we should acknowledge that in his Romans lectures Luther is not specially biased against the Jews; at one point he speaks somewhat in their defence, arguing against those (such as the theologians of Cologne) who entertain presumptuous pride against the Jews, those who display an amazing stupidity when they are so presumptuous as to call the Jews 'dogs', or accursed, or whatever they choose to call them: 'They should feel compassion for them, fearing that they themselves may have to take similar punishment.'[46]

However, it has to be admitted that the understanding of grace and works that Luther inherited from Augustine had already planted within it the seeds of anti-Judaism. In the nineteenth century, anti-Pelagianism was translated into anti-Judaism and thus assisted anti-Semitism. Stendahl is undoubtedly correct to see in Romans 9-11 'a warning against that kind of theological imperialism which triumphs in its doctrine of the justification of the ungodly by making Judaism a code word for all wrong attitudes toward God'.[47] We cannot go into the debate further here, but one modern outcome of Luther's theology is demonstrated in a debate between Ernst Käsemann and Markus Barth. Käsemann, like Luther, argued that 'the apostle's real adversary is the devout Jew'.[48] Barth wrote to him and begged Käsemann to withdraw these terrible remarks, so glaringly un-Christian in a post-Holocaust perspective, but Käsemann, great anti-Nazi theologian and great interpreter of Paul, nevertheless absolutely refused.[49]

To conclude on a positive note – what is so amazing is that Luther's interpretation of Paul has been so powerful and so persistent, even up to the present day. In this century Rudolf Bultmann re-interpreted Pauline Lutheranism in an individualistic, existentialist direction. In him we find the outcome and epitome of that developed condemnation of those who seek to justify themselves by keeping the Commandments. This was what Luther had already stressed in his 1535 lectures on Galatians: 'To want to be justified by works of the Law is to deny the righteousness of faith.'[50] According to Bultmann, man's effort to achieve his salvation solely by keeping the law leads him into sin, indeed this effort in the end is already sin – because sin is man's self-powered striving to under-gird his own existence in forgetfulness of his creaturely existence, to procure salvation by his own strength.[51]

In the post-Bultmannian era Ernst Käsemann, probably his most distinguished pupil and interpreter, corrected some aspects of his great teacher's theological opinions, and in some ways provided a more balanced version of Lutheran Paulinism for the second half of this century. Käsemann sought to put less emphasis on the individual and to avoid an acosmic understanding of salvation.[52]

Like Luther, Käsemann turned to the Old Testament to interpret the righteousness of God. Like Luther, he interprets it theologically, in terms of God's faithfulness to the covenant and to the creation: 'God's power reaches for the world, and the world's salvation consists in the fact that it is led back under God's dominion.' *Dikaiosyne theou* is *Heilsetzende Macht* – the righteousness of God is salvation-creating power.[53]

Käsemann therefore succeeds in stressing both 'the gift-character' of faith and 'the power-character', but his great achievement is that he can dynamically unite the two: 'The gift can never be separated from the Giver; it participates in the power of God, since God steps on to the scene in the gift. ... In and with the gift comes the presence of the Giver.' The task of the believer is to abide in the Lord in responsibility to his Lordship.[54] Käsemann concludes that what people have in salvation, therefore, is not something they can boast about, as if it could be held in isolation from the Giver. It is essentially a righteousness they can never call their own. With this, Martin Luther would be well satisfied.[55]

This paper is dedicated in deep gratitude to the late Professors Ernst Käsemann and Markus Barth, each of whom in his own way has enabled me to rediscover the Gospel according to Paul.

NOTES

1 Johannes Ficker's critical edition of Luther's *Roemerbriefvorlesung* (Weimar: Boehlau, 1938), vol. 56, was used as a basis for a new translation by Wilhelm Pauck in his *Luther: Lectures on Romans*, Library of Christian Classics, vol. XV (London: SCM Press, 1961). This will be the text of Luther's lectures mainly used in this essay, supplemented by Luther's *Works* vol. 25: *Lectures on Romans: Glosses and Scholia*, ed. by Hilton C. Oswald (St. Louis: Concordia, 1977).

2 See James Atkinson, *Martin Luther and the Birth of Protestantism* (Harmondsworth: Penguin Books, 1968), p. 108.

3 On this see Hugh Anderson, *Jesus and Christian Origins: A Commentary on Modern Viewpoints* (New York: Oxford University Press, 1964), pp. 63-70.

4 Barth was not completely uninterested in these 'subsidiary disciplines', but his real interest lay elsewhere, in the theological content of the biblical documents; this emerges clearly in Karl Barth, *The Epistle to the Romans*, English trans. from the 6th German edn (London: Oxford University Press, 1933), p. 15.

5 Peter Gorday, *Principles of Patristic Exegesis* (New York & Toronto: Edwin Mellen Press, 1983), p. 20.

6 Ibid., p. 21.

7 Ibid., p. 263, no. 23.

8 Pauck, p. xlii.

9 *De spiritu et littera*, ed. by F. Urba & J. Zycha, Corpus Scriptorum Ecclesiasticorum Latinorum, 60 (Vienna: 1913), pp. 153-229.

10 Gorday, p. 21.

11 Ibid., p. 266.

12 Pauck, pp. 235-6.

13 Ibid., p. li.

14 Ibid., p. 216.

15 David C. Steinmetz, *Luther in Context* (Grand Rapids: Baker Books, 1995), pp. 70-1, and Pauck, p. 216. On Luther's indebtedness to Augustine, see Steinmetz's essay, 'Luther and Augustine on Romans 9' in *Luther in Context*, pp. 12-22.

16 Pauck, pp. xl-xli.

17 Ibid., p. xxix.

18 Ibid., p. xxxiii.

19 Ibid., pp. xxx-xxxiv.

20 Ibid., p. xxxi.

21 Ibid., p. 288 (my emphasis).

22 John Reuchlin, *De Rudimentis hebraicis* (Pforzheim: T. Anselm, 1506); S. Faber, *Epistolae Pauli Apostoli* (Paris: 1512). Erasmus' Greek New Testament was published on the first of February, 1516; on this see *Das Buch der Basler Reformation. Zu ihrem vierhundertjaehrigen Jubilaeum im Namen der evangelischen Kirchen von Stadt und Landschaft Basel*, ed. by D. E. Staehelin (Basel: Helbing & Lichtenhahn, 1929), pp. 8ff.

23 Pauck, p. xxxiii.

24 Ibid., p. xxvii.

25 Ibid., pp. xxiv, xxxiii, and 16.

26 Ibid., p. xxxiv.

27 Ibid., p. xxxiv.

28 Ibid., pp. 17-18.

29 Ibid., pp. xlv-xlvi.

30 Ibid., p. xliv. See also Gordon Rupp, *The Righteousness of God: Luther Studies* (London: Hodder & Stoughton, 1963), pp. 160-1.

31 Pauck, pp. 312-14. Oswald (n. 1 above), pp. 428-9.

32 Pauck, pp. 47-8.

33 Ibid., p. 48.

34 Ibid., pp. 5-6.

35 Steinmetz, *Luther in Context* (n. 15 above), pp. 108-9. Steinmetz notes that despite its importance for the history of the Church, relatively little attention has been devoted to Pauline interpretation by historians. The figure of Abraham was of crucial significance but was

diversely interpreted as implying either continuity or discontinuity,depending on which reformed group was debating the issue.'Abraham and the Reformation', Steinmetz, pp. 32-46.

36 K. Stendahl, *Paul among Jews and Gentiles* (London: SCM Press, 1977), p. 87.

37 Stanley K. Stowers, *A Rereading of Romans: Justice, Jews and Gentiles* (New Haven & London: Yale University Press, 1994), pp. 1-15, 126-7, 258-60, 326-7.

38 Pauck, p. lxvi.

39 F. Watson, *Paul, Judaism and the Gentiles* (Cambridge: University Press, 1986), pp. 66-7.

40 Ibid., p. 64.

41 Pauck, pp. 60-1.

42 Pauck, pp. 260-5.

43 E. P. Sanders, *Paul and Palestinian Judaism* (London: SCM Press, 1977), pp. 1-12.

44 E. P. Sanders, *Paul, the Law and the Jewish People* (Philadelphia: Fortress Press, 1983), p. 37.

45 On this see Manfred T. Brauch, 'Perspectives on "God's righteousness" in recent German discussion', an appendix included in Sanders, *Paul and Palestinian Judaism*, pp. 523-56.

46 Pauck, p. 314.

47 Stendahl, p. 132.

48 Ernst Käsemann, 'Paul and Israel', in *New Testament Questions of Today* (London: SCM Press, 1969), p. 184.

49 Markus Barth, *The People of God* (Sheffield: JSOT, 1983), p. 85, n. 5. Markus Barth mentioned to me the outcome of his letter in a private conversation.

50 Martin Luther, *Lectures on Galatians, Chapters 1-4*, Luther's Works, vol. 26 (St. Louis: Concordia Publishing House, 1963), pp. 253-4.

51 Rudolf Bultmann, *Theology of the New Testament*, vol. I (London: SCM Press, 1959), p. 264.

52 Ernst Käsemann, 'The Righteousness of God in Paul', in *New Testament Questions of Today*, pp. 168-82; p. 182.

53 Ibid., pp. 174, 182.

54 Ibid., pp. 173-6.

55 For a full discussion of Luther in relation to the origins of anti-semitism, see H. A. Oberman, *Wurzeln des Antisemitismus: Christenangst und Judenplage im Zeitalter von Humanismus und Reformation* (Berlin: Severin & Siedler, 1981), pp. 125-83.

'WITHOUT GREAT EFFORT, AND WITH PLEASURE'

SIXTEENTH-CENTURY GENEVAN BIBLES AND READING PRACTICES

Francis Higman

IN AN ARTICLE entitled 'Protestantism and Literacy in Early Modern Germany', Richard Gawthrop and Gerald Strauss proposed a revision of the traditional view that the Protestant Reformation had a significant and direct impact on literacy rates in areas affected by the movement.[1] They argued that although Luther at first encouraged Bible reading for all, from 1525 onwards he expressed this aspiration far less frequently, and by his actions he 'effectively discouraged, or at least failed effectively to encourage, an unmediated encounter between Scripture and the untrained lay mind'.[2] Contrary to supporting the reading of the Scriptures by all, Luther placed at the centre of general lay education two things: the (oral) catechism, controlled by the pastors; and the sermon, which provided an interpretation of the Bible dispensed by qualified specialists. In schools in Lutheran regions, Bible study was envisaged only for selected students in the higher classes, in Latin and Greek. It was not intended for the more open classes for younger pupils, where 'Bibles were scarcely to be found among the assigned books, only the [Lutheran] catechism' (p. 37). Gawthrop and Strauss conclude that the Reformation did not produce a significant change in literacy rates in the German population; this occurred only two centuries later, under the impact of Pietism.

The article focuses exclusively on Lutheran regions of Germany; Gawthrop adds a note that the situation in Calvinist regions may have been different. Indeed, the whole article seems to correspond so little to the prevailing image of the Calvinist Reformation that we need to ask the same questions of that area as the authors asked about Lutheranism. Did the Calvinist Church similarly discourage Bible reading?

Several viable ways of answering this question may be suggested, and for the purposes of this article one single approach must be selected. I have therefore not examined inheritance inventories to establish the absence or presence of bibles or other texts. Neither have I analysed Calvinist school programmes to see what role the Bible played in the curriculum (although I do note in passing that in the prospectus for the Geneva school published in 1537 the study of the Bible, in French as well as in the original languages, was encouraged in several ways).[3] What I have done is to examine the numerous Bible editions produced in Geneva in the sixteenth century in the hope of identifying their editorial intentions. In particular, my concern is with the elements surrounding the text which may suggest a certain way of reading the text; it is these reading aids which will be my primary focus.[4]

My original intention was to study the evolution of the biblical reading aids through-out the century. However, it rapidly became clear that a detailed analysis of the subject would extend far beyond the bounds of a short article. Instead, I have chosen to go straight to the central piece of evidence, the key to the whole story: the octavo edition of the Bible produced in 1559 by the Genevan editors Nicolas Barbier and Thomas Courteau (Chambers 253).

Although the contents are for the most part pirated from other editions, the Barbier-Courteau Bible today stands as a landmark edition. The format is the first thing of note. The volume measures 190 × 125 mm, and is 55 mm thick – almost a pocket edition. Within these small boundaries are contained the complete text of Scripture and an appendix of the metrical psalms of Marot and Bèze (including their music), the Genevan liturgy, and Calvin's *Catechism*.[5] The contrast with the more usual folio bibles of the period is striking. A folio bible at that time cost around 30 sols, more or less a week's wage for a Genevan workman, and therefore out of his price range. An octavo bible, on the other hand, could be bought for about two days' wages; even an impover-ished artisan could purchase a copy by dint of a few weeks' saving.[6] Octavo editions of the Bible are in fact a significant characteristic of Genevan sixteenth-century printings: Bettye Chambers lists fourteen such editions, as compared with three from Lyons and two from elsewhere. We may contrast this with eleven Genevan folio editions, com-pared with thirteen from Lyons and nine from elsewhere. It seems, therefore, that there was a clear policy in Geneva to make scripture widely available in affordable editions.

The next noteworthy feature is the title-page of the volume, which reads:

LA BIBLE,

QVI EST

Toute la saincte Escriture, ascauoir le vieil & nou-
ueau Testament:

DE NOVVEAV REVEVE, AVEC AR-
gumens sur chacun liure, nouuelles annotations en marge, fort vti
les: par lesquelles on peut sans grand labeur, obtenir la vraye in
telligence du sens de l'Escriture, auec recueil de grande doctrine.

*Il y a aussi quelques figures & cartes chorographiques de grande vtilite, l'vsage
desquelles pourrez voir en l'espistre suyuante.*

The title-page does not merely offer the name of the book, it provides an entire pro-gramme, including the text, arguments for each book, marginal notes, maps, and plans, 'by means of which one can, without great effort, obtain true understanding of the sense of the Scriptures, with a summary of important doctrine'. We shall treat the implications of this programme below.

The presentation of the text itself also reveals the agenda of the editors. The begin-ning of each book of the Bible is marked by a large capital letter, and each chapter by a smaller capital. Moreover, the text is divided into verses, which facilitate orientation.[7] Preceding the biblical text of each individual book is the 'argument', printed in italics to differentiate it from the text of the Scripture; in addition there is a summary at the beginning of each chapter. In the margins are annotations, in italics, and cross-

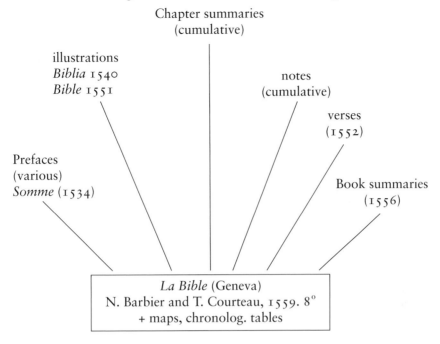

Fig. 1. Sources of study aids in the Barbier-Courteau Bible

references to other biblical passages in roman type. It is already clear that this is a text not only to be read, but to be studied.

Further aids surround the scriptural text. Before the beginning of the Old Testament is a series of prefaces, a summary, and a list of the canonical and apocryphal books of the Bible. At the end (or bound at the beginning in some copies) are: a table giving the meaning of proper names in Hebrew, Aramaic, Greek, and Latin, a *recueil d'aucuns mots difficiles* (a type of theological word-book), and an index which constitutes a short concordance. In addition there are several illustrations to aid the reader: a reconstruction of Noah's Ark which explains various details of the structure (Pl. 2); representations of the Tabernacle and Solomon's Temple (Pl. 3, 4); and geographical maps – the first edition in which they appear (Pl. 5). Finally, to further the understanding of the history of the Jews, or the travels of St Paul, chronological tables are also provided (Pl. 6). All these reading aids imply a particular way of reading the Bible. They draw attention to the literal meaning of the sacred text, encouraging the reader to concentrate on the historical truth of the book, rather than on dwelling on allegorical interpretations, as was the case in mediaeval exegesis. A pattern of 'guided reading' is beginning to emerge (see fig. 1).

As can be imagined, this accumulation of secondary material did not happen all at once; it instead represents the culmination of a long process, during which these diverse elements were added to the Bible gradually. To take one of the aforementioned pictures as an example, Noah's Ark has frequently attracted the attention of Bible illustrators. One frequently finds pictures intended to stimulate the imagination of the reader, as in the 1530 Bible by Martin Lempereur of Antwerp (Chambers 51; Pl. 7), or that published in 1553 by Jean de Tournes of Lyons (Chambers 177). However, the text of Genesis mentions an ark, not a boat, as was portrayed by Lempereur and de Tournes; how is this term to be understood? Nicolas of Lyra had already asked the question two centuries earlier in his commentary on the Bible, printed by Froben in 1504 (Pl. 8). Certain other illustrated bibles also represent the ark as being something other than a boat.

However, for the luxurious Latin *Biblia* produced in Paris by the royal printer Robert Estienne in 1540, the great humanist printer consulted Hebrew specialists, notably the *lecteur royal* François Vatable, in order to produce a 'scientific' illustration (Pl. 9); note the letters and annotations which seek to further the reader's comprehension.[8] From this Latin edition, the same illustration of the ark passed into Estienne's French Bible (Geneva, 1553; Chambers 172), and was later copied by other editors, including (in reduced format) Barbier and Courteau. A similar provenance can be traced for the representation of the tabernacle: Nicolas of Lyra provided a sketch of the forecourt of the tabernacle (Pl. 10), and Lempereur offered a rather uninteresting picture (Pl. 11); it is only in the hands of Robert Estienne that a more sophisticated rendering is achieved (Pl. 12). The illustration of Solomon's Temple was also taken over from Estienne's detailed illustration, rather than the rather simplistic versions of earlier bibles. A similar filiation may be traced for each of the elements of the Barbier-Courteau Bible. The sole exception is the maps, which were here published for the first time; they were subsequently copied extensively.[9]

A word must be added on the annotations, which constitute the most delicate part of the entire story. In the sixteenth century, as in any other period, one rarely finds an entirely plain biblical text. There are almost always cross-references to parallel passages provided. From the beginning of translation into modern languages, philological notes are also supplied, which indicate alternative readings, and explain obscure words (what is 'gopher wood', of which the Ark was built?) or expressions (who are 'the sons of God' in *Genesis* 6?). In the Genevan Bibles of the 1550s and 1560s, however, there is a marked increase in a different type of annotation, which makes explicit the editorial intention to provide a 'guided reading'. One of the most striking examples occurs in the second chapter of St James's Epistle, a text which posed a serious problem for many reformers. The text repeatedly asserts that we are saved by works and not by faith alone:

2.14: What doth it profit, my brethren, if a man say he hath faith, but have not works? can that faith save him?

2.24: Ye see that by works a man is justified, and not only by faith.

Yet St Paul repeatedly affirms that the basis of man's salvation is faith alone, not works – for example, in Ephesians 2.8-9: 'For by grace are ye saved through faith; and that not of yourselves: it is the gift of God: not of works, lest any man should boast.' There appears to be a direct contradiction between the apostles; and the reformers all regarded the epistles of Paul as the central exposition of Christian doctrine. How therefore is James to be accommodated? Martin Luther's answer was to call *James* a 'recht strohische Epistel' (in his preface to the German New Testament of 1524). Robert Estienne's 1553 Bible offers at the beginning of the chapter only a brief, and accurate, summary: 'la foi sans les oeuvres est nulle et morte'; no annotations are provided on this matter. Other editors, for example Jean Crespin (1555, Chambers 207) and Nicolas Barbier (1556, Chambers 221), seek to twist the sense by declaring in the introductory 'argument' that the text is concerned with charity; they do not, however, intervene in the text itself. On the other hand, the Barbier-Courteau Bible of 1559 provides 2.14 with the marginal annotation: 'I! entend une cognoissance de Dieu nue et froide'; in verse 24, 'justifie' is glossed 'cognu et approuvé juste devant les hommes', and 'par la foy' is glossed 'par une nue et vaine cognoissance de Dieu'. The effect of these annotations is to suggest that James is not talking about *saving* faith in the Pauline sense, but about a mere *knowledge* of God (verses 14 and 24), and that he is not talking about justification *by faith* in the Pauline sense (in verse 24) but about a social reputation for justice in human society. These formulations are in fact a brutal summary of the two pages which Calvin devoted, in his commentary on *James*, to the problem of reconciling James and Paul.

This type of annotation, which occurs throughout the biblical text, goes beyond a linguistic explanation, and sets forth the 'correct' doctrine to be extracted from the text by the reader. The Barbier-Courteau edition in fact constitutes a complete teaching manual: readers can study ancient history (the chronological tables), biblical geography (the maps), Temple architecture and utensils, priestly vestments, and so on; this book offers the means to acquiring a basic but comprehensive theological education. The editors were well aware of the value of their volume. In the preface 'L'Imprimeur aux lecteurs' it is made clear that the Word of God contained in the Scriptures is the necessary basis for all study. Many people wish to embark on such a course, but do not have access to the places where the necessary teaching is dispensed; others cannot obtain copies of 'good and pure expositors of scripture', or cannot read them because they are in Latin. To solve these problems:

je leur ay preparé une aide et un moyen fort propre pour supleer ce qu'il leur defaut. En premier lieu, pour avoir plus claire intelligence de ce qu'on lira, vous avez un argument sur chacun livre, lequel contient en somme ce qui est traitté en iceluy, avec le but et intention où il pretend; et en outre, des annotations en marge prises et recueilles des purs autheurs, et plus entiers et fideles expositeurs des sainctes Escritures, tant anciens que nouveaux. Au moyen de quoy il sera fort facile d'avoir sans grand travail, la vraye intelligence des passages difficiles desdites Escritures avec contentement, comme si on avoit long temps travaillé en lisant les autheurs et expositeurs susdits.[10]

He goes on to explain the value of the maps and chronological tables, in actuality providing a complete theological course in one portable volume.

To give a rapid, and very over-simplified, glimpse of the later development of the story, one can see from the *Bibliography of French Bibles* the filiation of subsequent editions, in large and small format, in Geneva, Lyons, Antwerp, and Paris (see fig. 2). A highly significant factor is the strong reaction – especially among Catholic editors – against the over-abundant annotation of the period *c*. 1560.[11] Both the Louvain Bible (Antwerp: Christophe Plantin, 1578; Chambers 439) and Sebastien Honorati's Bible (Lyons, 1582; Chambers 465) retain some prefaces, and anodyne versions of certain chapter and book 'arguments', in addition to the chronological tables, maps, dictionaries, and concordances at the end. Annotation of the texts themselves is, however, reduced to cross-references. As Honorati clearly states: 'j'ay … faict sortir en lumiere

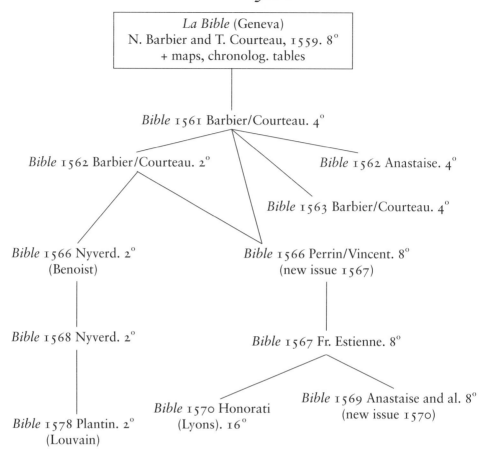

Fig. 2. Schematic summary of later sixteenth-century French Bible editions

ceste [édition] cy, sans gloses, additions ny distractions qui la puissent rendre suspecte'.[12] Clearly the overgrowth of annotation, in particular of doctrinally orientated annotation, had come to be associated with controversial theology rather than with biblical study, and a reaction set in – not only from Catholic editors, but also among Calvinists; the famous 1588 Bible of the Geneva Company of Pastors also eliminated most of the interpretative annotations.

Gawthrop and Strauss offered us a simple alternative: either individual uncontrolled reading of the biblical text, or an oral catechism, dominated by the pastors. The Genevan lesson appears to be different: individual study is encouraged, but controlled through the critical apparatus. The accumulation of reading aids aims at the 'correct' understanding of the text: images which appeal to the imagination are excluded; in their place is a solid historical reading backed up by 'scientific' illustrations and elements of interpretative commentary in the annotations; all this in octavo form, at a price anyone can afford.

Sixteenth-Century Genevan Bibles and Reading Practices

Beyond the general principle, suggested in the Geneva school prospectus, that the study of scripture is a good thing for all, there is a simple explanation for the proliferation of these small but encyclopedic editions in Geneva around the year 1560. Before 1555 there was no reformed church in France organized on Genevan principles. In 1562, seven years later, a survey indicated that there were 2150 churches and some three million believers.[13] In principle each of these churches had to have at least one pastor; where could the qualified personnel come from, when the entire Genevan church had only sixteen pastors at the time?[14] It seems to me that bibles in the line of the Barbier-Courteau edition were designed to provide one part of an answer to that question.

The argument that these small, encyclopaedic bibles were intended to remedy a specific and urgent need is reinforced if we take into account the appendices to the biblical text in the Barbier-Courteau edition, which have scarcely been mentioned in the present article: the metrical psalms of Marot and Bèze, the liturgy, and the catechism. The whole represents a complete do-it-yourself kit for church life and worship. It is known that many of the earliest pastors were 'home-grown', arising from the local community, and without much formal education.[15] These small bibles were an ideal way to give access under controlled conditions to the laity, and especially to those members of the laity who were to become pastors.

As Gawthrop and Strauss imply, no one in the 'magisterial' Reformation could envisage unlimited and uncontrolled access to scripture; Calvin above all was conscious of the need to supervise the orthodoxy of the doctrines being preached from the pulpit. But, unlike the Lutheran solution proposed by Gawthrop and Strauss, the Calvinist answer seems to lie in a conscious encouragement of generalized access to the Bible (witness the multiplication of small-format, relatively cheap editions), but accompanied by a panoply of study aids and elements of guided reading which could ensure conformity to the official doctrine on the part of the faithful. One seems justified in concluding that the attitude of the sixteenth-century Calvinist Church towards Bible reading was thus radically different from that of Lutheran regions.

NOTES

1 *Past and Present*, 104 (1984), 31-55.

2 See pp. 34-5.

3 For details of this see *L'Ordre et maniere d'enseigner en la Ville de Geneve au College* (Geneva: Jean Girard, 1537), pp. [8]-[9]: 'Tous les jours, ordinairement devant qu'on se mette à table, l'ung d'eulx list à haulte voix ung chapitre de la Bible en Françoys, et tous les autres l'escoutent. Estans à table ilz disent chacun une sentence de la saincte escriture et ce en diverses langues, ung chacun selon sa capacité. Apres qu'on a desservy … ilz prennent ung chacun selon ce qu'il est desja fondé en aucune langue, des livres de la saincte escriture c'est à savoir ou en Grec ou Latin, ou en Françoys, ou aussi en Ebrieu s'il est question du vieil testament. Adonc, afin que l'entendement d'ung chacun se recree joyeusement en chose saincte et honneste, l'ung des regens, comme delaissant ceste gravité ordinaire de maistre, expose couramment de Latin en Françoys quelque propos de ladicte escriture saincte: … puis apres il propose et presente familierement aux enfants le Latin, selon la maniere et ordre qu'il l'a declairé: et iceulx le tournent en Françoys comme chacun en a peu retenir en sa memoire. … Mesme les enfans sans estudier ne travailler proufitent beaucoup en la saincte escriture.'

4 I owe a great debt of gratitude to Bettye Thomas Chambers. Without her monumental *Bibliography of French Bibles: Fifteenth- and Sixteenth-Century French-Language Editions of the Scriptures*, Travaux d'Humanisme et Renaissance (henceforth THR) 192 (Geneva: Droz, 1983), the present study would have been impossible, or at least far more difficult. I give references below for all French-language editions of the Bible in the form 'Chambers 177'.

5 The miniaturization is achieved by the use of very small type: twenty lines of text measure 47 mm in depth, whereas twenty lines of a folio Bible may measure 96 mm (R. Estienne, 1553) or 121 mm (the 1588 *Bible des pasteurs*).

6 These prices are based on the inventory of Laurent de Normandie's bookshop (1569), published by H.-L. Schlaepfer, 'Laurent de Normandie', in *Aspects de la propagande religieuse*, ed. by G. Berthoud et al. (Geneva: Droz, 1957), pp. 176-230. Wage rates are taken from P. Chaix, *Recherches sur l'imprimerie à Genève de 1550 à 1564*, THR 16 (Geneva: Droz, 1954). The wage/price relationship may not be accurate, since the book prices may possibly be wholesale, but the folio/octavo price relationship remains valid.

7 Verses were first introduced by Robert Estienne in the early 1550s.

8 On Robert Estienne see Elizabeth Armstrong, *Robert Estienne, Royal Printer: an historical study of the elder Stephanus*, rev. edn (Appleford: Sutton Courtenay Press, 1986).

9 See Catherine Delano Smith & Elizabeth Ingram, *Maps in Bibles, 1500-1600*, THR 256 (Geneva: Droz, 1991) for full details. This study tracks the later history of the four maps in the Barbier-Courteau edition: a map of the route of the Exodus, imitated in 59 later editions Europe-wide; a map of Canaan and of the twelve tribes of Israel, imitated 51 times; a map of the Holy Land in the time of Christ, imitated 65 times; and a map of the eastern Mediterranean and the journeys of St Paul, imitated 48 times.

10 'I have prepared for them just the aid and means needed to make up for what is lacking. First, to have a clearer understanding of what one is going to read, there is an "argument" for each book, which says briefly what is treated in it and what is its intention; moreover, there are marginal annotations selected from the purest authors and most solid and faithful expositors, ancient and modern, of holy scripture. By means of which, without great effort, and with pleasure, it will be very easy to acquire a true understanding of the difficult passages of the said scripture, as if one had laboured for a long time in reading the aforementioned authors and expositors' (fol. *2r-v).

11 Only René Benoist, in his Paris editions of 1566 and 1568, maintains a copious annotation, applying the same technique as did the Genevans, but in reverse: that is to say, he gives annotations expounding the Catholic interpretation against those who misuse Holy Scripture.

12 'I have brought out this edition without glosses, additions or distractions which might have rendered it suspect.'

13 See Émile G. Léonard, *Histoire générale du protestantisme* (Paris: Presses universitaires de France, 1982), 3 vols, II, p. 110.

14 See Robert M. Kingdon, *Geneva and the Coming of the Wars of Religion in France, 1555-1563*, THR 22 (Geneva: Droz, 1956).

15 Bernard Palissy, for example, in his *Recepte veritable* of 1563, describes how the church in Saintes was founded by a group of artisans who gathered for Bible study and for mutual exhortation.

'THE LAW AND THE GOSPEL'

THE EVOLUTION OF AN EVANGELICAL PICTORIAL THEME IN THE BIBLES OF THE REFORMATION

Andrew Pettegree

FOR STUDENTS of the Reformation movement, one of the most interesting and absorbing questions has been how the teachings of the Reformation became disseminated among the broad mass of the population.[1] Protestantism is the religion of the Book, but as the Evangelical movement broadened its appeal beyond the urban patriciate and clerical elite, inevitably it confronted the problem of how its key messages would be generalized among an essentially non-literate population.

Several solutions have been postulated as to how a movement which emphasized the primacy of 'the Word' could overcome this barrier. Recent writings have stressed the importance, alongside the printed book, of the sermon, and it is certainly the case that a generation of charismatic local preachers played a crucial role in ensuring that the central tenets of Luther's attack on the old Church hierarchy were known and discussed in their own localities.[2] Even without such local leadership, reading members of the lay population could play their part by expounding and making known Luther's teaching among their friends and workmates: in this respect reading members of non-literate circles might play an important part in the communication process.[3] Reinforcing their efforts were the illustrations which appeared in many early Evangelical works. Many of such texts and broadsheets made use of visual material as a means of reinforcing core messages, in particular the contrast between the corruption of the old Church and the unadulterated simplicity of the new Evangelical order.[4] This, a central part of the first appeal of Luther's teaching in Germany, was reiterated in woodcuts and engravings of great ingenuity and force. Any reader who perused Lucas Cranach's *Passional Christi und Antichristi*, a series of 26 paired woodcuts in which the corruptions of the papal monarchy were contrasted with the gospel story, would have been in no doubt as to its central message, even before they had read Philip Melanchthon's accompanying text.[5]

This use of the graphic arts was certainly one of the most innovative aspects of the Reformation book. What had previously been an elite artifact was transformed to assist cultural transmission at a quite different social level; in terms of communication this was quite revolutionary. Given the importance of the visual medium, however, it is perhaps one of the most remarkable (and poorly explained) aspects of the development of the Evangelical movement, that the use of such visual material was soon largely abandoned. The relationship between the Reformation and the visual arts was by no means unambiguous. The rejection of many cultic elements of traditional Catholicism called into question the role of religious pictures and sculpture in worship, and in the early decades of the Reformation local communities often marked their rejection of this culture and its substitution by the 'pure word of the gospel' by 'cleansing' their churches of the rejected religious art.[6] In the first generation of the Reformation, Luther's personal conservatism, his distaste for any sort of disorder, and perhaps not least the exceptionally fine work which the graphic artists offered for the Evangelical cause in Germany in the age of Dürer and Cranach, made distinct limits to the Protestant rejection of visual culture. This became less the case as Luther's movement gave ground to the more radical force of Calvinism in the second half of the century. The Swiss reformers had always taken a more sceptical view of the role of religious art than had Luther, and this tradition was continued in Calvin's writings. His thought left little room for the pictorial representation of sacred objects, in church or in private worship.[7] The effect of his teaching was swiftly felt in countries where his teaching became the dominant strand within the Protestant movement.[8]

Some sense of this is necessary to explain the virtual absence of illustration in Protestant works of the second, Calvinist generation. In the middle decades of the sixteenth century, Protestant Evangelism enjoyed a second enormous surge of activity. Inspired by the spreading influence of Calvinism on the international stage, previously subdued Evangelical movements in France, the Netherlands, Scotland, and England suddenly found their voice; for a time it seemed as if the new Reformed movement might sweep all before it. This new movement generated a tidal wave of new Protestant publishing. In France in the years immediately before and during the first decade of the wars of religion, the printing presses of Geneva, Paris, and provincial France poured out a phenomenal volume of religious literature, both dogmatic and liturgical works for the rapidly-expanding French Huguenot churches, and polemic between the rival confessions.[9] However, only a tiny proportion of this literature made use of illustration.[10] This was true of both the polemical literature which so excoriated and infuriated French Catholics (there seems to have been no French equivalent to the German satirical woodcut broadsheet), and the more earnest literature of instruction. French Genevan Bibles, for instance, contained no illustration beyond a small number of technical maps and diagrams.[11]

In the Netherlands, the contrast was if anything even more stark. In the first generation of the Reformation the less closely regulated Dutch printing industry had published a large number of editions of vernacular scripture, many of them richly illustrated in the German tradition.[12] Most, indeed, drew directly on German prototypes for woodcut series heavily dependent on those designed for German and Swiss Bibles by such masters as Cranach, Holbein, and Dürer. However, in the second half of the century Dutch publishers in effect turned their backs on this lucrative and graphically rich tradition. From the first publications of the Bible in the new Reformed tradition, illustration was virtually excluded.[13]

Further investigation of the output of Dutch Evangelical printers reveals a similar pattern. As was the case with Genevan and French Calvinism, the earlier persecutions of Dutch Evangelicals had stimulated the growth of a new exile printing industry, safely outside the borders of the Netherlands. One such centre was at Emden, in north Germany, which in the middle decades of the sixteenth century emerged as an important centre of north-German Calvinism.[14] Stimulated by a massive immigration of religious refugees from the Netherlands, the Emden church swiftly took on the role as a mother church for the young Dutch Calvinist congregations, providing the small secret churches with printed materials for teaching and worship. In the process Emden became the principal centre of Dutch Reformed printing, before the establishment of permitted presses in the independent northern Netherlands after 1572. In the course of my work studying the emergence of Dutch Calvinism I have compiled a register of Dutch works published in Emden, and the level of output from the area was a remarkable achievement: even in a town which previously had had little or no tradition of a local printing industry, the émigré printers who settled in Emden were soon turning out works of the highest quality, and of some sophistication. However, in contrast to the publications of the first generation of churches in Lutheran Germany, these works were published almost entirely without illustration. The printer's craftsmanship was confined to the creation of a handsome artifact through the arrangement of different sorts of type.

In this context, it is interesting to direct close attention to one of the few surviving pieces of illustrative work associated with Emden, the magnificent Bible title-page first introduced in Gellius Ctematius's edition of the Liesvelt Bible in 1559 (Pl. 13). The history of the publication of this edition, emerging after a series of false starts which almost ruined Ctematius's printing house, has been well told elsewhere,[15] and here we want to direct our attention only to the title-page woodcut. In the context of the previous production of Emden's presses, mostly small-format works intended for clandestine importation and circulation in the Netherlands, it would have made a striking impression. Most interesting to us is that it re-introduced, into the very different context of a largely Calvinistic society, one of the great original themes of Reformation iconography: the Law and the Gospel.

The Law and the Gospel theme can be traced back to the first decade of the Evangelical movement in Germany, and to the workshop of Lucas Cranach. Cranach, the court painter to Frederick the Wise in Wittenberg, was already a prosperous and established figure by the time of the Reformation, turning out a variety of largely conventional religious paintings for courtly and aristocratic patrons.[16] But there is little doubt that almost from the first years of Luther's dramatic denunciation of papal and clerical power, Cranach became a committed and enthusiastic supporter of the new doctrines. When in 1521 Luther was forced to take refuge in the Wartburg after his condemnation at the Diet of Worms, it was to Cranach that he unburdened himself in a hurried letter scribbled *en route*; in less troubled times, printer and reformer would both stand as godparent to each other's children.[17] Cranach's personal admiration for Luther is evident not least in his remarkable series of portraits of the Reformer, which admirably document Luther's personal journey from rebel monk to patriarch of the Reformation.[18] In the process, Cranach produced some memorable images of real propaganda value and became an inventive and versatile publicist for the new movement. In addition to his conventional painting, Cranach also invested in the new growth industry of printing, and his workshop was soon heavily involved in the production of woodcut illustrations and title-page borders, many of which would adorn editions of Luther's writings.[19] The measure of Cranach's commitment to Luther's cause is indicated by his involvement in the scathingly anti-papal *Portraits of the Papacy* (1545), a clear indication that in the production of Reformation propaganda, printer and reformer worked closely together.

In the process, Cranach prospered. His business took full advantage of the vast increase in Wittenberg publishing, resulting from Luther's fame and prodigious literary output, a phenomenon which swiftly made Wittenberg one of Germany's principal centres of book production.[20] By the time of his death in 1553, Cranach was one of the most wealthy and influential of Wittenberg's citizens.

The Reformation had a profound impact on the work of the Cranach workshop. Although the business continued to work for Catholic patrons (inevitably so, given the complicated politics and geography of Reformation Germany), there was a distinct falling off of many traditional types of religious painting, such as pictures of saints and Marian devotional paintings.[21] In their place new themes emerged, such as the pictorial representation of the core doctrine of Justification of Faith, the allegory of sin and redemption known as the Law and the Gospel.

The iconographic scheme of this picture seems to have been worked out by Cranach towards the end of the first decade of the Reformation: certainly by 1528-9, when Cranach painted the subject in two different versions, it was already a mature design. The two designs are subtly different, and both would have a distinguished career in the pictorial art of the Evangelical movement. In the first version, known through a picture now in the Schlossmuseum at Gotha (Pl. 14), the major elements of the theme are already clear.[22] The two sides of the picture are filled with scenes from, respectively, the Old and New Testament, divided by a tree. On the left, the side of the Old Law, a man is harried into Hell by Death and the Devil, while Moses and the Prophets display the tablets of the Law. In the background the Fall is represented through Adam being tempted by Eve in the garden of Eden, while the people of Israel are shown worshipping the brazen serpent. The whole scene is presided over by the figure of Christ in Judgement. On the right side a man is pointed towards salvation through Christ on the Cross, while in the foreground Christ is shown rising from the tomb. To reinforce the message, the tree dividing the picture is shown fertile on the side of the new law, withered on the side of the old.

The woodcut of 1529 follows the same basic design, though with various elements re-arranged: the scene of the Israelites worshipping the serpent, for instance, here appears on the right side (Pl. 15).[23] The Prague picture, however, introduces several significant changes, which on the whole serve to simplify the design (Pl. 16).[24] Here Man is represented by a single figure, now pointed towards redemption by the prophet Isaiah and John the Baptist. The left side is far less crowded, with the man pursued into hell here replaced by the more static device of an entombed skeleton. Moses is now relegated to the far background, shown receiving the tablets of the law in the top corner.

It seems clear enough that the Gotha type represents Cranach's original design, not least because the conception can be traced back to a pen-and-ink sketch with a hand-written dedication of Cranach to the Duchess Catherine, wife of Duke Henry the Pious.[25] Although rudimentary in nature, most of the elements of the Gotha design are already present in this sketch; as it achieved its final shape Cranach added the tree which provides the central barrier and strengthens the antithesis. In the woodcut this was made explicit by the introduction of biblical citations, on the side of the Law, Romans 1.18: 'For the wrath of God is revealed from heaven against all ungodliness and unrighteousness of men', and on the side of the Gospel Isaiah 7.14: 'The Lord himself will give you a sign. A virgin shall conceive, and bear a son.' The citations strengthen the supposition that the Wittenberg Reformers were personally involved in the design of the Law and Gospel motif. The theme of the picture – that sinful man is justified by faith and not by his adherence to the old law – was absolutely central to Luther's teaching, and the programmatic nature of the design, supplied in the woodcut and at least one painted version with accompanying biblical texts, suggests that the Reformers played an active role in the picture's devising. Such cooperation between preacher and artist would not have been unusual, as we have already noted in the case of Cranach's *Passional Christi und Antichristi*, in this case through texts supplied by Philip Melanchthon. Elsewhere in his correspondence Melanchthon made reference to his custom of providing Cranach with pictorial ideas from the Bible.[26]

Luther's interest in Cranach's work is easily comprehensible. Quite apart from the Reformer's intuitive perception of the importance of printing for the dissemination of his new teachings, the Law and Gospel design proved to be one of the strongest original visual encapsulations of Luther's core doctrine of justification. Not surprisingly, it was soon being adapted from original painting and woodcut to serve also as a book title-page, the first instance of which came as early as 1528, when an edition of Luther's Easter sermons made use of a rather rudimentary version of the 'Prague' version of the theme provided by the Cranach workshop.[27] This, admittedly, is a somewhat unsuccessful production: compositionally rather cluttered, it loses much of the clarity of the painted version, doubtless a reflection of the difficulties of re-working a theme originally developed in a landscape mode to the portrait (upright) format of the book. Generally speaking, the Cranach workshop made greater use of the original 'Gotha' design. This seems first to have been used for the purposes of book illustration for a bible title-page of 1536, and here most of the compositional elements do seem to have been successfully integrated, though within a rather squat format. The design achieved its definitive form with the publication of the Luther Bible of 1541 (Pl. 17).[28] Here the border around the bible title lettering is successfully used for a strong upward narrative progression. On the left, the man harried into Hell is surmounted by scenes of Adam and Eve, the Brazen Serpent, and Christ in Judgement, carefully arranged one above another. On the right the eyes of the repentant sinner are directed straight to the crucified Christ, with a dramatic resurrection occupying the central portion of the right border. The title lettering rises through the tree in the centre, but the space at the top of the page is utilized to show the clear difference between its flourishing and dead branches.

In this form the *Gesetz und Genade* theme has become a highly successful piece of Protestant iconography, reminiscent in its strong narrative shape of the title-page designed by Hans Holbein the Younger for the Coverdale Bible of 1535, which combined contrasting views of the Old and New Law with a flattering motif designed to indulge Henry VIII's sense of his dominant influence over religious change in England.[29] However, the appearance of the Wittenberg Luther Bible did not mark the final victory of the Gotha over the Prague type of the Law and Gospel theme. Rather, the Prague design received a new lease of life, thanks largely to a brilliant compositional re-organization by the Regensburg artist Erhard Altdorfer. In 1533 Altdorfer was commissioned by the north German printer Ludwig Dietz to provide a title-page illustration for the first complete *niederdeutsch* version of the Luther Bible. Altdorfer provided Dietz with a reworked version of the Cranach 'Prague' type design, taking advantage of its greater compositional simplicity to produce a title-page of great elegance and force (Pl. 18).[30] Altdorfer injects into the picture a much greater sense of dramatic activity, with Christ rising dramatically from the grave to conquer death on the right-hand side, and Moses receiving the Tablets of the Law in the top left-hand corner. The size of the central tablet is greatly reduced, leaving far more space for the border and an elaborate representation of the foliage of the Tree of Life. This ornate construction reflects the greater impact on Altdorfer of both Renaissance form and the influence of the Danube school of which his brother, the better known Albrecht Altdorfer, was the leading exponent.[31]

Altdorfer's title-page proved to be an extremely influential representation, particularly in those countries closest, geographically and spiritually, to the north German areas where Dietz's Bible had circulated. The woodcut was copied in the Magdeburg Bible of 1538, the Danish Bible of 1550, and, most importantly for our purposes, the English Bible of 1537, the so-called 'Matthew's Bible'.[32] This latter version is important, not only because it provides another fine representation of Altdorfer's title-page, but also because it provides the vital link, through Antwerp, between Cranach's original design and the later Emden presses. The Matthew's Bible was the work of the important Antwerp press of Mattheus Crom, a printer who turned out a large number of English vernacular Protestant works at a time when the religious climate in England made the production of Evangelical literature in England hazardous and uncertain.[33] The strong tradition of the graphic arts in Antwerp meant that there would have been little difficulty in finding an artist capable of providing a faithful but elegant version of the Altdorfer design. The Law and Gospel theme was by this time well known to Antwerp's printers: a smaller simplified version of the theme is used in the bottom title-page border block of two Antwerp editions of the French Bible translation of Jacques Lefèvre d'Étaples, published in 1530 and 1534 by Martin de Keyser.[34] A version of de Keyser's woodcut appeared in several further Antwerp editions during the next decade.[35]

It was almost certainly through Antwerp that the design made its way to Emden and to Ctematius's workshop. Close personal connections linked the Emden presses and the former Evangelical printing houses of Antwerp. When Charles V renewed his campaign against heresy in the mid-1540s, several of the leading Antwerp printers previously active in the production of Evangelical literature found it prudent to suspend their activities, and a number sought a safer working environment in London. Among them were Steven Mierdman, Mattheus Crom's partner and brother-in-law, and Nicolaes van den Berghe, Ctematius's later partner in Emden.[36] In 1553 both Mierdman and van der Berghe would move on to Emden, along with Ctematius, to form the core of the new publishing houses established there by the incoming exiles. The Antwerp connection played an important part in the success of the new industry in Emden. The new Emden printing houses almost certainly obtained most of their printing materials from Antwerp, and the early editions published on their presses included a large number of reprints of early Dutch Evangelical works first popularized in Antwerp in the 1520s and 1540s.[37]

Ctematius's choice of the Liesvelt Bible in 1559 is a case in point. The Liesvelt Bible, first published in 1526, represented a milestone for the Dutch Evangelical movement, providing the nascent Netherlandish Evangelical communities with a complete Dutch translation of Luther's text.[38] It was an immediate success from the time of its first edition of 1526, going through numerous reprints and taking on a steadily more Evangelical character. Its popularity persisted, despite its eventual condemnation by the Netherlandish authorities and the execution in 1545 of the printer/translator Jacob van Liesvelt.[39] For the 1538 edition the printer adopted – quite exceptionally for this series of editions – a version of the Law and Gospel title-page, closely related, if not identical, to the version of the Altdorfer design used in the Matthew's Bible of 1537.[40]

The publication of the Liesvelt Bible was taken up again almost as soon as the exiles had established themselves abroad, with two editions in 1556 and 1558, one apparently published in Wesel, the other by the Emden press of Mierdman and Galliart.[41] It was small wonder then that Ctematius, seeking to break into a market which promised steady profits, should turn to the most popular Dutch translation then available.

Ctematius's first use of the Law and Gospel title-page, on the 1559 edition of the Liesvelt Bible, thus represented an important development for his press. For some years before this, Ctematius and his associates has been attempting to bring to the press a new Bible translation, and the search was now all the more urgent with the further success of a second Dutch Bible published in 1558 by the rival Emden press of Jan Galliart and Steven Mierdman.[42] But the signs were not altogether auspicious: the previous involvement of the Ctematius press in a major Bible project, Jan Utenhove's ill-starred attempt to create a new translation of the New Testament derived from the original Greek, had been a complete disaster, bringing the press to the brink of ruin and causing considerable bad blood with others financially involved in the project.[43] So it may have been that in proposing a new edition of the Leisvelt Bible Ctematius was looking for a reliable seller in a well-established market, trading on the well-known popularity of the Leisvelt translation in Dutch Evangelical circles.

If this was the case, the strategy was a conspicuous success. Although a lavish and well-produced book, the 1559 Liesvelt Bible sold out sufficiently quickly that a new edition was necessary in 1560; further editions followed in 1562, 1564, and 1569.[44] The Law and the Gospel title-page was a feature of all five editions, in a new woodcut version of the Altdorfer design, recut for Ctematius by Arnold Nicolai of Antwerp. Nicolai was an engraver at this point in the service of Christopher Plantin at Antwerp, and his rendering of the title-page follows closely the design of the Altdorfer and Matthew's Bible versions, though the figures are if anything finer and more delicate.[45] The title-page makes this one of the most imposing and impressive books of the Emden printing industry.

It is not possible in a short article of this sort to trace the subsequent history of the Law and the Gospel motif, though this would be an interesting subject in itself.[46] The subject remained one of enduring interest for Protestant artists, and continued to serve in book woodcut illustrations and paintings until well into the seventeenth century. A more immediate (if ultimately unfathomable) question is how to gauge the effect of the use of this theme as a bible title-page on the readers of the fine Liesvelt Bibles published in Emden. What would they have made of this design, perhaps all the more striking and imposing because for the most part the Evangelical books they would have owned would have been small-format catechisms and liturgical books with no illustration whatsoever? Virtually no other books published in Emden have a title-page of this sophistication; none have any text illustrations.

How would Dutch readers have responded to this rare sortie into visual polemic? Would they have appreciated the theological sophistication of the design, or would they have had no more than a very general sense of its grandeur and inspirational quality? And what of the printer: did he choose this title-page for the simple commercial reason that it identified this as a Bible translation long popular with his potential readers? This is an important question, because Ctematius was himself an important and influential member of the local Calvinist congregation, and he would not necessarily have felt comfortable as the publisher of a bible which had a large following among members of other Evangelical groups, not least Anabaptists. (This popularity was largely on account of an index devised by Galliart which helpfully referenced themes of interest to them.)[47] Perhaps Ctematius was attracted to the publication of a new edition of the Liesvelt Bible only by the precarious financial situation of his business; in this context it is interesting, and perhaps significant, that after the success of the first edition Ctematius in fact resigned publication of the Liesvelt series to the rival house of Galliart and Mierdman. He was able to do this because his own new translation, building on the work undertaken for the failed Utenhove translation of 1556, was now in the process of production; with its publication in 1562 Dutch Calvinists at last had a translation of their own with which they could feel reasonably comfortable.[48]

Jan Galliart would have had no such scruples. The new editions of the Liesvelt Bible took their place in Galliart's list among a much more eclectic body of work than that of the Calvinist Ctematius: these included a number of the most substantial works of the German spiritualist author Sebastian Franck.[49] Franck had a considerable following in the Netherlands, a fact reflected in the quantity of his work published by Galliart. These, too made use of substantial title-page illustrations of a similar conceptual type.[50]

This, however, was the extent of Emden's contribution to the original graphic art of the Reformation book. Later editions of Ctematius's work made use of a neat oval design, illustrating the printing-house motto; in the larger editions, such as the Deux-Aes Bible of 1562, this was surrounded by a more ornate border.[51] But for the most part Emden books continued to eschew illustration, a preference on the whole followed by the Dutch printers, who took on the mantle of Emden's presses when the Dutch churches became established back in the free Netherlands. The Law and Gospel title-page remained, in this respect, a curious and solitary sortie into the biblical visual arts.

What then was its purpose: decorative or pedagogic? Perhaps it is the later use by Galliart, rather than its first adoption by Ctematius, which is in this respect the critical indicator. Galliart's eclectic taste in the texts he published suggests that he had no very precise theological agenda in the adoption of the Law and Gospel title-page; his use of the title-page was probably largely opportunistic. This lack of theological clarity in the employment of illustrative materials seems to be part of a more general pattern. Bart Rosier, who has undertaken the fullest and most fundamental investigation of illustration in Dutch Bibles, is ultimately drawn to the conclusion that there is no clear correlation between the confessional orientation of a particular edition of the Bible and the illustrations it employed. Illustrations moved back and forth between Protestant and Catholic versions with little apparent pattern or clear didactic purpose. This indeed was to be the ultimate fate of the Law and the Gospel title-page, which would subsequently be used in two Antwerp Catholic Bibles of the 1560s. The title-page woodcuts were newly cut, but retained the same essential design features.[52]

The Evolution of an Evangelical Pictorial Theme

Even without this final twist in the tale, the history of this ingenious and popular Evangelical design is full of interest for the student of Reformation iconography. Yet even before this unexpected denouement – the use, apparently uncontroversial, in Catholic bibles – enough has been said to cast an interesting light on the more general debate concerning the role of visual images in the transmission of Evangelical ideas. Can such images function, as has been argued, as teaching aids for the illiterate, thus spreading the range of those who had access to the Reformation doctrines? The evidence presented here suggests we should be extremely cautious before pursuing such a line of argument with any real conviction. It is not just the fact that the second, Calvinist generation of the Reformation orchestrated a genuine mass movement at a time when Evangelical publishing was largely abandoning the earlier illustrative tradition, although this is surely instructive. One should also consider the function and status of the images themselves. By and large, illustrated books tended to be among the most expensive and lavish editions (indeed, the woodcuts were themselves one of the most costly items). This was true of bibles also, with the larger folio editions generally among the most illustrated. But designs like the Law and the Gospel were also iconographically complicated. Like many such pieces of woodcut art, they employed visual references hardly likely to be self-evident to those of meaner education (something that was equally true, incidentally, of many of the polemical prints of the first Lutheran generation).[53] The conclusion to which one is drawn is that the woodcuts which decorated the Protestant book-culture of the sixteenth century achieved their most powerful impact only in social circles which enjoyed relatively high literacy and education. If one is looking for the key to the dissemination of ideas among a genuine mass movement, one must focus on a genuine mass media;[54] in the sixteenth century the visual arts were hardly in a position to perform this function.

Nevertheless, even exercising this proper caution, the development and endurance of the Law and the Gospel motif, and especially its re-appearance in this popular series of Emden Bibles, is not without interest and some significance. For although Emden played a vital role as the nursery of Dutch Calvinism – the movement of the second wave of the Reformation – the continued success of the Law and the Gospel theme demonstrates the extent to which these developments were rooted in the achievement of the first generation. Emden's Dutch Reformed community had sturdy roots in the earlier movement stifled by the persecution of Charles V.[55] The continuing popularity of the Liesvelt Bible, and the close connections with Antwerp's graphic artists revealed in this episode, are a reminder of the extent to which Emden's printers and reformers built on the achievements of the earlier generation. Emden's printing industry was in many respects the direct heir of the generation of Antwerp printers who had flourished in the 1530s and 1540s, until Charles V's clamp-down on Evangelical activity closed their presses. Sometimes the connections were direct and personal, as in the case of Steven Mierdman, and Ctematius's first partner in Emden, Nicolaes van den Berghe.

A single illustrated title-page can raise as many questions as it solves. To point out the importance of the graphic arts for the dissemination of Evangelical doctrines does not answer the question of how these visual texts were 'read', or even the extent to which they were understood. Much work remains to be done in probing the full significance of illustration for the dissemination of ideas in an age of widespread illiteracy. But it is clear that even while rejecting so much of the visual aspects of late

Andrew Pettegree

mediaeval religion, Protestantism had found a place for art, developing new themes and also what were substantially new modes of communication. Nothing makes this clearer than the enduring popularity of the Law and the Gospel, an intricate iconographic construction original to the first generation of the reform.

NOTES

1 For the debate on this question see especially the essays collected in Hans-Joachim Köhler, *Flugschriften als Massenmedium der Reformationszeit* (Stuttgart: Klett-Cotta, 1981). Also R. W. Scribner, *For the Sake of Simple Folk: Popular Propaganda for the German Reformation*, new edn (Oxford: Clarendon Press, 1994; first published Cambridge: University Press, 1981) and Mark Edwards, *Printing, Propaganda, and Martin Luther* (Berkeley: University of California Press, 1994).

2 Bernd Moeller, 'Was wurde in der Frühzeit der Reformation in den deutschen Städten gepredigt?', *Archiv für Reformationsgeschichte*, 75 (1984), 176-93.

3 R. W. Scribner, 'Oral Culture and the Transmission of Reformation Ideas', in *The Transmission of Ideas in the Lutheran Reformation*, ed. by Helga Robinson-Hammerstein (Dublin: Irish Academic Press, 1989), pp. 83-104.

4 See Scribner. For the importance of the concept of *Rein Evangelium*, see Heinrich Richard Schmidt, *Reichstädte, Reich und Reformation. Korporative Religionspolitik 1521-1529/30* (Stuttgart: Steiner Verlag Wiesbaden, 1986).

5 Lucas Cranach, *Passional Christi und Antichristi* (Wittenberg: Johann Rhau-Grunenberg, 1521). Karin Groll, *Das 'Passional Christi und Antichristi' von Lucas Cranach d. A.* (Frankfurt: P. Lang, 1990). All twenty-six woodcuts are illustrated in Gerald Fleming, 'On the origins of the Passional Christi und Antichristi and Lucas Cranach the elder's contribution to Reformation polemics in the iconography of the Passional', *Gutenberg Jahrbuch* (1973), 351-68.

6 Lee Palmer Wandel, *Voracious Idols and Violent Hands. Iconoclasm in Reformation Zurich, Strasbourg and Basel* (Cambridge: University Press, 1995).

7 John Calvin, *Institutes of the Christian Religion*, ed. by J. T. McNeill, Library of the Christian Classics, 20/21 (Philadelphia: Westminster Press, 1960), book 1, chapter 11: 'It is unlawful to attribute a visible form to God, and generally whoever sets up idols revolts against the true God.'

8 Carlos Eire, *War against the idols. The Reformation of Worship from Erasmus to Calvin* (Cambridge: University Press, 1986).

9 The classic literature on this subject is still Robert Kingdon, *Geneva and the Coming of the Wars of Religion* (Geneva: Droz, 1956). There exists at present no full listing of sixteenth-century French printed books, an omission which is presently being corrected for religious literature by the St Andrews University Sixteenth Century French Religious Book project. The project's data files, which now include information on some 16,000 editions, inform the remarks which follow.

10 Phillip Benedict, 'Of Marmites and Martyrs. Images and Polemics in the Wars of Religion', in *The French Renaissance in Prints from the Bibliothèque Nationale de France* (Los Angeles:Grunwald Center for the Graphic Arts, University of California, Los Angeles, 1995), pp. 108-37.

11 Catherine Delano-Smith & Elizabeth Morley Ingram, *Maps in Bibles, 1500-1600. An Illustrated Catalogue* (Geneva: Droz, 1991).

12 Bart A. Rosier, *The Bible in Print. Netherlandish Bible Illustration in the Sixteenth Century*, 2 vols (Leiden: Foleor, 1997).

13 Rosier, I, pp. 45-7.

14 This paragraph follows my *Emden and the Dutch Revolt. Exile and the Development of Reformed Protestantism* (Oxford: Clarendon Press, 1992).

15 H. F. Wijnman, 'Grepen uit de geschiedenis van de Nederlandse emigrantendrukkerijen to Emden', *Het Boek*, 36 (1963-4), 140-68, 37 (1965-6), 121-51.

16 The standard works on Cranach are Max Friedländer & Jakob Rosenberg, *The Paintings of Lucas Cranach* (Ithaca, NY: Cornell University Press, 1978) and Dieter Koepplin & Tilman Falk, *Lukas Cranach*, 2 vols (Basel: Birkhäuser 1974). See also now *Lucas Cranach. Ein Maler-Unternehmer aus Franken*, ed. by Claus Grimm and others (Augsburg: Hans der Bayerischen Geschichte; Regensburg: F. Pustet, 1994).

17 Luther to Cranach's daughter Anna in 1520; Cranach to Luther's first son Johannes in 1526.

18 Martin Warnke, *Cranachs Luther. Entwürfe für ein Image* (Frankfurt: Fischer, 1984).

19 Lucas Cranach, *Cranach im Detail. Buchschmuck Lucas Cranachs des Alteren und seiner Werkstatt*, ed. by Jutta Strehle (Wittenberg: Drei Kastanien Verlag, 1994).

20 Mark Edwards, 'Statistics on Sixteenth-Century Printing', in *The Process of Change in Early Modern Europe*, ed. by Philip Bebb & Sherrin Marshall (Athens, OH: Ohio University Press, 1988), pp. 149-63.

21 Andreas Tacke, *Der katholische Cranach* (Mainz: P. von Zabern, 1992).

22 See also here *Gesetz und Genade. Cranach, Luther und die Bilder* (Eisenach: Museum der Wartburg, 1994): the Gotha version is illustrated at p. 45. Friedländer & Rosenberg, no. 221.

23 The woodcut is illustrated in *Gesetz und Genade*, p. 44, Koepplin, no. 353. Surviving examples in London, British Library, and Weimar, Schlossmuseum.

24 Friedländer & Rosenberg, no. 221C, where it is described as a workshop production in a poor state of repair.

25 Illustrated in Friedländer & Rosenberg, p. 24 (fig. 9). The original is in Dresden, Kupferstichkabinett.

26 Friedländer & Rosenberg, p. 113.

27 Martin Luther, *Auslegung der Evangelien vom Advent bis auff Ostern sampt viel anderen Predigten* (Wittenberg: G. Rhaw, 1528). *Gesetz und Genade*, no. 42.

28 Heimo Reinitzer, *Biblia deutsch. Luthers Bibelübersetzung und ihre Tradition* (Wolfenbüttel: Herzog August Bibliothek, Wittig, 1983), no. 103. The cover illustration shows a fine coloured version of the title-page. The woodcut is generally attributed to Lucas Cranach the Younger.

29 A. W. Pollard & G. R. Redgrave, *Short Title Catalogue of Books printed in England, and of English Books printed abroad, 1475-1640*, 2nd edn revised by K. F. Pantzer *et al.*, 3 vols (London: Bibliographical Society, 1976-91), STC 2063; John N. King, *Tudor Royal Iconography* (Princeton: University Press, 1989), p. 55. Holbein was clearly aware of the iconographical significance of Cranach's Law and Gospel theme, which he painted himself on at least one occasion (painting in Edinburgh, National Gallery of Scotland). F. Grossman, 'A religious allegory by Hans Holbein the Younger', *Burlington Magazine*, 103 (1961), 191-4.

30 Reinitzer, p. 167 (no. 96).

31 Christopher S. Wood, *Albrecht Altdorfer and the origins of landscape* (London: Reaktion, 1993); Jacqueline Guillaud & Maurice Guillaud, *Altdorfer and fantastic realism in German Art* (New York: Rizzoli International, 1985).

32 STC 2066. Illustrated in R. B. McKerrow & F. S. Ferguson, *Title-page Borders used in England and Scotland, 1485-1560* (London: Bibliographical Society, 1932), p. 32.

33 Crom's English work is listed in STC index volume, which lists seventeen volumes between 1536 and 1544. See also H. F. Wijnman, 'De Antwerpse hervormings-gezinde drukker Mattheus Crom en zijn naaste omgeving', *De Gulden passer*, 11 (1962), 105-24. For the

general context of English Protestant printing in Antwerp see also now *Antwerp, Dissident Typographical Centre. The role of Antwerp printers in the religious conflicts in England (16th century)*, exhibition catalogue (Antwerp: Plantin-Moretus Museum, 1994).

34 Bettye Thomas Chambers, *Bibliography of French Bibles: Fifteenth- and Sixteenth-Century French-Language Editions of the Scriptures,* Travaux d'Humanisme et Renaissance 192 (Geneva: Droz, 1983), nos. 51, 62.

35 As for instance J. Seritius, *Lexicon Graeco-Latinum* (1539/40), and Vorsterman's Dutch Bible editions of 1534 and 1542. A. A. den Hollander, *De Nederlandse Bijbelvertalingen, 1522-1545* (Nieuwkoop: de Graaf, 1997), pp. 423 (no. 53), 487 (no. 7). Numerous other bible editions made use of the other blocks in the title-page border, replacing the bottom block with a more neutral decorative scheme. Ibid., p. 397 (no. 46).

36 On Mierdman and van den Berghe (Nicolas Hill) in England see STC, vol. 3 (index of printers), E. G. Duff, *A Century of the English Book Trade* (London: Bibliographical Society, 1948), pp. 72-3, 105. Andrew Pettegree, *Foreign Protestant Communities in Sixteenth-Century London* (Oxford: Clarendon Press, 1986), pp. 88-93.

37 As for instance Pettegree, *Emden* (n. 14 above), nos 13, 39, 40, 59. For the standard types used in Emden, see H. D. L. Vervliet, *Sixteenth-Century Printing Types of the Low Countries* (Amsterdam: 1968).

38 C. C. de Bruin & F. G. M. Broeyer, *De Statenbijbel en zijn voorgangers: nederlandse bijbelvertalingen vanaf de Reformatie tot 1637* (Haarlem: 1993), pp. 94-103. Also Den Hollander.

39 On van Liesvelt, Jean-François Gilmont, 'L'imprimerie et la Réforme aux Pays-Bas, 1520-c.1555', and A. G. Johnston & Jean-François Gilmont, 'L'imprimerie et la Réforme à Anvers', in *La Réforme et le livre*, ed. by Jean-François Gilmont (Paris: Éditions du Cerf, 1990), pp. 161-214.

40 Rosier (n. 12 above), fig. 478.

41 Pettegree, *Emden*, app. no. 41. Paul Heinz Vogel, 'Der niederländische Bibeldruck in Emden, 1556-1568', *Gutenberg Jahrbuch* (1961), 162-71, no. 1. De Bruin & Broeyer, pp. 163-7.

42 Vogel, no. 3.

43 Pettegree, *Emden*, pp. 89-92. De Bruin, pp. 167-76.

44 Pettegree, *Emden*, app. nos 91, 99, 115, 132, 199.

45 Plate one. Wijnman, p. 146.

46 For examples of the use of the theme later in the century, see *Gesetz und Genade*, nos 44, 46. See also Susanne Urbach, 'Eine unbekannte Darstellung von "Sündenfall und Erlösung" in Budapest und das Weiterleben des cranachschen Rechtfertigungsbildes', *Niederdeutsche Beiträge zur Kunstgeschichte*, 28 (1989), 33-63. There is a fine version of the theme by Hans Holbein, with several interesting compositional variations, in the National Gallery of Scotland in Edinburgh: see no. 28.

47 Pettegree, *Emden*, pp. 92-3. Wijnman, pp. 145-7. Ctematius adopted Galliart's index in his own edition of the Liesvelt Bible.

48 Pettegree, *Emden*, app. no. 118. On the 'Deux-Aes' bible, de Bruin & Broeyer, pp. 180-91.

49 Klaus Kaczerowsky, *Sebastian Franck Bibliographie* (Wiesbaden: Pressler, 1976), nos A56, 57, 82, 111, 126, 132, 133, 148.

50 As for instance Sebastian Franck, *Die Gulden Arck* (Louvain: A. M. Bergagne, 1560), Pettegree, *Emden*, app. no. 100.

51 Illustrated in Paul Heinz Vogel, 'Der Druckermarken in den Emdener Niederländischen Bibeldrucken, 156-1568', *Gutenberg Jahrbuch* (1962), 456-8 (no. 1). Also de Bruin & Broeyer, p 188.

52 Rosier (n. 12 above), figs 480, 481.

53 See for instance Luther and Erasmus with the Divine Mill (Illustrated in Scribner, p. 104),

which depended for its force on an understanding of references to a number of different iconographic traditions.

54 Such as, for instance, song. For the powerful role of communal singing in the Huguenot movement see, *inter alia*, Pierre Pidoux, *Le psautier huguenot du XVIe siècle, Mélodies et documents*, 2 vols (Basel: Éditions Baerenreiter, 1962). Stanford W. Reid, 'The Battle Hymns of the Lord. Calvinist Psalmody of the Sixteenth Century', in *Sixteenth Century Essays and Studies*, vol. II, ed. by Carl Meyer (St Louis: Foundation for Reformation Research, 1971), pp. 36-54.

55 On the early Reformation in the Netherlands, see Alastair Duke, *Reform and Reformation in the Low Countries* (London: Hambledon Press, 1990) and C. Ch. G. Visser, *Luther's geschriften in de nederlanden tot 1546* (Assen: Van Gorcum & Company, 1969).

POLITICS AND POLEMICS
IN ENGLISH AND GERMAN
BIBLE ILLUSTRATIONS

Tatiana C. String

THE NOTION that 'for the common people, things enter sooner by the eyes than by the ears' has often been applied to the question of how the illiterate populace was instructed in Reformist doctrine. For the Lutheran Reformation, pamphlets and broadsheets have been examined and understood to have been powerful tools in a propaganda campaign against the church.[1] I would like to argue a case which modifies that overall picture, demonstrating that the English Reformation must not be seen simply as a projection of the same expectations.[2] An examination of the use of images in the English Reformation provides contradictory and ambiguous information about the power of images and their prominence in early Tudor society. My examples lie in the woodcut illustrations of Antichrist in the Apocalypse cycle of the first printed English Bibles. These provide a rare opportunity for direct comparisons and contrasts between the uses made of images in the German and English Reformist programmes.

The English identification of the pope as Antichrist may be found in the writings of John Wyclif, William Tyndale, and Thomas Cranmer.[3] Each recognized the Antichrist of the Apocalypse as the pope in Rome. While Wyclif and Tyndale were not concerned to make this identification for political gain, Thomas Cranmer, during Henry VIII's dispute with Rome over his divorce from Catherine of Aragon, saw the tradition of the papal Antichrist as an opportunity to further attack and discredit the English King's adversary.[4] Since the English Reformation focused on the removal of papal authority, which was to be replaced by royal supremacy over the Church of England, a steady stream of anti-papal materials in various media was prepared to support the King's cause. Printed books and spectacles underlined the ills of the papacy and the need for the triumph of the monarchy.[5] Richard Morison, one of Henry's chief apologists, in his 1539 *Discourse on Law* wrote of the need to employ these specific media – printed books and spectacles – as well as plays and songs, to inculcate and 'drive into the people's heads' the abuses of the papacy.[6]

Conflating the pope with Antichrist was not difficult for the English Reformers; they built on a knowledge of Antichrist that was readily available in the pre-Reformation era. Popular texts, intended for a wide English readership, such as Wynken de Worde's 1525 publication, *Here begynneth the byrthe and lyfe of Antechryst,* were full of specific language about the corrupt power of Antichrist.[7] He was described as a world leader who could preach the Gospels, having been well taught by Lucifer. He was the composite Antichrist of the Bible: the Beast of the Apocalypse, the Antichrist as prophesied in the Book of Daniel, and as described in I John. Falseness, deceit, beguilement, and pride were repeated as traits of this pre-Reformation Antichrist, and this perception formed the basis on which the Reformers could create their anti-papal allusions.

Intentionally similar language is employed to characterize the pope by Miles Coverdale in the first complete printed Bible in English in 1535.[8] In Coverdale's epistle to the king, he describes the contemporary pope as a usurper, as deceitful and secretive, and in all possible ways antithetical to God. He is antithetical to Henry as well, as Coverdale informs the King: 'his stealynge away of youre money for pardons: his disceavyng of youre subiectes soules with his develyshe doctrunes and sectes of his false religions: his bloudsheddyng of so many of your graces people …'.[9]

But it was Cranmer who finally articulated the link between the general pre-Reformation image of Antichrist and the anti-papal sentiment that was being promoted at the English court. In 1536 Cranmer preached a high-profile, well-attended sermon at Paul's Cross in which his major theme was the identification of the Pope as Antichrist. This was to remain one of Cranmer's favourite *topoi*.[10] Thus linking the Pope's contemporary abuses with the power-hungry evils of Antichrist became a useful theme in English political theory. The idea was propagated by making the leap from the familiar, recognizable, general evil to the newly-recognized, specific, contemporary enemy. From this point onwards, countless citations to the papal Antichrist may be found.

At first glance, then, it would seem likely that the English Reformers would look for ways to expand this argument by making the association in visual terms as well. This had certainly been exploited by the German Reformers.[11] Despite the many differences in reforms in England and Germany, Cranmer and Thomas Cromwell sought to manipulate some of the major themes of Luther's battle with Rome and emulated the means by which these themes had been communicated by the German Reformers. The repudiation of the papacy and the revelation of the pope as Antichrist were among the elements adopted from the German Protestants to serve the English brand of Reformation.

These shared concerns, however, in the end did not lead the English Reformers to adopt the type of visual propaganda so successfully employed by Luther and his supporters. Unlike the situation in Germany, there is no evidence of a comparable English campaign that used illustrated anti-papal broadsheets or polemical prints. The English anti-papal books and pamphlets which abounded are all unillustrated. The text of a work like *A Litel Treatise ageynst the Mutterynge of some Papists in Corners* almost demands a visual parallel, but the reader is left unsatisfied.[12] Instead, the only illustrations that English Reformers used are those found in printed bibles. The availability of a vernacular bible accessible to the widest English readership, or at least viewership, based on the insistence of the authority of scripture, was another key element adopted by the English Reformers from the German Protestants.

With that in mind, it is now useful to examine the German material in order to explore the possibilities it created for those drawing upon it. Since bible illustrations were the one sure visual tool that was to be employed by the English Reformers, it seems reasonable to suppose that they would take full advantage of this medium to highlight their most important messages. For example, when choosing woodcuts for an Apocalypse cycle in the English New Testament, printed around the same time that Cranmer preached about the papal Antichrist, the obvious choice as a suitable model for English Reformers would have been the series in Martin Luther's *September-testament* (1522), in which Lucas Cranach's woodcuts of the Harlot of Babylon (Pl. 19) and the Beast of the Apocalypse (Pl. 20) are adorned with papal tiaras.[13] This is an unequivocal visual statement of the perversion of Christ's Church by Rome. These figures had been invested with references to Antichrist since their inception, and here Cranach's adaptations added a further layer of contemporary meaning.

In the Book of Revelation the associated powers of evil appear in the last days in three guises. The Beast who confronts the visitors to the temple in Chapter 11 ascended from the bottomless pit to make war, conquer, and kill. This Beast is thought to be the Antichrist prophesied in Daniel. The seven-headed beast of Chapter 13 is the Beast of Rome, given its power by the dragon, or Satan. It has represented the Roman Empire since the writing of the Revelation. Chapter 17 identifies the third antithetical figure, 'the great whore that sytteth upon many waters, wyth whome have commytted fornicacion the kynges of the erthe, and the inhabyters of the erthe are droncken wyth the wyne of her fornicacion'.[14] She is the evocation of Rome in all its decadence. The Great Whore, along with the Beast of Rome, demanded complete submission of her subjects. Holding the golden cup, she is the seductress who offers the power of empire.[15] The opulent garb is described in highly pictorial language that emphasizes her seductive appearance: 'And the woman was arrayed in purple and scarlet colour, and decked with gold and precious stones and pearls, having a golden cup in her hand full of abominations and filthiness of her fornication'; this visual description was mimicked by German print-makers, albeit in black and white.

Cranach's provocative interpretation of the Harlot and the Beasts with triple crowns transforms the more general Antichrist images in Albrecht Dürer's earlier bestselling Apocalypse series of 1498. Virtually all sixteenth-century Apocalypse series owe their composition to Dürer's definitive designs. His authoritative adaptations of St John's vision consolidated the tradition of Apocalypse imagery and gave life to the abstract notion of living in the last days. The wave of prophecy and Apocalyptic fever in which it was created provided a huge market for such images, hence their familiarity and immediate recognizability. They were reproduced and repeated in series by Hans Burgkmair and Georg Lemberger as well as Cranach.

So easily recognizable were the images of the Harlot and the Beasts as Antichrist that Lucas Cranach was able to take the next step of investing them with specific contemporary references to the papacy. Cranach knew that Dürer had provided models that were sufficiently familiar that, once transformed, they could be employed in the Lutheran cause. Cranach's polemical illustrations were part of a long line of Lutheran anti-papal woodcuts, such as the *Passional Christi/Anti-Christi*, the scathing comparison of Christ and the pope. However, by December 1522 Lucas Cranach retracted his provocative stance and physically altered the Apocalypse woodcuts so that the tiaras in the now re-titled *Dezembertestament* were cut down to benign non-papal coronets in each instance (Pl. 21, 22). The explanations which have been offered for this dramatic reversal vary, but it seems that the explicitness of the Reformers' attack was too offensive to those Luther and Cranach needed to appease. It is clear from Cranach's alterations, however, that the initial assigning of the papal tiaras to the traditional references to Antichrist was both a highly charged and a very deliberate allusion.

Despite Cranach's reworking of his own woodcuts, papal tiaras did not disappear from German Bibles. His cycle proved to be nearly as influential as Dürer's, and was repeatedly imitated in both versions, with and without the triple crowns and their resonant symbolism. For instance, a series attributed to Hans Holbein which appears in bibles from 1524 employs tiaras, as does a 1534 series in a bible printed by Hans Lufft.

Let us return to the English material. When the opportunity finally arose to include woodcuts in the printed editions of the English-language New Testament, first by William Tyndale, then by Miles Coverdale, the woodcuts chosen to illustrate these volumes were not those with papal tiaras based on the original Cranach series or on Holbein's patterns. Instead, these volumes used illustrations based on the Apocalypse images in Cranach's second series, those in the altered *Dezembertestament*. That is, the Harlot of Babylon (Pl. 23) and the Beasts in Tyndale's 1536 New Testament derive from Cranach's altered blocks and wear only coronets, thereby completely removing any direct reference to the papal Antichrist.[16]

The implication of this – that the publisher of the Bible had little or no interest in the exact nature of the illustrations – is further reinforced by the example of the Harlot and the Beasts in Coverdale's New Testament of 1538 (Pl. 24, 25, 26).[17] Here, the images are printed from woodcuts in which the former papal tiaras have actually been cut away, indicating not the following of an existing design based on Cranach's second series, but intentionally altered woodcuts, which suggests that the printer who chose the illustrations for this publication was not specifically intent on conveying an anti-papal message. More importantly, it also shows how apparently little interest was invested in choosing appropriate illustrations in the first place. If consulted, Coverdale himself surely would have opted for an overt anti-papal reference which would have corresponded with his barrage of anti-papal writing. Apparently, however, the woodcuts used by the printer who put the volume together, 'Matthew Crom. of Antwerpe' in this case, were simply those that were available to him at the time and place of publication. On the basis of the stylistic disparity of these examples, I believe that it is even clear that this is a 'mix and match' set of illustrations.[18] Owning woodcuts like these was expensive enough and would undoubtedly have left little opportunity for choice. Yet, considering the fact that Coverdale's publication on behalf of the King of England was printed in the midst of a vicious anti-papal campaign, this seems an incredible missed opportunity.

It is important to recognize at this point that no native print industry was developed in England to accommodate the particular needs of the early Reformation. The English-language Bibles and persuasive texts of the 1530s were most often printed on the Continent. When the Bibles were illustrated, they generally used German woodcuts, or at least German designs. The 1535 Coverdale Bible, for example, is patterned on a 1534 German Bible using the same woodcuts by Sebald Beham.[19] The so-called 'Matthew's Bible' of 1537[20] bears a frontispiece by Erhard Altdorfer and its Apocalypse series is modelled on Cranach's *Dezembertestament*. Hans Holbein was in England at this time, working with Miles Coverdale, so specifically anti-papal illustrations should have been readily available, or could easily have been commissioned from Holbein himself. Holbein had already designed the title-page for the 1535 Coverdale Bible, but was not employed to design woodcuts for Coverdale's New Testament, nor was he asked to retrieve a set of his own previously-executed Apocalypse woodcuts. There is evidence that anti-papal subjects existed as images in England at this time. For instance, Henry VIII's posthumous inventories reveal that the King owned a painting showing himself triumphing over the seven-headed Beast of Rome that wears a triple crown, as well as another painting depicting the Harlot of Babylon.[21] However, since viewing of these paintings was restricted to the royal palaces, they could not have been effective tools in a propaganda campaign, nor were they apparently ever re-used as models for prints that could have been disseminated to alert the English public to Henry's religious and political supremacy over Rome.

What this indicates is that only the title-pages at the front of the Coverdale Bible and the Great Bible were specially conceived to communicate specific political and theological messages. They are intentional in depicting Henry VIII's newly-established dual role as Supreme Head of both Church and State. By contrast, the internal illustrations of these bibles, the New Testaments, and the 'Matthew's Bible' seem to have been considered substantially less important and in the nature of afterthoughts. This is especially notable in the example of the Apocalypse woodcuts just discussed and their lack of appropriateness to their publications. Henrician writers never mention the importance or even the existence of bible illustrations. In Coverdale's prologue to the reader of the Great Bible, for example, he explains that he has included aids for understanding this new vernacular Bible, 'what is meant by certayn signes and tokens that we have set in the Bybble', but there is no mention of the numerous woodcuts punctuating the text. If images were to function as 'unlearned men's books', where can we find reference to them?

After considering these examples, it emerges that the illustrations have been haphazardly chosen, and that there is little which specifically relates to the Englishness of these bibles. Except for the title-pages, which credentialize each publication, the choices of scenes illustrated in the bibles do not relate to Henry VIII's supremacy or his triumph over the papacy. In addition, we learn that Henrician patronage of the arts did not extend to a print industry. Today this seems a missed opportunity to provide the English populace with more charged visual messages corresponding to the fiery words they were hearing or reading. However, as these examples show, the early English Reformers were not always as uniformly calculating as they have been made out to be by later scholarship.[22]

This leads us to a conclusion that raises issues about English visual culture in the sixteenth century. The primary means by which the majority of the English people were 'inculcated' with political and theological propaganda were not pictorial; pictures had never been one of the traditional means for disseminating such messages to the English populace. When Luther wrote his version of 'into the common people things sooner enter by the eyes than by the ears', the reference was to pictures.[23] The Germans cunningly exploited the possibilities of the print medium by linking general, familiar visual references to the newly important image of the pope as Antichrist. They were intentional in the use of symbolism and were aware of the loaded messages they were sending out. In a period in which eschatology was a very real concern, the German Reformers manipulated the fears and confusion of the people for their own particular reforming ends. When the same phrase was used in England by Richard Morison, that 'things sooner enter by the eies than by the ears', the reference was to plays.[24] Morison's advice to Henry, cited at the beginning of this paper, on how to drive anti-papal messages into the people's heads, listed the means as: playing it in plays, singing it in minstrels' songs, teaching it in schools, and printing it in books. Pictures are not mentioned.

NOTES

1 The literature on this subject is extensive, as demonstrated by Linda Parshall & Peter Parshall, *Art and the Reformation, an Annotated Bibliography* (Boston: G. K. Hall, 1986). Among the most authoritative studies of Lutheran propaganda are: Robert Scribner, *For the Sake of Simple Folk: Popular Propaganda for the German Reformation*, new edn (Oxford: Clarendon Press, 1994; first published Cambridge: University Press, 1981); Keith Moxey, *Peasants, Warriors and Wives* (Chicago: University of Chicago Press, 1989); Carl Christensen, *Art and the Reformation in Germany* (Athens, OH: Ohio University Press, 1979), and *Princes and Propaganda* (Kirksville, Missouri: Sixteenth Century Journal Publishers, 1992); and Christiane Andersson & Charles Talbot, *From a Mighty Fortress: Prints, Drawings and Books in the Age of Luther, 1483-1546*, ex. cat. (Detroit: Institute of Art, 1983).

2 Studies such as Roy Strong's *Holbein and Henry VIII* (London: Routledge & Kegan Paul, 1967) and John King's *Tudor Royal Iconography* (Princeton: University Press, 1989) suggest a coordinated campaign of Reformation propaganda in England. By contrast, see Sydney Anglo, *Images of Tudor Kingship* (London: Seaby, 1992) and Tatiana C. String, 'Henry VIII and the Art of the Royal Supremacy' (unpublished Ph.D. dissertation, University of Texas at Austin, 1996).

3 Richard Kenneth Emmerson, *Antichrist in the Middle Ages: a Study of Medieval Apocalypticism, Art, and Literature* (Seattle: University of Washington Press, 1981), pp. 1-31; Richard Bauckham, *Tudor Apocalypse: Sixteenth-Century Apocalypticism, Millenarianism, and the English Reformation* (Appleford: Sutton Courtenay Press, 1978), pp. 94-5.

4 Diarmid MacCullough, *Thomas Cranmer, A Life* (New Haven & London: Yale University Press, 1996), p. 150.

5 Geoffrey Elton's 'Propaganda' chapter in *Policy and Police: The Enforcement of the Reformation in the Age of Thomas Cromwell* (Cambridge: University Press, 1972) remains the most lucid discussion of the print campaign. See now also String, 'Henry VIII and the Art of the Royal Supremacy', pp. 22-45.

6 British Library, Royal MS 18. A.L., fols 15-19. The transcription of the entire manuscript appears in Jonathan Woolfson, 'English Students at Padua, 1480-1580' (unpublished Ph.D. thesis, University of London, 1995).

7 STC 670.

8 STC 2063.

9 fol. iii^v.

10 MacCullough, pp. 150-1.

11 See especially Scribner, pp. 148-89.

12 STC 19177.

13 *Das Newe Testament Deutsch* (Wittenberg: [Melchior Lotther], September, 1522).

14 I am quoting from the text of the 1539 Great Bible.

15 In addition to the traditional Antichrist reference, Rosemary Muir Wright, in *Art and Antichrist in Medieval Europe* (Manchester: University Press, 1995), pp. 180-212, has recently shown that in medieval manuscripts the Harlot had also been conflated with guardian figures, amazons, Jezebel, Luxuria, and fallen women.

16 STC 2835.

17 STC 2836.

18 Especially given that figure 8 is a derivation of Holbein's Apocalypse cycle, while figures 6 and 7 are unrelated.

19 Fragments of the Coverdale Bible and the German Bible printed in Frankfurt by Christian Egenolph are bound together in the British Library as 3051.ff.10 to illustrate their close relationship.

20 STC 2066.

21 *Three Inventories of the Years 1542, 1547, and 1549-50 of Pictures in the Collections of Henry VIII and Edward VI*, ed. by W. A. Shaw (London: G. Allen & Unwin, 1937), p. 35 and p. 43; *The Inventory of King Henry VIII: Society of Antiquaries MS 129 and British MS Harley 1419*, ed. by David Starkey (London: Harvey Miller: Society of Antiquaries, 1998), p. 238 and p. 239.

22 Especially Strong and King (n. 2 above).

23 *D. Martin Luthers werke. Kritische Gesamtausgabe* (Weimar: H. Böhlaus Nachfolger, 1883-1978), vol. 10/ii, 458, as cited by Scribner (n. 1 above), p. 244, note 42.

24 BL, Royal MS 18. A.L., fol. 19.

THE REVELATION AND EARLY ENGLISH COLONIAL VENTURES

Andrew Hadfield

THE VIEW that English colonial activity in the Americas in the late sixteenth and early seventeenth centuries was motivated primarily by the desire for profit has become something of an historical commonplace. The exhortationary pamphlets produced during this era are often dismissed as propaganda exercises, in which no one earnestly believed.[1] However, while it is undoubtedly true that many of those who actually travelled to the Americas were more interested in plundering Spanish shipping or attempting to make the early colonies somehow pay for themselves, it needs to be made clear that many of the propagandists were not cynically manipulating a gullible populace. Instead they felt that there were urgent reasons why England should be more keen to develop colonies than had hitherto been the case.[2] Enthusiasts for colonial ventures such as Richard Hakluyt and Theodor De Bry, I would suggest, were inspired by cogent political and religious fears. They felt that if the threat of Catholic Spain were not countered, the true Protestant faith, which had only just been re-established after years of spiritual darkness, could well founder; the end of the world would be imminent. The struggle, as many saw it, could not be contained within Europe, but would also involve a confrontation with the might of the Spanish in the New World. Spanish colonies would have to be overthrown and replaced with Protestant – principally English – ones. This would enable Spanish trade routes to be cut off, preventing the shipment of gold back to Spain, and so curtailing her wealth and power within Europe. In addition, the native Americans could be converted to the Protestant faith, enlarging Christ's true empire.[3] Hence from the outset English colonial activity had a significant religious dimension, and was often cast as a Protestant enterprise. Colonial ventures, I would argue, were specifically inspired by the recent Protestant emphasis on the Book of Revelation. Although the Revelation of Saint John has 'been a source of scandal to many both ancient and modern ... it remains the most influential of all apocalyptic texts'.[4]

The Geneva translation of the Bible, prepared by the Marian exiles in Geneva in the 1550s, included a detailed commentary on the Book of Revelation.[5] This was a controversial book for many Reformers in the first half of the sixteenth century, but one which the Geneva Bible made especially significant for subsequent English readers. The commentary used was heavily based on John Bale's *The Image of Both Churches* (*c.* 1545?), which divided the Protestant sheep from the Catholic goats in the last days before the return of Christ.[6] Bale, like many others, felt that the end of the world was imminent, and argued that a particularly vigorous effort was required by Protestants to save as many souls as possible before Christ's return to earth. Previous history was

145

regarded as one in which the false Church of Rome had swamped and repressed – but never obliterated – the true apostolic church of Christ. Only in the last days had the truth become clear to believers. As Katherine Firth points out, Bale's commentary was both specific in detail (referring to the persecutions of Domitian and Boniface VIII at points) and 'avoided any periodization according to the order of the text or its images'.[7] What was clear was that the battle with the Antichrist had just begun, and would continue until history was ended by Christ's intervention. Bale's commentary was hugely influential, providing a key for reading a Protestant history which could include details and events, yet was flexible enough to be adapted to a variety of schemes. The Geneva Bible included a commentary that was confined by reasons of space, but which was, in essence, the same as that of Bale.[8]

This interpretation of history could easily be mapped on to the European struggle between Protestant England and Catholic Spain in the wake of the Papal bull of 1570, which declared that loyal Catholics could legitimately depose Elizabeth. The Bale/Geneva reading of world history was made more plausible for many Protestants after the Massacre of St Bartholomew's Day in France (23 August 1572); the fear that such apocalyptic slaughter could be visited on the English if they failed to halt Spain's advance in the Americas lay behind much colonial literature in the 1580s.[9] In addition, as the English saw it, the colonial venture offered them opportunities both to enlarge the Protestant empire and to transform the nature of English national identity.

A case in point is Bartolomé de Las Casas's *Brevíssima Relación de la Destrucción de las Indias*, which was translated into English in 1583 by the unknown 'M.M.S.' as *The Spanish Colonie, or the Briefe Chronicle of the Acts and Gestes of the Spaniards in the West Indies, called the New World for the space of xl. yeares*.[10] Las Casas's text is best known as the work which depicted the horrifying slaughter the *conquistadors* inflicted upon the Americas. This characterization formed the basis of the Black Legend, which constituted an attempt by the English to vilify Spanish colonialism by highlighting and exaggerating the atrocities committed by the Spanish in the Americas in order to emphasize their own good intentions and virtuous practice and the desire of the natives to be ruled by Protestant Englishmen.[11]

The date of the English translation of *Brevissima Relacion*, over thirty years after the original publication, is interesting. The text was obviously thought to be relevant to the English people of the 1580s, perhaps as never before. One reason may perhaps be found in the preface to *The Spanish Colonie*, which characterizes the Spanish as the most barbarous and cruel nation in the world, and urges the peoples of the Low Countries to wake from their sleep and realize the terrible nature of the enemies they face in their struggle for independence.[12] The text can be read as having a European dimension in its urgent plea for the defense of the Protestant Low Countries against the encroachments of the Catholic Spanish empire within Europe. As such, it undoubtedly aims to persuade English readers of the necessity of helping their religious brethren. This was a frequent plea of English Protestants throughout Elizabeth's reign, who attacked (what they saw as) the Queen's dangerous parsimony in refusing to lend anything beyond the most rudimentary military aid to the Dutch.[13] Hence, the translator explicitly refers the atrocities of *The Spanish Colonie* back to a European context, perhaps evoking a memory of the recent St Bartholomew's Day Massacre.

For English audiences, the massacre was the story of a wicked Catholic plot against innocent Protestants. This crucial component of the Black Legend flattened out the disputes within Catholic Spain so that a straightforward Protestant/Catholic dichotomy could be established.[14] The text includes a catalogue of brutalities (fol. Q2^v), consisting of plundering gold, random massacres, feeding rebel Indians to dogs,[15] dismembering, a whole variety of other tortures, along with the enslavement of huge numbers, resulting in the death of more Indians than Spaniards who had ever lived. The catalogue suggests to the reader an apocalyptic vision of a future Europe overrun by the evil Spanish before they, in turn, meet their judgement. Las Casas claims that the wickedness of Francisco Pizarro is of such immense proportions that the full extent of it will only be revealed on the Day of Judgment (fol. K3^r).[16] More pointed still are the claims made by the Spanish authors, in the material which M.M.S. has appended to his translation of Las Casas, that the Spanish never condemned martyrs within Europe to greater torments than were experienced by the Indians they forced to mine metals for them (fol. P3^v). Mining, which was a common image of Hell, here serves as a dire warning that the Spanish experience in the New World will encourage them to return to Europe to rule with even greater ferocity and cruelty, unless they are stopped by resolute opposition.[17]

Therefore it is not without significance that the *Brevissima Relacion* was translated as *The Spanish Colonie*, or that it appeared in 1583, by which time the first concerted English efforts to establish colonies in the New World were well under way. These efforts were backed up by a significant number of exhortationary and propagandist treatises, an outburst of intellectual activity which highlighted the conspicuous lack of interest in the Americas of recent years.[18] The two most significant Elizabethan publications on the Americas were Thomas Harriot's *A Briefe and True Report on the New Found Land of Virginia* (1588, 1590) – which will be discussed later – and Richard Hakluyt's major compilation of English voyages, *The Principall Navigations, Voiages and Discoueries of the English Nation* (1589).[19] In addition to his *Principall Navigations*, Hakluyt also wrote a pioneering work, which has become known as *A Discourse of Western Planting* (1584).[20] This influential tract promoted the colonization of the Americas as a means to supplant Spain's empire in the New World. The wealth from the Americas could be used to increase the power of the English empire; in addition, the idle hands of England could be put to work in the colonies. Hakluyt takes his argument further and directly links the need to undercut Spain's power with the spread of Protestantism: the Indians would be converted to the Protestant, and not the Catholic, cause. The political loyalties of the native peoples would be implicit in their religion.

Hakluyt commences his argument with an assertion of the need to establish the reformed religion in the Americas, but in doing so he draws attention to the inadequacies of England. The Spanish have successfully converted numerous Indians, 'Of which acte they more vaunte in all their histories and Chronicles, then of anythinge els that ever they atchieved' (p. 216). However, of the ministers of the Gospel sent by the French into Florida, the Genevans into Brazil, and 'also those of our nation that went with ffrobsher, Sir ffraunces Drake, and ffenton, … in very deede I was not able to name any one Infidell by them converted' (p. 217). Hakluyt makes the connection between material success and the conversion of the infidels, neatly eliding the spiritual and the economic:

Unto the Prince and people that shalbe the occasion of this worthie worke, and shall open their coffers to the furtheraunce of this most godly enterprise, God shall open the bottomless treasures of his riches and fill them with aboundance of his hidden blessinges. (p. 216)

It is later made clear that the 'hidden blessings' promised include 'the Revenewes and customes of her Majestie' (pp. 268-70): moral righteousness and wealth were working in harmony.

The problem, according to Hakluyt, is that England is failing on two counts, and domestic matters are hobbling hopes of glory abroad. First, there has been no state encouragement for colonization. Hakluyt points out that God 'hath his tyme for all men, whoe calleth some at the nynthe, and some at the eleventh hower': this concern – that the apocalypse is impending – gives urgency to the suggestion that the time for converting is imminent, if it is to happen at all. There is a desperate need for the Queen to act: 'And if it please him to move the harte of her Majestie to put her helping hande to this godly action she shall finde as willing subjectes of all sortes as any other prince in all christendome' (p. 217).

However, not all the blame can be directed at Elizabeth; her subjects' lack of success in expanding overseas also results from a divided nation:

But also many inconveniences and strifes amongest ourselves at home in matters of Ceremonies shalbe ended: For those of the Clergye which by reason of idlenes here at home are nowe always coyninge of newe opynions, havinge by this voyadge to sett themselves on worke in reducing the Savages to the chefe principles of our faith, will become lesse contentious, and be confined with the truth in Rellgion alreadie established by aucthoritie: So they that shall beare the name of Christians shall shewe themselves worthye of their vocation, so shall the mouthe of the adverserie [i.e., the Spanish] be stopped, so shall contention amongest Bretheren be avoyded, so shall the gospell amonge Infidells be published (pp. 217-18).

National renewal and the colonial enterprise were thus interrelated goals.[21] Hakluyt reasons that just as Elizabeth has to speculate in order to accumulate wealth, so will the nation have to expand in order to unify itself and check the advance of the forces of Antichrist. Furthermore, the establishment of colonies in the Americas would force idle ministers to direct their energies towards a more productive enterprise, making the destructive disputes, which have torn the nation apart, an impossible luxury.[22]

The religious concerns of Hakluyt should not surprise us. He was from a family of divines and was ordained a priest before he became interested in colonialism and travel literature.[23] In fact it would be odd had he not perceived England's colonial mission in terms of the apocalyptic theory of history outlined by John Bale and the commentary accompanying the Geneva Bible, a relationship too few commentators have chosen to emphasize.[24]

The apocalyptic concerns of the Geneva Bible also resonate through the second colonial work under consideration – Thomas Harriot's *A Briefe and True Reporte of the New Found Land of Virginia*. While the text of the *Briefe and True Reporte* first appeared in 1588, the most significant edition was undoubtedly that published by the exiled Belgian printer Theodor de Bry in 1590, translated from the Latin by Richard Hakluyt the younger. Harriot's work was the first part of de Bry's multi-volume collection of New World voyages, *America*, and in 1590 was published in a folio edition, separately reproduced in four languages (Latin, English, French, and German).[25]

148

Appended was a series of drawings by the English artist John White, who had sailed with Sir Richard Grenville's expedition in 1585.[26] The edition was dedicated to Walter Raleigh, as originator of the Roanoke colony.[27]

Harriot's text remains virtually the same in all editions, but the significance clearly alters according to the context, betraying very different agendas. De Bry's magnificent editions aim as much to celebrate English success in the Americas as to assess the importance of the discovery of the new continent. Evident is a strongly anti-Spanish bias, which is hardly surprising given de Bry's own religious views, his narrow escapes from persecution, and his age (early forties) at the time of the St Bartholomew's Day Massacre. However, what is most significant is his framing of Harriot's narrative in an explicitly theological framework.[28]

The introduction to the collection of appended drawings makes the religious context clear, perhaps demanding that the reader return to reinterpret Harriot's text in a deeper, more allegorical manner.[29] The series is introduced by an engraving of Adam and Eve before the Fall, which has been attributed to de Bry himself (Pl. 27). They reach to pick the apples, with the serpent entwined around the tree between them. In the foreground a lion lies next to a mouse, and a panther prowls on one side of the tree with a rabbit on the other, symbolizing the harmony of nature before the Fall. The background is divided in two by the tree: on the left, a mother nurses a baby; on the right, a man tills the ground with a staff, symbolizing the division of the sexes after the Fall and God's injunction in Genesis 3.19: 'In the sweat of thy face shalt thou eat bread, till thou return unto the ground.' The meaning of the picture is ambiguous: has mankind rediscovered the Garden of Eden in the Americas, even if Indian society is more georgic than pastoral? Or is the European discovery of the peoples of the New World a violation, a forced entry into an earthly paradise, which will lead to its destruction? As the iconography of the developing project makes clear, Protestant colonialism has the potential to establish a new Garden of Eden, through peaceful co-existence with the natives, and their conversion to the true faith. In contrast, Spanish Catholic colonialism can lead only to dark visions.[30] Of course, either vision depends on the cooperation of the Indians in question; however, it is significant that de Bry generally represents those colonized by Spanish Catholics as far more ferocious than those colonized by French or English Protestants.

The engravings and commentaries establish Virginia as a land of plenty, which is administered in a civil and sophisticated manner by the natives.[31] To take one example, Pl. 28 shows 'An ageed manne in his winter garment', standing in front of a well-ordered fortified village. To either side are fields of abundant corn; in the background a line of carefully planted and pruned trees separate the village from the river, on which Indian canoes are paddled. The accompanying commentary describes primarily the garment of the old man, but concludes with an acknowledgment that the surrounding details bear considerable significance: 'The contrye abowt this plase is soe fruit full and good, that England is not to bee compared to yt.'[32]

However, Pl. 29 provides a less optimistic representation of the Indians. 'Their manner of fishynge in Virginia' shows a canoe in the foreground, with two Indians using nets to catch the abundant supply of various fish in the water. In the background are a number of natives wading in the water, using spears and a series of large nets, to force the fish nearer to their doom. Although Harriot's commentary recognizes the skill of the Indians ('There was neuer seene amonge us soe cunninge a way to take fish withall'), the conclusion reveals that the question of religion, so lightly dismissed in de Bry's opening epistle, is an ever-present problem:

Dowbteles yt is a pleasant sighte to see the people, somtymes wadinge, and goinge somtymes sailinge in those Riuers, which are shallowe and not deepe, free and liuinge frendlye together of those thinges which god of his bountye hath giuen unto them, yet without giuinge hym any thankes according to his desarte. So sauage is this people, and depriued of the true knowledge of god. For they haue none other then is mentionned before in this worke. (p. 56)[33]

Evidently, the primitive georgic way of life enjoyed by the Indians has severe limitations, as well as obvious advantages. As the sequence continues the emphasis on the limitations increases.

The text concludes with a group of five engravings: 'Som Picture, Of The Pictes which in olde tyme dyd habite one part of the great Bretainne'. These are advertised as being by 'The Painter of whom I have had the first Inhabitans of Virginia' (i.e. John White), and are apparently based on pictures found in an old English chronicle, 'for to showe how that the Inhabitants of the great Bretainnie haue bin in times pase as sauuage as those of Virginia' (p. 75).[34] The engravings show three pictures of Picts: a naked war-like man, covered in body painting, holding a spear and the severed head of a vanquished enemy in one hand (as the commentary makes clear), with another severed head beside his feet in the foreground (Pl. 30); a Pictish woman, similarly naked and body-painted, carrying three spears; and the daughter of the Picts (Pl. 31), legs crossed at the calf, reclining on a spear and staring to her left in a wary, aggressive manner (Pl. 32). The two neighbours of the Picts represented in the last two of the five engravings are not identified, but they appear to be more civilized than the Picts: they wear clothes which cover their genitals; the man does not retain his enemies' severed heads; and they look out to the side of the engraving rather than staring directly at the observer in a hostile manner.

Furthermore, it could be argued that the Picts are all seen to have turned their backs on civilization, which is represented in the backgrounds of their pictures. The man has no obvious connection with the village, or the ships which sail in the river behind him. The woman would appear to be excluded from the castles on the hills behind her; indeed they may have been erected to keep her out, especially if one bears in mind that the stated purpose of the engravings was to show that the Picts were as savage as the Virginian Indians – savage peoples do not, as a rule, build castles. The daughter of the Picts could also be regarded as being at odds with the orderly village behind her. The 'neighbours unto the Picts' are integrated with their backgrounds. The three figures in the background of the first engraving wear the same clothes as the main figure, indicating that they may all come from the same village on the far shore, and may have built the large ocean-going boats (significantly larger than those in the first two pictures) sailing away on the sea, possibly towards new lands. The woman is also obviously from the village behind her, a settlement that may be intended to recall the shelter in the prefatory engraving of Adam and Eve.

What is the point of de Bry's comparison between the savagery of the Virginian Indians and the peoples of ancient Britain? The evidence from the engravings is ambiguous, even leaving aside the problem of interpreting the details as simply changes made for the convenience of the engraver or printer.[35] This is in part because we are not told the identity of the neighbours of the Picts. It would appear most likely that the neighbours are, in fact, the Britons, but it is significant that de Bry's text chooses not to name them. The iconography of the engravings clearly indicates that one group of peoples, the Picts, are savages in need of civilizing. The other group, the Britons, have established the rudiments of agricultural life, and look out towards the New World, ready to colonize and civilize others, if not now then in the future.

Such an interpretation of ancient British life suggests a number of possibilities for the cultural encounter between the new Britons (the English) and the Virginian Indians. The Indians may be compared to the Picts; much is made of the body-painting of both peoples, and the practice links the two sequences of pictures, as the final one in the Indian series shows the tattoos used by the Virginians (Pl. 33, 'The Marckes of sundrie of the Chief mene of Virginia'). This suggests that the English are like the Britons, having to build a new Britain (in the Americas) by conquering and absorbing a savage race; remember also that the ancestors of the English were shown building ships and sailing westwards.[36]

However, this straightforward contrast between civilized and savage does not accord with the representation of the Indians in the sequence, who are shown to be civil, possessing many superior aspects to the English, which their Old World counterparts would do well to imitate. The point is, perhaps, that the possibilities for the future of 'New Britain' – and, indeed, the world – are not fixed, as the engraving of Adam and Eve suggested. Britain's past may well be a guide to the future; alternatively, the future may point back even further, to the harmony experienced by mankind in the Garden of Eden. The civilized but pagan inhabitants of the Americas may explode the old dichotomies between civil and savage, leading to a future society beyond the brutalities of the Old World. On the other hand, the possibility that such divisions will be simply rediscovered and reinforced should not be ruled out. Either way, the discovery of the Americas is represented by de Bry as an apocalyptic event (as in Hakluyt's *A Discourse of Western Planting*); it constitutes the discovery of new wonders, which cannot be quantified or classified within the realms of Western knowledge, scientific or other-wise.[37] The content has gone beyond the form; the identities of the colonizers are called into question as much as those of the colonized.[38]

Harriot's actual report registers this awareness of a knowledge, which has changed all certainties, demanding that the English rethink their own identities and historical genealogy in order to meet the challenge of the New World. The Indians are represented as being open to persuasion that their own explanations of events are not necessarily the best. Having described their religion, Harriot comments: 'Wherein they were not so sure grounded, nor gaue such credite to their traditions and stories but through conuersing with us they were brought into great doubts of their owne, and had no small admiration of ours' (p. 27). This open-mindedness leads to a moment of great embar-rassment after Harriot has explained the contents of the Bibles to the Algonquians. Their excessive zeal for the truth makes them profane the Book as a sexual rather than a religious object, as if somatic sensation can replace intellectual effort:

And although I told them the booke materially & of it self was not of anie such vertue, as I thought they did conceive, but onely the doctrine therein contained; yet would many be glad to touch it, to embrace it, to kiss it, to hold it to their brests and heades, and stroke ouer all their bodie with it; to shewe their hungrie desire of that knowledge which was spoken of. (p. 27)

While the first description illustrates a tolerance, which contrasts favourably with the brutal zeal of internecine European politics, the second opens out the problem once again, representing the Algonquians as a benign, confused, and inferior people in need of the guidance of their cultural superiors. One moment the Indians are savage critics, morally superior to their European counterparts, the next they are reduced to helpless savages. The gap between the two peoples expands and contracts in a series of rapid movements.

However, the report ends, quite deliberately, with a phenomenon which no one can explain, the death of hostile Indians after the visits of the English.[39] In fact, events would seem to confirm the simultaneous bemusement of both English and Indians alongside an efficacious serendipity, leaving the text balanced between success and failure (the actual position of English colonial ventures in the period). The Algonquians are convinced that the English can kill whom they please, without weapons, and ask them to help them to destroy their enemies. Although the English refuse (arguing that such entreaties are ungodly, and that all should try to live together and wait for God to act), the Indians' longing becomes reality, leaving the colonizers in a more powerful position than before. This allows them to retain the moral high ground:

Yet because the effect fell out so sodainly and shortly after according to their desires, they thought neuerthelesse it came to passe by our meanes, and that we in using such speeches unto them did but dissemble the matter, and therefore came unto us to giue thankes in their manner that although wee satisfied them not in promise, yet in deedes and effect we had fulfilled their desires. (p. 29)

Although the two peoples misunderstand each other, events conspire to leave both satisfied; the Algonquians get rid of their enemies, and the English affirm their colonial power. Nevertheless, the gratitude of the Indians rests on their perception of the English as duplicitous; hinting that future discord may result between the two peoples, thus leaving the encounter in a state of precarious balance.[40]

Perhaps the most important point for the European reader is that the text concludes not with a discussion of the identity of the newly-discovered peoples, but of the English colonizers, linking the text neatly to the series of pictures concluding with the representations of the ancient inhabitants of Britain. The final page of Harriot's report lists the various opinions of the Indians as to the nature of the English: some suggest they are not born of women, but are a race of immortals; some prophesy that more English will come to kill the Indians in future years (a chillingly accurate prediction); others hold that they are ethereal creatures, who shoot invisible bullets at Indians who have angered them. It is the Indians who are posing the questions, not the English; this is a surprising inversion of expected norms, indicating that what is at stake in the text is the future of the world in the wake of the discovery of the New World, not simply colonial domination. This apocalyptic reading has roots in, and takes its force from, the historical schema outlines in the glosses to the Geneva Bible.

The historical schema outlined in the Geneva Bible had enormous influence when it became 'the edition preferred by Elizabethans seeking an accurate English translation'.[41] The Calvinist-inspired version with its extensive commentary helped to impose a Protestant outlook on wide sections of the population.[42] John Bale's apocalyptic reading of world history became enshrined in Elizabethan consciousness and culture. As the works of M.M.S., Richard Hakluyt, Thomas Harriot and John White demonstrate, such a reading had a significant influence on plans for colonial expansion in the Americas. The struggle for political and religious hegemony in Europe was being played out in another continent.

NOTES

1 See, for example, J. H. Andrews, *Trade, Plunder and Settlement: maritime Enterprise and the Genesis of the British Empire, 1480-1630* (Cambridge: University Press, 1984), introduction.

2 In addition to Andrews, see Angus Calder, *Revolutionary Empire: The Rise of the English-Speaking Empires from the Fifteenth Century to the 1780s* (London: Cape, 1981); David Beers Quinn, *England and the Discovery of America, 1481-1620: From the Bristol Voyages of the Fifteen Century to the Pilgrim Settlement at Plymouth: The Exploration, Exploitation, and Trial-and-Error Colonization of North America by the English* (London: George Allen & Unwin, 1974). Karen Kuppermann makes the case that there was a vast difference between the preconceptions of colonial planners in England and colonists in Virginia in the early seventeenth century, in *Settling with the Indians: The Meeting of English and Indian Cultures in America, 1580-1640* (Totowa, NJ: Rowman & Littlefield, 1980).

3 I make this case at greater length in *Literature, Travel and Colonial Writing in the English Renaissance, 1545-1625* (Oxford: Clarendon Press, 1998), ch. 2.

4 Bernard McGinn, 'Early Apocalypticism: the ongoing debate', in *The Apocalypse in English Renaissance thought and literature*, ed. by C. A. Patrides & Joseph Wittreich (Manchester: University Press, 1984), p. 21.

5 For details of this community see Christina H. Garrett, *The Marian Exiles: A Study in the Origins of Elizabethan Puritanism* (Cambridge: University Press, 1938, repr. 1966). On the Geneva Bible see Katherine R. Firth, *The Apocalyptic Tradition in Reformation Britain, 1530-1645* (Oxford: University Press, 1979), pp. 122-4.

6 Bale's tract is first thought to have appeared in the mid-1540s: see STC 1296.5 (Antwerp: Mierdman?, 1545?). Three further editions went to press within a decade: STC 1297 (Antwerp: [S. Mierdman for] R. Jugge, 1548?); STC 1298 (Antwerp: [S. Mierdman for] J. Day & W. Seres, *c.* 1550), and STC 1299 (London: J. Wyer, 1550).

7 Firth, p. 122.

8 John King, *English Reformation Literature: The Tudor Origins of the Protestant Tradition* (Princeton: University Press, 1982), p. 429; Firth, p. 122. On the apocalyptic tradition and the crucial role of Bale see J. F. Mozley, *John Foxe and his Book* (London: SPCK, 1940); William Haller, *Foxe's Book of Martyrs and the Elect Nation* (London: Cape, 1963); V. Norskov Olsen, *John Foxe and the Elizabethan Church* (Berkeley: California University Press, 1973); L. P. Fairfield, *John Bale: Mythmaker for the English Reformation* (Indiana: Purdue University Press, 1976); Richard Baukham, *Tudor Apocalypse, from John Bale to John Foxe and Thomas Brightman* (Oxford: Sutton Courtney Press, 1978); Hadfield, *Literature, Politics and National Identity: Reformation to Renaissance* (Cambridge: University Press, 1994), ch. 2.

9 See Hadfield, *Literature, Travel*, pp. 70-111.

10 Bartolomé de Las Casas, *A Short Account of the Destruction of the Indies*, trans. by Nigel Griffin with an introduction by Anthony Pagden (Harmondsworth: Penguin, 1992).

11 See William S. Maltby, *The Black Legend in England: The Development of Anti-Spanish Sentiment, 1558-1660* (Durham, NC: Duke University Press, 1971).

12 Bartolomé de Las Casas, *The Spanish colonie, or briefe chronicle of the acts and gestes of the*

Spaniardes, trans. by M.M.S. (London: Thomas Dawson for William Brome, 1583), fols Q2^v-Q3^v. All subsequent references to this edition are provided in parentheses after the text.

13 See Maltby, pp. 15-16. On Anglo-Dutch relations and the claims of English Protestants for greater intervention, see John Guy, *Tudor England* (Oxford: University Press, 1988), pp. 281-9; Charles Wilson, *Queen Elizabeth and the Revolt of the Netherlands* (London: Macmillan Press, 1970), *passim*.

14 Las Casas, *Short Account*; Pagden, 'Introduction', p. xxiv; Maltby, ch. 2.

15 Most famously in the case of the woman who refused to submit to rape by the Spanish.

16 For details of Pizarro's conquest of Peru (1530-5), see the classic account of William H. Prescott, *History of the Conquest of Peru* (London: Bickers, 1878); Leslie Bethell, *The Cambridge History of Latin America, Vol. I: Colonial Latin America* (Cambridge: University Press, 1984), pp. 177-85.

17 For mining as an image of Hell see John Milton, *Paradise Lost*, I.684:

> 'by him [Mammon] first
> Men also, and by his suggestion taught,
> Ransack'd the Center, and with impious hands
> For Treasures better hid. Soon had his crew
> Op'n'd into the Hill a spacious wound
> And digg'd out ribs of Gold. Let none admire
> That riches grow in Hell; that soil may best
> Deserve the precious bane.'

18 For example: Martin Frobisher made three (unsuccessful) attempts in search of the North-West passage (1576-8); Francis Drake circumnavigated the globe (1577-80); Humphrey Gilbert wrote *Discourse of a Discoverie for a New Passage to Cataia* (London: H. Middleton for R. Jhones, 1576), and made voyages to Newfoundland where he attempted to establish colonies (1582-3). In order to publicize these voyages, George Peckham published his *A true Report of the late discoveries* (London: J. C. for J. Hinde, 1583). Also published in this period was Richard Willes' *The History of Trauayle in the West and East Indies* ([London]: R. Jugge, 1577), a new edition of Peter Martyr's *Decades of the New World* ([London]: G. Powell [for] R. Jugge, 1555). Publications dealing with the English colonization of America are extensive. The list given here is based on information provided in Samuel Eliot Morison, *The European Discovery of America: The Northern Voyages, A.D. 500-1600* (New York: Oxford University Press, 1971), chs xv-xx; William Gilbert Gosling, *The Life of Sir Humphrey Gilbert: England's First Empire Builder* (London: Constable, 1911); John Parker, *Books to Build An Empire* (Amsterdam: N. Israel, 1965), ch. 8; Mary C. Fuller, *Voyages in Print: English Travel to America, 1576-1624* (Cambridge: University Press, 1995); *The Roanoke Voyages, 1584-1590: Documents to Illustrate the English Voyages to North America under the Patent Granted to Walter Raleigh in 1584*, ed. by David Beers Quinn, 2 vols (London: Hakluyt Society, 1955); Karen Ordhal Kupperman, *Roanoke: The Abandoned Colony* (Totowa, NJ: Rowman & Littlefield, 1984).

19 Harriot's work was first published in London by Robinson in 1588 (STC 12785). Two years later another edition appeared, translated from Latin by Hakluyt: STC 12786 ([Frankfurt]: T. de Bry, 1590). For *Principall Navigations* see STC 12625 ([London]: G. Bishop & R. Newberie, deputies to C. Barker, 1589).

20 Richard Hakluyt the Younger, 'A Discourse of Western Planting', in *The Original Writings and Correspondence of the Two Richard Hakluyts*, ed. by E. G. R. Taylor (London: Hakluyt Society, 1935), pp. 211-26. All subsequent references in parentheses in the text.

21 See the reading of Hakluyt's enterprise in Richard Helgerson, *Forms of Nationhood: The Elizabethan Writing of England* (Chicago: University of Chicago Press, 1992), ch. 4. 'The Voyages of a Nation', pp. 149-91.

22 For a similar argument used with respect to Irish colonies, see *Calendar of State Papers Domestic Series, Addenda, 1566-79*, (Nendeln: Kraus, 1967), pp. li-liv. A convenient overview of contemporary religious developments and Elizabeth's reactions to them is described in W. P. Haugaard, *Elizabeth and the English Reformation* (Cambridge: University Press, 1968).

23 See DNB article and *The Hakluyt Handbook*, ed. by David Beers Quinn, 2 vols (London: Hakluyt Society, 1974), I, pp. 263-331.

24 An exception is James P. Helfers, 'The Explorer of the Pilgrim? Modern Critical Opinion and the Editorial Methods of Richard Hakluyt and Samuel Purchas', *Studies in Philology*, 94 (1997), 160-86.

25 See Theodor de Bry, *America* (Frankfurt: T. de Bry, 1594). A convenient selection is contained in *Discovering the New World, Based on the Works of Theodor De Bry*, ed. by Michael Alexander (London: London Editions, 1976). A book-length structural analysis is provided in Bernadette Bucher, *Icon and Conquest: A Structural Analysis of the Illustrations of De Bry's Great Voyages*, trans. by Basia Miller Gulati (Chicago: University of Chicago Press, 1981). All subsequent references to Thomas Harriot, *A Briefe and True Report of the New Found Land of Virginia* (1590), introduced by Paul Hulton (New York: Dover, 1972).

26 Harriot had written Latin captions to accompany White's drawings, which Hakluyt translated into English. White became governor of the Roanoke colony (in modern-day Virginia) in 1587, before being persuaded by his charges to return to England to plead for supplies and support. For an account of White's life and importance, see Kupperman, *Roanoke: The Abandoned Colony* (Totowa, NJ: Rowman & Littlefield, 1984); Kupperman, *Settling with the Indians*, ch. 7, *passim*; *The American Drawings of John White, 1577-1590*, ed. by Paul Hulton & David Beers Quinn, 2 vols (London: British Museum, 1964), I, pp. 12-24.

27 Interestingly, de Bry had probably been persuaded to publish Harriot's text by Richard Hakluyt the younger, whom he had met in London in 1587. On the probable sequence of events which led to de Bry's publication, and the close relationship between Harriot, Raleigh, Hakluyt, de Bry and White, see *The Roanoke Voyages, 1584-1590: Documents to Illustrate the English Voyages to North America under the Patent Granted to Walter Raleigh in 1584*, ed. by D. B. Quinn, 2 vols (London: Hakluyt Society, 1955); Alexander, *Discovering*, p. 64; *America 1585: The Complete Drawings of John White*, ed. by Paul Hulton (London: British Museum, 1984), pp. 17-21.

28 This is something of an irony, given Harriot's scandalous reputation in England at the time; see Stephen Greenblatt, 'Invisible Bullets', in *Shakespearean Negotiations: The Circulation of Social Energy in Renaissance England* (Oxford: Clarendon Press, 1988), pp. 21-65 (pp. 22-3); John Shirley, 'Sir Walter Raleigh and Thomas Harriot', in *Thomas Harriot: Renaissance Scientist*, ed. by John Shirley (Oxford: Clarendon Press, 1974), pp. 16-35 (pp. 23-4).

29 De Bry published other works which placed such demands upon the reader, and was clearly well-versed in the modes of Protestant allegory; see for example, the emblem book he published, *Iani Iacobi Boissardi Vesvntini Emblematum* (Frankfurt: T. de Bry, 1593).

30 See, for example, the engraving of the natives of Darien feeding liquid gold to the greedy Christians, or the Spanish atrocities reminiscent of the illustrations accompanying Las Casas's text, reproduced in Alexander, *Discovering*, pp. 136, 137, 144-5.

31 For commentary on the perceived sophistication of the societies of native Americans, see Karen O. Kupperman, *Settling with the Indians: the Meeting of English and Indian Cultures in America, 1580-1640* (Totowa, NJ: Rowman & Littlefield, 1980).

32 Harriot, *Brief and True Report*, p. 52.

33 For other disparaging comments on the Indians' lack of religion see plate XXI, 'Ther Idol Kivvasa' (which appears to be based on the observations of the French artist Jacques Le

Moyne in Florida, rather than John White in Virginia, and which may have been incorporated by de Bry to end the sequence of engravings with an attack on the Virginian Indians' idolatry (see *The Works of Jacques Le Moyne de Morguel*, ed. by Paul Hulton, 2 vols (London: British Museum, 1977), p. 216; Hulton & Quinn, I, pp. 93-4)). See also plate XXII, 'The Tombe of their Werowans or Cheiff Lordes'. Positive comments on their temperance, which Europeans would do well to imitate, accompany plates XV and XVI.

34 Engraving III, 'The truue picture of a yonge dawgter of the Pictes', is actually based on a painting by Jacques Le Moyne (*Works of Jacques Le Moyne*, II, plate 7). De Bry probably confused the collections he had acquired from the two artists; the remaining four pictures may well be based on lost work by Le Moyne; Hulton, 'Le Moyne and John White', in *Works of Jacques Le Moyne*, p. 211.

35 I have also left aside the question of the controlling intellect behind the text. De Bry may have worked in collaboration with Hakluyt, Harriot, or even Raleigh. Raleigh's belief in the existence of the Amazons, described in *The discoverie of the large, rich, and beautifull Empire of Guiana* (London: R. Robinson, 1596), may be connected to this engraving (Richard Hakluyt, *Principall Navigations* (1598), 12 vols (Glasgow: MacLehose, 1903), X, pp. 338-431 (pp. 366-8)).

36 The concept of a New Britain is implicit in the name 'Virginia', named after Elizabeth; later treatises such as William Strachey's *The Historie of Travell into Virginia Britania* (1612), ed. by Louis B. Wright & Virginia Freund (London: Hakluyt Society, 1953) made the comparison explicit. Strachey refers to Virginia as 'Nova Britania' (p. 10).

37 Stephen Greenblatt, *Marvelous Possessions: The Wonder of the New World* (Oxford: Clarendon Press, 1991), introduction.

38 On this frequently discussed question in post-colonial theory, see Homi Bhabha, 'Articulating the Archaic: Cultural difference and colonial nonsense', in Homi Bhabha, *The Location of Culture* (London: Routledge, 1994), pp. 123-38; Albert Memmi, *The Colonizer and the Colonized*, trans. by Howard Greenfield (New York: Orion, 1965), conclusion; and Robert Young, *Colonial Desire: Hybridity in Theory, Culture and Race* (London: Routledge, 1995).

39 The most famous explanation of Harriot's text is Stephen Greenblatt's argument that Harriot is testing out Machiavelli's hypothesis that religion is best used as an instrument of control over subject populations: 'Invisible Bullets' (n. 28 above), pp. 24-39. Greenblatt's essay is too well known to require further comment; it suffices to say that my argument here complements or extends Greenblatt's analysis.

40 Compare the story of the death of Captain James Cook; see Neil Rennie, *Far-Fetched Facts: The Literature of Travel and the Idea of the South Seas* (Oxford: Clarendon Press, 1995), pp. 129-36.

41 King (n. 8 above), p. 127.

42 Firth (n. 5 above), pp. 123-4.

IMAGINING TRANSLATION COMMITTEES AT WORK

THE KING JAMES AND THE REVISED VERSIONS

David Norton

An emissary has come from Miles Smith, Bishop of Gloucester, one of the translators of the King James Version, to Shakespeare who, with Ben Jonson, is enjoying sun, apples, and wine in a Stratford orchard. The emissary brings some of the work of the translators for Shakespeare to polish. Will asks Ben how 'Smith's crew' have gone about the first verse of Isaiah 60:

'Thus.' Ben read from the paper. '"Get thee up, O Jerusalem, and be bright, for thy light is at hand, and the glory of God has risen up upon thee."'

'Up-pup-up!' Will stuttered profanely. ... 'It may be mended. Read me the Coverdale of it now. 'Tis on the same sheet – to the right, Ben.'

'Umm – umm! Coverdale saith, "And therefore get thee up betimes, for thy light cometh, and the glory of the Lord shall rise up upon thee. ..."'

'Now give me the Douai and Geneva for this "Get thee up, O Jerusalem,"' said [Will] at last. 'They'll be all there.'

Ben referred to the proofs. ''Tis "arise" in both,' said he. '"Arise and be bright" in Geneva. In the Douai 'tis "Arise and be illuminated."'

'So? Give me the paper now.' Will took it from his companion, rose, and paced towards a tree in the orchard. ... Ben leaned forward in his chair. The other's free hand went up warningly.

'Quiet, man!' said he. 'I wait on my Demon! ... How shall this open? "Arise?" No! "Rise!" Yes. And we'll have no weak coupling. 'Tis a call to a City! "Rise – shine" ... Nor yet any schoolmaster's "because" – because Isaiah is not Holofernes. "*Rise – shine; for thy light is come, and – !*"'[1]

And so the KJV gradually appears, vividly Shakespearean.

This, condensed, is from Rudyard Kipling's last short story, '"Proofs of Holy Writ"' (1934). It is a brilliant imagining of some of the work that might have gone into the making of the KJV if Shakespeare had been involved in the process.[2]

For centuries lovers and scholars of the English Bible have been imagining and researching just how the KJV came to be what it is, and Kipling's story is the finest product of that theorizing.[3] Typically, that imagining proceeds from the kind of question that Kipling heard John Buchan pose, and which led to his story. Buchan thought

it was strange that such splendour had been produced by a body of men learned, no doubt, in theology and in languages, but including among them no writer. Could it be, he wondered, that they had privately consulted the great writers of the age, Shakespeare perhaps and Jonson and others.[4]

Great art requires a great artist: this is the premise that lies behind such a question. Great artists have been found for the Bible, from the inspiring Author of all things through Harold Bloom's possibly-female 'J' to Tyndale and Kipling's Shakespeare, but it has always been a stumbling block for lovers of the KJV that it is the work of committees, and committee prose – to say nothing of committee poetry – is notoriously bad.

Kipling's story is, of course, fiction, but we cannot escape from fiction in trying to picture the work of the KJV translators. Bringing together some of the extant evidence about the work of translation committees with the evidence of the work on the KJV will suggest how one might better imagine the KJV committees working. The most useful translation to set beside the KJV for this purpose is the Revised Version; it was to be the same kind of translation as the KJV. The first rule of that version was to keep the Bishops' Bible 'as little altered as the truth of the original will permit'.[5] Almost identically, the first rule of the RV was 'to introduce as few alterations as possible into the text of the Authorised Version consistently with faithfulness'.[6] Both sets of translators worked in committees, and both worked consultatively through several stages.

There is, therefore, ground for thinking that the way the RV committees worked might have been similar to the way the KJV companies worked. Let me pin up here a little of what is known of the way the RV translators worked. The account draws particularly on a detailed record of the meetings kept by Samuel Newth, variously Professor of Classics, Principal and Lee Professor of Divinity, New College, London.[7] The committee held ten monthly sessions a year (August and September were not used); each session was made up of four meetings, Tuesday to Friday, starting at 11 a.m. with prayer, three collects, the Lord's Prayer, and then, mundanely, minutes. There was a half-hour luncheon some time after 2 p.m., and then work went through till 6 p.m. The first meeting was held on 22 June 1870, and the New Testament was completed at 5 p.m. on 11 November 1880. In total there were 407 meetings, attended by an average of sixteen members (seventeen during the period of the first revision). Initially, they managed only seventeen verses in the course of six-and-a-half hours' work, that is, two-and-a-half verses an hour. As the work went on, however, this rate doubled to an average of five verses an hour.[8] The second revision went about three times as quickly, completing 109 verses a meeting (nearly seventeen verses an hour).

One of the things that Newth's notes reveal is the human side of the work.[9] Sometimes there was humour, sometimes animosity surfaced, sometimes there were arguments about formal procedure, and there were interruptions, both trivial and grave. Bad puns crept in. When Dean Alford suggested 'didst hide' in Matthew 11.25, Dr Kennedy asked, 'what is the objection to hiddest?' Ellicott, Bishop of Gloucester, retorted from the chair, 'because it is hideous'.[10] Similarly, when F. J. A. Hort proposed 'into the marriage feast' for Matthew 25.10, 'it was wittily whispered, "*into* the feast! Four & twenty blackbirds &etc".'[11] Another of the jokes hints at personal tensions between the translators: once when Canon Blakesley entered, Ellicott greeted him with, 'you will be sorry to hear that your Dean is unable to be here'. Newth observes that 'there was a spice of irony in this, as Bl[akesley] & Al[ford] are somewhat antagonistic in the Chapter at Canterbury'.[12]

There were several arguments about formal procedures and precise interpretation of the rules for the translation. Shortly after the beginning of the second revision of Matthew, F. H. Scrivener called attention to the rule by which changes in this latter work had to be approved by a two-thirds majority. He argued that the rule 'meant not two-thirds of voters, but two-thirds of those present. It was in consequence agreed that those who did not wish to be counted should back their chairs',[13] so symbolically absenting themselves.

The interruptions ranged from an international deputation to the Society for the Prevention of Cruelty to Animals being shown round the Jerusalem Chamber[14] (where most of the work was done), to sickness and death. Between prayer and the minutes on 9 December 1873, the 'chairman read a letter from Dr Scrivener stating that his wife was in a dying state. Also. Introduced Professor Palmer to the Company'.[15]

A single example of the work must suffice. For the most part, Newth's notes record, on the recto of the leaves, suggested readings and how the voting went on them. Pl. 34 is typical. From it we see that three things came to a vote in John 1.5, which reads in the KJV, *And the light shineth in darkness; and the darkness comprehended it not.* There was general agreement for *the darkness.* Westcott's suggestion, *overcame it not,* was carried eight to seven, and the marginal annotation, 'Or apprehended it not', found general agreement.[16] On the verso of the leaves Newth added other notes, occasionally bringing out the reasoning behind the suggested readings and translations. He did so on this occasion:

There was considerable discussion of οὐ κατέλαβεν. Sc[ott] proposed 'overcame it not' referring to ch XII.35, & contending that while καταλαμβ in mid[dle voice] = comprehend, it never did in act[ive voice]. He quoted also I K.18.44. W[estcott] concurred but suggested "intercepted it not", & pointed out that the verb is used in Plut[arch] in connexion with eclipses. Ho[rt] objected this meaning does not suit the context as the figure is not of the darkness overtaking or coming suddenly upon the light since the light is described as shining in the darkness.

Mem. Sc[ott]'s view is that taken by Chrysostom.[17]

In reading this, the initial presumption must be that this is still no more than a glimpse of 'considerable discussion'; other unrecorded suggestions may well have been made without finding enough support to go to a vote.[18] Newth records only the part of the discussion that contributed directly to the decision. Robert Scott, Master of Balliol, still famous as co-author of the Liddell & Scott *Greek-English Lexicon,* used his lexicographical knowledge in relation to the KJV's *comprehended it not* to show that that reading is without support elsewhere in Greek literature.[19] He was presumably arguing against a general inclination to retain the KJV reading, and this led him to multiply examples. So next he brought up a connected verse, John 12.35, where the same Greek verb is rendered in the RV, *that darkness overtake you not,* and then, impressively, moved on to the Septuagint, which has another active use of the verb at I Kings 18.44.[20] Bruce Foss Westcott, another formidable scholar among formidable scholars, remembered a passage from Plutarch[21] and took up the argument, making an unsuccessful attempt to bring out a figurative sense. This was duly refuted by his fellow editor of the Greek text, Hort, who brought the committee's attention back to the figurative meaning of the entire verse. We may deduce from the contradiction between the basic note and the record of the discussion that Westcott now took over Scott's reading and formally proposed it for a vote. We may further guess from the closeness of the vote that there was substantially more argument, very likely against Scott's and Westcott's position and for the KJV reading. This is implicit in the general agreement to put *or apprehended it not* in the margin. *Apprehended* would seem to be an intelligent compromise between Scott's argument and the desire to keep *comprehended*, intelligent because, in keeping with the verb's basic meaning, 'to lay hold or seize', it keeps the more physical sense of 'arrest'. Finally, Newth's last comment, that Scott's view is Chrysostom's, may be a later note of his own, a product of further research into the verse.

Such a discussion must have taken a good half hour or more. Newth's outline gives some flesh to the record of things voted on, enough for us to make what is, hopefully, a responsible but too brief imaginative effort at reconstruction.[22] At this point, it would be possible to proceed to a Kipling-like recreation of the discussion. All we would need would be to create the role of defender of the KJV, and to cast someone for it. Dean Stanley, who fought 'for every antique phrase which can be defended', and who characteristically 'put in an appearance when any very noteworthy passage ... came under notice', is the most likely candidate.[23]

There was still the second revision to come. For this we have not only the evidence of Newth's notes but also copies of the printed sheets from which the translators worked. These sheets give the text and margin as they emerged from the first revision. On them the translators have noted the changes made. Hort's copy[24] (Pl. 35) is dated: he received it on 14 September 1874, and it was revised on 26 January 1875. These sheets give a more graphic view of the work than Newth's record of readings and votes,[25] but contain no further information. The proposed reading, *overcame it not*, was reconsidered, and changed places with the marginal reading, *apprehended it not*. That some of the same ground was traversed is evident from the addition at this point of the main reference Scott used, John 12.35 in the Greek.

So much work in the end, then, produced no more than a change of one syllable, *apprehended* for *comprehended*, and a marginal alternative complete with a cross-reference. Translation and revision are hard and earnest tasks.

Turning to the KJV, we need to determine whether its six committees (two each at Westminster, Oxford, and Cambridge) are likely to have worked in the same way as the RV New Testament committee. Our first guide is 'The Rules to be observed in the Translation of the Bible'. Unless there is clear evidence to the contrary, we should assume that the companies closely followed these rules. Each member of the company, taking note of older English translations, was to make his own revision of the Bishops' Bible, then the members were to meet together and compare their work (rules 14, 1, 8). Finished work was to be sent to the other companies for consideration (rule 9); reasoned differences were to be sent back to the company, and resolved at a final general meeting if the company did not agree with them (rule 10).[26]

Under these rules, the KJV translators could have worked in substantially the same way as the RV translators. Before looking at the differences, it is worth settling whether they had enough time to labour as hard as their successors. They took between four and five years, from late 1604 to no later than the end of 1609, when the general meeting took over.[27] Two committees worked on the New Testament, the second Oxford company taking the larger part (Gospels, Acts, and Revelation, 5187 verses in all), and the second Westminster company taking the 2772 verses of the Epistles. If the second Oxford company, given the larger task, worked at the same pace and for the same hours as the RV New Testament committee, it would have needed about three years and nine months for the first revision, and fourteen months for the second revision, roughly five years in all. We cannot guess how much additional time was spent on reviewing the work of the other companies. Nevertheless, it was clearly possible for the KJV translators to work as slowly and as thoroughly as their successors. Indeed, the approximate coincidence of time encourages one to imagine that they did work similarly, meeting for days at a time on a regular basis, and subjecting both the original texts and the English to hard scrutiny.

The most substantial differences from the rules for the RV are the lack of provision for voting (one can presume, therefore, that there was no formal voting), and the number of companies – six against two. None of the KJV companies had more than ten members, and one should not assume that meetings were fully attended: the RV meetings were not, and in 1604 Lancelot Andrewes remarked in a letter that most of the first Westminster company were negligent.[28] Nor should one take for granted, as historians of the KJV have done so far, that the companies worked as single groups with parts of the Bible assigned to them. One late list of the translators (possibly drawing on information from John Bois after the work was completed) suggests that at least two of the companies subdivided their work: namely, that half of the first Westminster company took the Pentateuch, and half Joshua to II Chronicles, and that four members of the second Westminster company took the Pauline epistles, and three members 'the canonicall Eples'.[29] If the evidence of this list is credible, as I am inclined to think it is, we must imagine the companies working in groups that were sometimes as small as three members. Consequently, one can imagine the work to have proceeded quite informally, and with a greater degree of individuality than one normally associates with committee work.

Roughly half a century after the translation appeared, John Selden said that:

that part of the Bible was given to him who was most excellent in such a tongue (as the Apocrypha to Andrew Downes), and then they met together, and one read the translation, the rest holding in their hands some Bible either of the learned tongues or French, Spanish, Italian etc.; if they found any fault they spoke, if not he read on.[30]

This fits with the supposition of a fairly informal process in which particular individuals played a predominant part, but not with the rules given to the translators. From these we know that Downes was director of the second Cambridge company because he was Regius Professor of Greek at Cambridge. It is also known that each translator was to make his own revision and that the older English versions were consulted. Without other evidence, therefore, much weight cannot be given to Selden's evidence. Rather, since we are engaged in imagining, it may be used to suggest a difference from the RV, that at company meetings older English versions, original-language versions, and modern-language versions were available, and that individual translators might have had responsibility for keeping an eye on particular versions.

Kipling's example, the evidence of the Revised Version, and these few points of comparison make a basis for imagining the progress of one verse through the hands of the translators. But there must be some words of warning. In addition to imagining, I have made a number of compromises with what I think might have happened. For instance, my characters here speak English, whereas it is probable that Latin would have been used for preference. But perhaps the greatest limitation is that there is space here for only one example; a genuinely credible picture could emerge only from multiple examples which explore all the various kinds of evidence from the KJV. This example explores only the evidence of the changes visible in the text of the KJV, and a perhaps peculiar instance of the notes John Bois kept from the final general meeting.

Throwing scholarly caution aside, I take I Corinthians 4.9.[31] The scene is Westminster, late in 1605. An open fire, tended occasionally by a manservant, keeps the edge off the cold; candles penetrate the gloomy afternoon. Four men are seated around a large table. Ralph Hutchinson, for fifteen years president of St John's College, Oxford, is in his early fifties, but looks older. A cough shakes him now and then, and he sits closest to the fire. Death is close, but he defies it. Next to him sits John Spencer, in his mid-forties, his face still bright from a half-hour's walk from Newgate, where he is vicar at St Sepulchre's. Across from him is the youngest of the group, Roger Fenton, Rector of St Benet's Sherehog. He is already fashioning a reputation for his 'Treatise on Usury', though it is five years and more before it will be lent to the world at large. Chairman of the group is William Barlow, Dean of Chester. He too is in his very early forties, and is known for his royalist and anti-Puritan views. He was present at the Hampton Court conference at which James I approved the motion for a new translation of the Bible.

In front of Barlow are sheets from the Bishops' Bible on which he is entering the results of their deliberations. To his left is Stephens' Greek Testament, to his right his notes from his own work on the chapter. The others also have Stephens and sheets from the Bishops' Bible which they have worked over. Also on the table are an assortment of other Bibles, as well as a Vulgate and a Polyglot. On shelves there are other translations, including Luther's, and a range of theological works. The other translators have been assigned to keep a special eye on particular versions. Hutchinson has Rheims and the Vulgate, Spencer has Geneva and the Great Bible, while Fenton keeps an eye on Tyndale, Coverdale, and Matthew.

Barlow reads from the Bishops' Bible: '*For me thinketh that God hath set forth us which are the last Apostles, as it were men appointed to death. For we are made a gazing stock unto the world, and to angels, and to men.*' He looks round. Spencer catches his eye. 'The Genevans have *I think*,' Barlow remarks. 'Ay, the Papists follow them there,' adds Spencer. 'Me thinketh 'tis a proper expression,' says Barlow, who will have his little joke, and his companions smile indulgently. But he is diligent as well as a humourist; 'you will find *I think* again in the seventh and the tenth chapters, even in the Bishops' Bible'. He eyes his companions; they nod. He strikes out *me thinketh* and writes *I think* above it. Fenton quietly copies *For I think* into the second column of a neatly ruled sheet which he will shortly add to the pile of similar sheets beside him. When I Corinthians is finished these sheets will be carefully wrapped together and despatched to Oxford for comment, and then on to Cambridge.

'*Which are the last Apostles,*' muses Barlow. 'I like it not, for 'tis not the Greek, nor what St Paul meaneth. They are not the last apostles, but the last men in the eyes of God. τοὺς ἀποστόλους ἐσχάτους, *id est the apostles last*. St Paul writeth what he meaneth.' The others look uncertain. They have let the Bishops' phrase stand, for it is clear and reasonable. There is a sudden rustle as they look through their Bibles. Not one is identical to the Bishops', but most seem to understand the Greek in the same way. Hutchinson and Spencer are both about to contest Barlow, when Fenton, looking back and forth between his precious old copy of Tyndale and his Matthew's Bible, laying his rule under the line in the one and touching the other with his finger, says, 'tis here and here, not for the words, but for the meaning. Listen, 'tis the same in both: *Me thinketh that God hath set forth us which are Apostles, for the lowest of all, as it were men appointed to death.* These are no last Apostles. Master Tyndale keepeth open the apostolic succession, and him no papist.'

'He doth well,' says Barlow. 'Yet he keepeth not to the letter. ἐσχάτους is not, how sayeth he? *the lowest of all.* Nor is it Jerome's *novissimos.* 'Tis *last.*' He scribbles quickly on his copy, and goes on without looking up, 'What's next? *As it were men appointed to death.* So it is in all our old Bibles, eh?'

'Save for the papists,' interrupts Spencer. 'They have *deputed.* I wonder they follow not their own text. *Destinatos. As it were destinate to death.* How like you that?'

'A plague on your inkhorn,' is all the thanks he gets from Fenton for this, but Barlow, having had his way, is amused. 'It soundeth well, as doth *deputed to death.* Yet I think the sense be the same as *appointed.* Let *appointed* stand.'

'Nay,' splutters Hutchinson through a fit of coughing. Realizing he has banged his fist on the table, he remembers himself, and goes on more moderately, 'I grant you *the Apostles last* goeth to the letter, but doth *appointed?* I have laboured here. ἐπιθανατίους is no more than *condemned to death,* as a criminal is condemned.'

'Me thinketh,' says Barlow, still enjoying his joke, 'me thinketh you are too nice. Niceness with words is ever counted next to trifling.'

'I think this no trifle. What, to talk of the Apostles as criminals! *Appointed,* 'tis predestined, 'tis Spencer's *destinate,* 'tis papistical. I approve it not.'

'Now there's a word!' exclaims Fenton suddenly; he too wishes to make Barlow pay for his victory with *the Apostles last.* 'Approve': 'tis strong, 'tis the language of the lawyers, yet 'tis good too: our Lord is a man approved of God, Apelles is approved in Christ.[32] *Approved to death,* tried, esteemed, worthy, like our Lord.'

There is a prolonged debate. At last Barlow, muttering, 'appointed, approved, 'tis a small change,' writes it into his copy. He reads again, '*For we are made a gazing stock unto the world.* I like not *gazing stock.* The Greek hath θέατρον. Thy Rhemists have the answer here, eh, Spencer? *Spectacle.* Yet *spectacle* is not *theatre.*'

Spencer nods: 'From their Vulgar Latin, *spectaculum.* I saw the veriest spectacle not three days since, *King Lear* it was. But 'twas no gazing stock.'

The others look critically at him: his weakness for the theatre is well known. Tactfully, Fenton remarks that *gazing stock* is good old English, to be found in Tyndale, but now Hutchinson adds his voice to Barlow and Spencer's. 'Neither goeth to the very letter, but *spectacle* goeth close. Thou needest the Greek in the margin.'

At this they all nod. Barlow notes the changes in his copy, and Fenton completes his transcription of the whole verse into his columned manuscript.

The second scene takes place at Stationers' Hall in early autumn, 1610.[33] Andrew Downes, a tall, ruddy man with eyes that are sometimes lively, sometimes peevish, sits back in a chair with his feet on the table. Now in his sixties, his pioneering days as a

David Norton

Greek scholar at Cambridge long past, he is no longer sure of the eminence his fellows give him, and the burden of the wrongs he has borne is accumulating. Today his temper is as bad as ever; not for the first time, he has been summonsed to the meeting under threat of a *poursuivant* or officer with a warrant. Standing across the room from him is John Bois, some dozen years his junior and the best of his pupils. Fresh-faced and the picture of health, he is nevertheless a hypochondriac. As always when reading or studying the Bible, his head is uncovered. John Harmer, as long Regius Professor of Greek at Oxford as Downes has been at Cambridge, is also present.

The sheets of the Bishops' Bible on which Barlow wrote are in front of them. So is the columned manuscript that Fenton prepared for circulation. There have been a few additions to it, made by the other companies. Most of these are marked *Agreed*, and Barlow's sheets have been amended to take account of these agreements. The places not so marked are supposed to be the prime business of the three men, but they have long since taken licence to use their own judgement on anything they think appropriate.

Approved to death has not found agreement among the other companies, and is marked *To Be Resolved* on Fenton's manuscript. Bois has been looking into this and made notes for himself on it. From these he is lecturing his companions.

'So the Apostle thinketh of the gladiators in the circus or theatre. The learned Scaliger saith that those whom the Greeks call ἐφέδρους, the Romans call *sequutores*. Indeed they are followers. He noteth also the old glosses, which call ἐφέδρον *tertiarium*, that is, *a third man, one who taketh the place of one killed*.'

'So?' interrupts Downes, impatient that his old pupil is lecturing him. 'Paul writeth ἐσχάτους, not ἐφέδρους. Thy point?'

'Not mine, but Scaliger's. He citeth the Apostle here. The Greek tongue alloweth not τοὺς ἀποτόλους ἐσχάτους alone, so the Apostle must write ἀπέδειξεν ἐσχάτους ἡμᾶς τοὺς ἀποστόλους – he has placed us who are Apostles as if we are substitutes with the beasts, *bestiaros*. So ἐσχάτους here is truly ἐφέδρους. It fitteth the process and order of the text. And he saith more of these *bestiaros*, that they are not certainly doomed to death, as the Apostle saith, ἐπιθανατίους, but they are desperate men, hired for the spectacle. So they are called παράβολοι, adventurers, from which the Apostle takes his unique word, παραβολεύεσθαι in Philippians 2.30. Others read παραβουλεύεσθαι. 'Tis *to risk* or *take no thought for one's life*.'

'Enough, enough,' snorts Downes. 'I bow to the learned Scaliger.'

'What of the English?' asks Hutchinson. '*God hath set forth us the Apostles last, as it were approved to death*. Us the Apostles followers? Following? Substitutes?'

'*Last* it must be,' declares Downes. 'The figure is hidden in the English. These are the last gladiators, not condemned but valiant, approved, even to death. But how reads the English of Philippians?'

He turns over the pages, and reads, '*because for the work of Christ he was nigh unto death, not regarding his life*. That is, *taking no thought for his life*, παραβουλεύεσθαι, yet 'tis also *hazarding his life*, παραβολεύεσθαι. 'Tis good. Let it stand.'

Bois, who has been rubbing at his teeth, writes *Stet* against *approved to death*, and sets down his pen. He has added nothing in his notes to his passage from Scaliger.

'What a Mayday dance to do nothing!' exclaims Downes. 'Is it for this that they send me a *poursuivant*, to do nothing?'

Imagining Translation Committees at Work

There is one last scene, some six years later in the printing house of Robert Barker, the King's Printer. A compositor is setting this same verse of I Corinthians. In the copy he works from, *approved* is struck through, and *appointed* written in the margin. He follows his copy. The single word unique to the KJV has vanished.

NOTES

1 *The Sussex Edition of Kipling's Works*, 35 vols (London: Macmillan, 1937-9), XXX, pp. 346-8.

2 Shakespeare is supposed to have left his signature in the KJV: he was probably forty-six years of age when this story took place, so one goes to Psalm 46 and counts forty-six words from the beginning, and then one counts forty-six words from the end.

3 Kipling's prime source was the critic George Sainsbury. I discuss him and show Kipling's dependence on him in my *A History of the Bible as Literature*, 2 vols (Cambridge: University Press, 1993), II, pp. 323-6; I deal with the story itself at greater length in '"Proofs of Holy Writ"', myths of the Authorised Version: Kipling and the Bible', *Kipling Journal* 63 (December 1989), 18-27.

4 Hilton Brown, prefatory note to the *Strand Magazine* (1947) reprint of '"Proofs of Holy Writ"'. As given in Philip Mason, '"'Proofs of Holy Writ'"': an introduction', *Kipling Journal*, 62 (March 1988), 33.

5 The Instructions are frequently reprinted. I have followed A. W. Pollard, *The Holy Bible. A Facsimile ... of the Authorized Version ...* (Oxford: University Press, 1911), pp. 29-30.

6 Revised Version New Testament preface, p. viii.

7 'New Testament Company, Notes of Proceedings, Taken and Transcribed by Samuel Newth,' British Library, Add. MSS 36284-6. These notes are a fair copy begun by Newth in 1893 of his original pencil notes, British Library, Add. MSS 13279 etc. Official minutes of the meetings of the RV British New Testament committee were kept and presumably survive somewhere. I also draw here on Newth's *Lectures on Bible Revision* (London: Hodder & Stoughton, 1881), pp. 105-27.

8 Newth reports that 'the average did not rise above 35 verses a day' (Newth, p. 122). His notes confirm this: the first revision of John and Acts averaged thirty-six verses a day (forty for John, thirty-four for Acts).

9 A similar sense of the human side of translation committees can be gained from Basil Willey's account of the work on the New English Bible, especially his recreation of a sample discussion, 'On translating the Bible into modern English', *Essays and Studies*, n.s. 23 (1970), 1-17.

10 Newth's notes, I, fol. 20$^\mathrm{v}$.

11 Newth's notes, I, fol. 83$^\mathrm{v}$.

12 Newth's notes, I, fol. 26$^\mathrm{v}$.

13 Newth's notes, III, fol. 106$^\mathrm{v}$. Newth adds: 'this was a bit of scrupulosity on Scr's part. It was generally felt that it would be absurd not to leave a way open for any to remain neutral if they so wished, & still more to require them to leave the room whenever a division took place, & so the agreement was come to, as to the backing the chairs. I said to Scr. at the time, that this was a bit of pure formalism which would necessarily soon die, & that our former practice of reckoning by the number of votes would insensibly be resumed. And so it turned out.'

14 Newth's notes, III, fol. 122$^\mathrm{v}$.

15 Newth's notes, III, fol. 33$^\mathrm{v}$.

16 Newth's notes, II, fol. 39$^\mathrm{r}$. At this stage simple majorities were needed to carry a reading or a rendering; a two-thirds majority was required for changes in the second revision.

17 Newth's notes, II, fols 38ᵛ, 39ᵛ.

18 The one document to give all suggestions made is William Aldis Wright's notes of the discussions the RV Old Testament committee had on the first six chapters of Genesis, 'Proposed alterations in the Authorised Version', Cambridge University Library, Adv c 100 17¹. I give a description and sample of these in *A History of the Bible as Literature*, II, pp. 249-50.

19 Nevertheless, though nineteenth-century editions did not, Liddell & Scott now gives this verse (with several other citations) for the sense, *seize with the mind, comprehend*.

20 μὴ καταλάβῃ σε ὁ ὑετός; *lest the rain overtake thee*, The Septuagint ... *with an English Translation by Sir Launcelot Lee Brenton* (London: Bagster, n.d.).

21 Probably *De facie in orbe lunae*, 933A. I suggest he remembered this because there is no apt reference in Liddell & Scott. On other occasions, if not this one, the translators would have referred to the Lexicon. The following exchange between Ellicott, chairman of the company, and Scott depends on its being available (and clearly caused amusement): 'If I turn to your excellent lexicon & turn up κῆτος should I find a great fish given as the meaning, should I not find whale? Sc. I don't know. Curiously enough the meaning given in the Lexicon is any sea monster or huge' (Newth's notes, I, fol. 25ᵛ, in connection with Matthew 12.40).

22 We might enlist one other piece of evidence, of a sort not available in relation to the KJV. Westcott published a very substantial commentary on John known as 'The Speaker's Commentary', clearly written after the revision of John, that rehearses some of his arguments, *The Gospel According to St John: the Authorised Version. With Introduction and Notes* (London: B. F. Westcott [1881], 1898; reprinted from *The Holy Bible According to the Authorised Version, A.D. 1611, with an explanatory and critical commentary and a revision of the translation by Bishops and other clergy of the Anglical Church*, ed. by F. C. Cook, 12 vols (London: John Murray, 1871-88)), p. 5. I give Westcott's note in full to suggest how lengthy the discussion could have been:

> *comprehended* (**overcame**) *it not*] The verb in the original (κατέλαβεν) has received two very different renderings – *overcame* and *apprehended*. It is found again in a parallel passage, xii. 35, *that darkness overtake you not*; and also in an old reading of vi. 17, *the darkness overtook them*. In these cases the sense cannot be doubtful. The darkness comes down upon, enwraps men. As applied to light this sense includes the further notion of overwhelming, eclipsing. The relation of darkness to light is one of essential antagonism. If the darkness is represented as pursuing the light it can only be to overshadow and not to appropriate it. And this appears to be the meaning here. The existence of the darkness is affirmed, and at the same time the unbroken energy of the light. But the victory of the light is set forth as the result of a past struggle; and the abrupt alteration of tense brings into prominence the change which has passed over the world. It could not but happen that the darkness when it came should seek to cover all; and in this attempt it failed: *the light is shining in the darkness, and the darkness overcame it not*.
>
> This general interpretation of the word, which is completely established by the usage of St John (comp. I Thess. v. 4), is supported by the Greek Fathers; but the Latin version gives the rendering *comprehenderunt*, 'took hold of', 'embraced'. This sense, however, and that of 'understood' (expressed in the New Testament by the middle voice of the verb: Acts iv. 13, x. 34, xxv. 25; Eph. iii. 18) seem to be inconsistent with the image and foreign to the context. The darkness, as such, could not 'seize', 'appropriate', the light. In doing this it would cease to exist. And yet further, the notion of the historical development of revelation is not at present pursued. The great elements of the moral position of the world are stated: their combinations and issues are outlined afterwards. In this respect *v. 5* is parallel with 9-13, indicating the existence and continuance of a conflict which is there regarded in its contrasted issues. The whole phrase is indeed a startling paradox. The light does not banish the darkness: the darkness does not overpower the light. Light and darkness coexist in the world side by side.

23 Hort, letter of 7 July 1870; Ellicott, *The Times* (20 July 1881); both as given in Samuel Hemphill, *A History of the Revised Version of the New Testament* (London: Elliot Stock, 1906), p. 78; Newth's notes, II, fol. 117ᵛ.

24 Cambridge University Library, Adv b 100.52.

25 Close inspection shows that Hort had made some notes in advance of the meeting, including an alternative rendering of the last three words of verse 8, *of the light*. Evidently he proposed this alternative, but it did not get the two-thirds support necessary, so he struck it through. What appears to be the official copy of this page (Adv a 100 10) has the same notes from the meeting, including Hort's suggestion; the only word still legible under the crossing-out is 'Hort' at the beginning. This is the equivalent of a translator's initial followed by a proposed reading and a record of the vote in Newth's notes (I have not seen the notes for this part of the work).

26 One thing we know happened in addition to these processes: there was a final period during which Bishops Miles Smith and Thomas Bilson 'put the finishing touch to this version'; Report to the Synod of Dort, 20 November 1618; as translated in Pollard (n. 5 above), p. 142.

27 Here I follow Ward Allen, translator and editor, *Translating for King James: notes made by a translator of King James's Bible* (Nashville: Vanderbilt University Press, 1969), pp. 5-8.

28 'This afternoon is our translation time, and most of our company are negligent,' 30 November 1604; as given in Gustavus S. Paine, *The Men Behind the King James Version* (1959; Grand Rapids, Mich.: Baker Book House; repr. 1977), p. 72.

29 British Library, Harley MS 750, fols 1ʳ-1ᵛ. This manuscript continues with a copy of 'The Rules to be obserued in Translation' and then of Bois's notes. This latter copy was unknown to historians of the KJV, so it is likely that the list of translators with which it begins was also unknown. I report the discovery of this manuscript, show its link with Bois, and analyse how the Bois notes differ from the published version in 'John Bois's Notes on the Revision of the King James Bible New Testament: a New Manuscript', *The Library*, sixth series 18.4 (December 1996), 328-46.

The authenticity of the Bois notes argues the overall credibility of this manuscript, and it is difficult to see how or why the information about the companies would have been invented if it were not correct. The uniqueness of the manuscript would be a worry were it not that this manuscript gives the only one of the surviving lists that demonstrably could have drawn on knowledge of how the work actually proceeded rather than how it was meant to proceed. There is one other possible cause for worry. If this manuscript is reliable, the companies simply drew a line half way down the list of their members, assigning the top half to one part of the work, and the bottom half to the other part. All one can say here is that the manuscript would be more credible if the names were given in a significantly different order from that found in the other lists.

These are the divisions the manuscript gives: first Westminster company, Andrewes, Overall, Saravia, Clark, and Layfield for the Pentateuch, Tighe, Burleigh, King, Tomson, and Bedwell for Joshua to II Chronicles; second Westminster company, Barlow, Hutchinson, Spencer, and Fenton for the Pauline epistles, Rabbett, Sanderson, and Dakins for the canonical epistles. The manuscript also divides the second Cambridge company, but without indicating which parts of the Apocrypha each division took: Duport, Branthwait, and Radcliffe, and Ward, Downes, Bois and Ward.

30 *Table Talk of John Selden*, ed. by Frederick Pollock (London: Quaritch, 1927), p. 10 (modernized).

31 In terms of the origins of particular parts of the verse, it may be divided up thus:

KJV	Others
For I thinke	Gen, R; others; me thinketh
that God hath set forth vs	T, Gt, Gen, Bs'; R: that God hath shewed us
the Apostles last,	T: which are Apostles; Gt: (which are the last Apostles); Gen: the laste Apostles; Bs': which are the last Apostles; R: Apostles the last

as *it were*	All, unitalicized
approued	T, Gt, Gen, Bs': appointed; R: deputed
to death. For wee are	T, Gt, Gen, Bs'; R: because
made	Gen, Bs', R; T, Gt omit
a †spectacle	R; T, Gt, Gen, Bs': gazingstock
vnto	T, Gt, Gen, Bs'; R: to
the world, and to	All
Angels, and to men.	Bs'; T, Gt, Gen: the Angels, and to men; R: Angels and men
†Gr. theater.	

32 Acts 2.22, Romans 16.10.

33 The following is based on Allen, pp. 45, 115-16, and my 'John Bois's Notes', 336-7, 339.

BIBLIOGRAPHY

Alexander, Michael, ed., *Discovering the New World, Based on the Works of Theodor De Bry* (London: London Editions, 1976)

Allen, Ward, ed. & trans., *Translating for King James: notes made by a translator of King James's Bible* (Nashville: Vanderbilt University Press, 1969)

Alvarez, Roman & M. Carmen-Africa Vidal, eds, *Translation, Power, Subversion* (Clevedon, UK: Multilingual Matters, 1996)

Anderson, Hugh, *Jesus and Christian Origins: a Commentary on Modern Viewpoints* (New York: Oxford University Press, 1964)

Andersson, Christiane & Charles Talbot, *From a Mighty Fortress: Prints, Drawings and Books in the Age of Luther, 1483-1546*, ex. cat. (Detroit: Institute of Art, 1983)

Andrews, J. H., *Trade, Plunder and Settlement: Maritime Enterprise and the Genesis of the British Empire, 1480-1630* (Cambridge: University Press, 1984)

Anglo, Sydney, *Images of Tudor Kingship* (London: Seaby, 1992)

Anglo, Sydney, *Spectacle Pageantry and Early Tudor Policy* (Oxford: Clarendon Press, 1969)

Antwerp, Dissident Typographical Centre: the role of Antwerp printers in the religious conflicts in England (16th century), ex. cat. (Antwerp: Plantin-Moretus Museum, 1994)

Arber, Edward, ed., *The First Printed English New Testament, translated by William Tyndale*, facsimile (London: Selwood Printing Works, 1871)

Armstrong, Elizabeth, *Robert Estienne Royal Printer: an historical study of the elder Stephanus*, rev. edn (Appleford: Sutton Courtenay Press, 1986)

Articles to be enquyred in the visitation, in the fyrste yeare of the raygne of our moost drad soveraygne Lady, Elizabeth (London: R. Jugge & A. Cawood, 1559)

Atkinson, James, ed. & trans., *Luther: Early Theological Works*, The Library of Christian Classics, vol. XVI (London: SCM, 1962)

Atkinson, James, *Martin Luther and the Birth of Protestantism* (Harmondsworth: Penguin Books, 1968)

Augustine of Hippo, *De Spiritu et Littera*, ed. by F. Urba & J. Zycha, Corpus Scriptorum Ecclesiasticorum Latinorum, 60 (Vienna: Hoelder-Pichler-Tempsky, 1913)

Barnstone, Willis, *The Poetics of Translation: History, Theory, Practice* (New Haven & London: Yale University Press, 1993)

Barth, Karl, *The Epistle to the Romans*, trans. from 6th German edn (London: Oxford University Press, 1935)

Barth, Markus, *The People of God* (Sheffield: JSOT Press, 1963)

Bassnett, Susan & André Lefevere, eds, *Translation, History and Culture* (London: Cassell, 1990)

Bassnett-McGuire, Susan, *Translation Studies* (London: Routledge, 1991)

Bauckham, Richard, *Tudor Apocalypse: Sixteenth-Century Apocalypticism, Millenarianism, and the English Reformation* (Appleford: Sutton Courtenay Press, 1978)

Bebb, Philip & Sherrin Marshall, eds, *The Process of Change in Early Modern Europe* (Athens, OH: Ohio University Press, 1988)

Berry, Lloyd E., ed., *The Geneva Bible: a Facsimile of the 1560 Edition* (Madison: University of Wisconsin Press, 1969)

Bibliography

Berthoud, G., *Aspects de la propagande religieuse* (Geneva: Droz, 1957)

Bethell, Leslie, *The Cambridge History of Latin America, Vol. I: Colonial Latin America* (Cambridge: University Press, 1984)

Bhabha, Homi, *The Location of Culture* (London: Routledge, 1994)

La Bible (Geneva: Jean Girard, 1540)

The bible and holy scriptures conteyned in the olde and newe testament (Geneva: R. Hall, 1560)

La Bible nouvellement translatée (Basel: J. Hervage, 1555)

La Bible, Qui est toute la Saincte Escripture (Geneva: Robert Estienne, 1553)

Biblia Sacra (Stuttgart: Württembergische Bibelanstalt, 1975)

Biblia Sacra ex Sebastiani Castellionis interpretatione eiusque postrema recognitione (Basel: J. Oporinus, 1551, 1556)

The boke of psalmes, where in are conteined praiers (Geneva: R. Hall, 1559)

Brewer, J. S., James Gairdner, & R. H. Brodie, eds, *Letters and Papers, Foreign and Domestic, of the Reign of Henry VIII, 1509-1547*, 21 vols (London: Longman, 1862-1910)

Brink, Jean R., ed., *Privileging Gender in Early Modern England*, Sixteenth Century Essays and Studies 23 (Kirksville, MO: Sixteenth Century Journal Publishers, 1993)

Brinkelow, Henry, *The complaynt of Roderyck Mors for the redresse of certen wicked lawes* ([Strassburg: W. Köpfel, 1542?])

Brinkelow, Henry, *The lamentacion of a christian against the citie of London, made by R. Mors* ([Bonn]: L. Mylius, 1542)

Bucher, Bernadette, *Icon and Conquest: a Structural Analysis of the Illustrations of De Bry's Great Voyages*, trans. by Basia Miller Gulati (Chicago: University of Chicago Press, 1981)

Bultmann, Rudolf, *Theology of the New Testament*, vol. 1 (London: SCM Press, 1959)

Butterworth, Charles C., *The English Primers (1529-1545): Their Publication and Connection with the English Bible and the Reformation in England* (Philadelphia: University of Pennsylvania Press, 1953)

Butterworth, Charles C., *The Literary Lineage of the King James Bible, 1340-1611* (Philadelphia: University of Pennsylvania Press, 1941)

Butterworth, Charles C., & Allan G. Chester, *George Joye, 1495?-1553: a Chapter in the History of the English Bible and the English Reformation* (Philadelphia: University of Pennsylvania Press, 1962)

Calder, Angus, *Revolutionary Empire: the Rise of the English-Speaking Empires from the Fifteenth Century to the 1780s* (London: Cape, 1981)

Calendar of State Papers Domestic Series, Addenda, 1566-79 (Nendeln: Kraus, 1967)

Calvin, John, *Institutes of the Christian Religion*, ed. by J. T. McNeill, Library of the Christian Classics, 20/21 (Philadelphia, PA: Westminster Press, 1960)

Calvin, John, *Sermons of John Calvin, upon the songe that Ezechias made after he had bene sicke, and afflicted by the hand of God, conteyned in the 38. Chapiter of Esay*, trans. by 'A.L.' (London: John Day, 1560)

Cameron, James K., ed., *The First Book of Discipline* (Edinburgh: St Andrews Press, 1972)

Campbell, William S., *Paul's Gospel in an Intercultural Context: Jew and Gentile in the Letter to the Romans* (Frankfurt & New York: Peter Lang, 1992)

Chaix, P., *Recherches sur l'imprimerie à Genève de 1550 à 1564*, THR 16 (Geneva: Droz, 1954)

Chambers, Bettye Thomas, *Bibliography of French Bibles: Fifteenth- and Sixteenth-Century French-Language Editions of the Scriptures*, Travaux d'Humanisme et Renaissance 192 (Geneva: Droz, 1983)

Christensen, Carl, *Art and the Reformation in Germany* (Athens, OH: Ohio University Press, 1979)

Christensen, Carl, *Princes and Propaganda* (Kirksville, MO: Sixteenth Century Journal Publishers, 1992)

Bibliography

Christie, R. C., *Etienne Dolet: the Martyr of the Renaissance*, rev. edn (Niewkoop: B. De Graaf, 1964)

Collinson, Patrick, *Godly People: Essays on English Protestantism and Puritanism* (London: Hambledon Press, 1983); first published in *Studies in Church History*, 2 (1965)

Cook, F. C., ed., *The Holy Bible According to the Authorised Version, A.D. 1611, with an explanatory and critical commentary and a revision of the translation by Bishops and other clergy of the Anglical Church*, 12 vols ([London: John Murray, 1871-88])

Coverdale, Miles, *Biblia The bible, that is, the holy scripture* ([Cologne?] E. Cervicornus & J. Soter?, 1535)

Coverdale, Miles, *Remains of Myles Coverdale*, ed. by George Pearson, Parker Society 14 (Cambridge: University Press, 1846)

Cranach, Lucas, *Cranach im Detail. Buchschmuck Lucas Cranachs des Alteren und seiner Werkstatt*, ed. by Jutta Strehle (Wittenberg: Drei Kastanien Verlag, 1994)

Cranach, Lucas, *Passional Christi und Antichristi* (Wittenberg: Johann Rhau-Grunenberg, 1521)

Daniell, David, ed., *Tyndale's New Testament* (New Haven & London: Yale University Press, 1989)

Daniell, David, ed., *Tyndale's Old Testament* (New Haven & London: Yale University Press, 1992)

Daniell, David, *William Tyndale: a Biography* (New Haven & London: Yale University Press, 1994)

Das Newe Testament Deutsch (Wittenberg: [Melchior Lotther], September 1522)

Dasent, John Roche, ed., *Acts of the Privy Council of England*, n.s. 1 (London: Eyre and Spottiswoode, 1890)

de Bruin, C. C. & F. G. M. Broeyer, *De Statenbijbel en zijn voorgangers: nederlandse bijbelvertalingen vanaf de Reformatie tot 1637* (Haarlem: Nederlands Bijbelgenootschap, 1993)

de Bry, Theodor, *America* (Frankfurt: T. de Bry, 1594)

de Bry, Theodor, *Iani Iacobi Boissardi Vesvntini Emblematum* (Frankfurt: T. de Bry, 1593)

Delano-Smith, Catherine & Elizabeth Morley Ingram, *Maps in Bibles, 1500-1600: an Illustrated Catalogue* (Geneva: Droz, 1991)

de Las Casas, Bartolomé, *A Short Account of the Destruction of the Indies*, trans. by Nigel Griffin with an introduction by Anthony Pagden (Harmondsworth: Penguin, 1992)

de Las Casas, Bartolomé, *The Spanish colonie, or briefe chronicle of the acts and gestes of the Spaniardes*, trans. by M.M.S. (London: Thomas Dawson for William Brome, 1583)

den Hollander, A. A., *De Nederlandse Bijbelvertalingen, 1522-1545* (Nieuwkoop: de Graaf, 1997)

Derrida, Jacques, *Of Grammatology*, trans. by Gayatri Spivak (Baltimore: Johns Hopkins University Press, 1976)

De Vreese, W. L. & G. J. Boekenoogen, *Woordenboek der Nederlandsche Taal* ('s Gravenhage & Leiden: Martinus Nijhoff, A. W. Sijthoff, 1910)

Dolet, Etienne, *La maniere de bien traduire d'une langue en aultre* (Lyon: Étienne Dolet, 1540; facsimile repr. Geneva: Slatkine, 1972)

Dove, Linda, 'Women at Variance: Sonnet Sequences and Social Commentary in Early Modern England' (unpublished doctoral thesis, University of Maryland at College Park, 1997)

Dowling, Maria & Joy Shakespeare, 'Religion and Politics in mid Tudor England through the eyes of an English Protestant Woman: the Recollections of Rose Hickman', *Bulletin of the Institute of Historical Research*, 55 (1982)

Duff, E. G., *A Century of the English Book Trade* (London: Bibliographical Society, 1948)

Duffy, Eamon, *The Stripping of the Altars* (New Haven & London: Yale University Press, 1992)

Duke, Alastair, *Reform and Reformation in the Low Countries* (London: Hambledon Press, 1990)

Bibliography

Eadie, John, *The English Bible*, 2 vols (London: Macmillan, 1876)

Edwards, Mark, *Printing, Propaganda, and Martin Luther* (Berkeley: University of California Press, 1994)

Eire, Carlos, *War against the idols: the Reformation of Worship from Erasmus to Calvin* (Cambridge: University Press, 1986)

Elton, Geoffrey, *Policy and Police: the Enforcement of the Reformation in the Age of Thomas Cromwell* (Cambridge: University Press, 1972)

Emmerson, Richard Kenneth, *Antichrist in the Middle Ages: a Study of Medieval Apocalypticism, Art, and Literature* (Seattle: University of Washington Press, 1981)

English Recusant Literature 1558-1640, vol. 127 (Menston, Yorkshire: Scolar Press, 1973)

Faber Stapulensis, Johann, *Epistolae Pauli Apostoli* (Paris: Henri Estienne, 1512)

Fairfield, L. P., *John Bale: Mythmaker for the English Reformation* (Indiana: Purdue University Press, 1976)

Felch, Susan M., *The Collected Works of Anne Vaughan Lock*, Medieval & Renaissance Texts & Studies Series, vol. 185, Renaissance English Text Society, vol. 21 (Tempe, AZ: Medieval and Renaissance Texts and Studies Center, 1998)

Felch, Susan M., '"Deir Sister": the Letters of John Knox to Anne Vaughan Lok', *Renaissance and Reformation/Renaissance et Reforme*, 19, no. 4 (1995)

Firth, Katherine R., *The Apocalyptic Tradition in Reformation Britain, 1530-1645* (Oxford: University Press, 1979)

Fisher, John, *A Sermon had at Paulis* (London: T. Berthelet, 1526)

Fisher, John, *This treatyse concernynge the fruytfull saynges of Dauyd the kynge & prophete in the seuen penytencyall psalmes* (London: Wynkyn de Worde, 1508)

Fleming, D. Hay, *The Last Days of John Knox, by... Richard Bannatyne*, Knox Club Publications: 35 (Edinburgh: Knox Club, 1913, 10)

Fleming, Gerald, 'On the origins of the Passional Christi und Antichristi and Lucas Cranach the elder's contribution to Reformation polemics in the iconography of the Passional', *Gutenberg Jahrbuch* (1973)

Forshall, Josiah & Frederic Madden, eds, *The Holy Bible, containing the Old and New Testaments, with the Apocryphal Books, made from the Latin Vulgate by John Wycliffe and his Followers*, 2 vols (Oxford: University Press, 1850)

Foucault, Michel, *The Archaeology of Knowledge*, trans. by A. M. Sheridan Smith (New York: Harper & Row, 1972)

Foxe, John, *Acts and Monuments*, ed. by Stephen R. Cattley (London: R. B. Seeley & W. Burnside, 1841)

Foxe, John, *Acts and Monuments*, ed. by George Townsend (New York: AMS, 1965)

Franck, Johannes, *Altfränkische Grammatik*, ed. by Rudolf Schützeichel, 2nd edn (Göttingen: Vandenhoeck & Ruprecht, 1971)

Franck, Sebastian, *Die Gulden Arck* (Louvain: A. M. Bergagne, 1560)

Frei, Hans, *The Eclipse of Biblical Narrative: A Study in Eighteenth and Nineteenth Century Hermeneutics* (New Haven & London: Yale University Press, 1974)

The French Renaissance in Prints from the Bibliothèque Nationale de France (Los Angeles: Grunwald Center for the Graphic Arts, University of California, Los Angeles, 1995)

Friedländer, Max & Jakob Rosenberg, *The Paintings of Lucas Cranach* (Ithaca, NY: Cornell University Press, 1978)

Fulke, William, *A Defence of the Sincere and True Translations of the Holy Scriptures into the English Tongue, Against the Cavils of Gregory Martin* (London: H. Bynnemann, for G. Bishop, 1583), ed. by Charles Hartshorne, Parker Society 17 (Cambridge: University Press, 1843)

Fuller, Mary C., *Voyages in Print: English Travel to America, 1576-1624* (Cambridge: University Press, 1995)

Bibliography

Garrett, Christina H., *The Marian Exiles: a Study in the Origins of Elizabethan Puritanism* (Cambridge: University Press, 1938, repr. 1966)

Gawthrop, Richard & Gerald Strauss, 'Protestantism and Literacy in Early Modern Germany', *Past and Present*, 104 (1984)

Gelbert, J. P., *Magister Johann Bader's Leben und Schriften Nicolaus Thomae und seine Briefe: ein Beitrag zur Reformationsgeschichte der Städte Landau, Bergzabern und der links-rheinischen Pfalz, zur Feier des fünfzigjährigen Jubiläums der kirchlichen Union* (Neustadt a.d.R.: Verlag von Gottschick-Witter's Buchhandlung, 1868)

Gesetz und Genade. Cranach, Luther und die Bilder (Eisenach: Museum der Wartburg, 1994)

Gilmont, Jean-François, *La Réforme et le livre* (Paris: Éditions du Cerf, 1990)

God's Outlaw: the Story of William Tyndale, dir. by Tony Tew (a Grenville Film Production in association with Channel Four, undated)

Gorday, Peter, *Principles of Patristic Exegesis* (New York & Toronto: Edwin Mellen Press, 1983)

Gosling, William Gilbert, *The Life of Sir Humphrey Gilbert: England's First Empire Builder* (London: Constable, 1911)

Greenblatt, Stephen, *Marvelous Possessions: the Wonder of the New World* (Oxford: Clarendon Press, 1991)

Greenblatt, Stephen, *Renaissance Self-Fashioning* (Chicago: University of Chicago Press, 1980)

Greenblatt, Stephen, *Shakespearean Negotiations: the Circulation of Social Energy in Renaissance England* (Oxford: Clarendon Press, 1988)

Grimm, Claus, ed., *Lucas Cranach: ein Maler-Unternehmer aus Franken* (Augsburg: Hans der Bayerischen Geschichte; Regensburg: F. Pustet, 1994)

Grimm, H. J., ed., *Martin Luther's Works: The Career of the Reformer*, vol. 31 (Philadelphia: Fortress Press, 1957)

Grimm, Jacob & Wilhelm, *Deutsches Wörterbuch* (Leipzig: S. Hirzel, 1889)

Groll, Karin, *Das 'Passional Christi und Antichristi' von Lucas Cranach d. A.* (Frankfurt: P. Lang, 1990)

Grossman, F., 'A religious allegory by Hans Holbein the Younger', *Burlington Magazine*, 103 (1961)

Guggisberg, Hans R., *Sebastian Castellio 1515-1563* (Göttingen: Vandenhoeck & Ruprecht, 1997)

Guillaud, Jacqueline & Maurice Guillaud, *Altdorfer and fantastic realism in German Art* (New York: Rizzoli International, 1985)

Guy, John, *Tudor England* (Oxford: University Press, 1988)

Hadfield, Andrew, *Literature, Politics and National Identity: Reformation to Renaissance* (Cambridge: University Press, 1994)

Hadfield, Andrew, *Literature, Travel and Colonial Writing in the English Renaissance, 1545-1625* (Oxford: Clarendon Press, 1998)

Hakluyt, Richard the Younger, *The Principall Navigations, Voiages and Discoueries of the English Nation* ([London]: G. Bishop & R. Newberie, deputies to C. Barker, 1589)

Hakluyt, Richard, *Principall Navigations* (1598), 12 vols (Glasgow: MacLehose, 1903)

Haller, William, *Foxe's Book of Martyrs and the Elect Nation* (London: Cape, 1963)

Hammond, Gerald, *The Making of the English Bible* (Manchester: Carcanet New Press, 1982)

Harriot, Thomas, *A Briefe and True Report of the New Found Land of Virginia* (1590), introduced by Paul Hulton (New York: Dover, 1972)

Hasler, P. W., ed., *The History of Parliament: The House of Commons 1558-1603*, vol. 3 (London: The History of Parliament Trust, 1981)

Haugaard, W. P., *Elizabeth and the English Reformation* (Cambridge: University Press, 1968)

Helfers, James P., 'The Explorer of the Pilgrim? Modern Critical Opinion and the Editorial Methods of Richard Hakluyt and Samuel Purchas', *Studies in Philology*, 94 (1997)

Bibliography

Helgerson, Richard, *Forms of Nationhood: the Elizabethan Writing of England* (Chicago: Chicago University Press, 1992)

Hemphill, Samuel, *A History of the Revised Version of the New Testament* (London: Elliot Stock, 1906)

Hogrefe, Pearl, *Women of Action in Tudor England* (Ames, IA: Iowa State Univ. Press, 1977)

The Holy Bible: The Authorized or King James Version of 1611 now reprinted with the Apocrypha, 3 vols (London: Nonesuch Press, 1963)

Hopf, C., *Martin Bucer and the English Reformation* (Oxford: Blackwell, 1946)

Hughes, Paul L. & James F. Larkin, eds., *Tudor Royal Proclamations* (New Haven & London: Yale University Press, 1964), vol. 1

Hulton, Paul, ed., *America 1585: the Complete Drawings of John White* (London: British Museum, 1984)

Hulton, Paul, ed., *Work of Jacques Le Moyne* (London: Trustees of the British Museum, 1977)

Hulton, Paul & David Beers Quinn, eds, *The American Drawings of John White, 1577-1590*, 2 vols (London: British Museum, 1964)

Illuminations (New York: Schocken, 1969)

Janton, Pierre, *John Knox (ca. 1513-1572): l'homme et l'oeuvre* (Paris: G. de Bussac, 1967)

Johnston, George, 'Scripture in the Scottish Reformation', *Canadian Journal of Theology*, 9 (1963)

Jones, Norman L., *Faith by Statute: Parliament and the Settlement of Religion, 1559* (London: Royal Historical Society, 1982)

Jones, Richard Foster, *The Triumph of the English Language: a Survey of Opinions Concerning the Vernacular from the Introduction of Printing to the Restoration* (California: Stanford University Press, 1953)

Joye, George, *An Apologye made by George Joye to satisfye (if it maye be) w. Tindale* (London: John Byddell, 27 February 1535)

Joye, George, *George Joye confuteth/ Winchesters false Articles* (Antwerp: Catherine Van Endhoven, 1543)

Joye, George, *Jeremy the Prophete* (Antwerp: Catherine Van Endhoven[?], May 1534)

Joye, George, *A present consolacion for the sufferers of persecucion for ryghtwysenes* (Antwerp: S. Mierdman, September 1544)

Joye, George, *The prophete Isaye* (Antwerp: Martin de Keyser, 10 May 1531)

Joye, George, *The prouerbes of Solomon ... Here foloweth the boke of Solomon called Ecclesiastes* (London: Thomas Godfray, c. 1535)

Joye, George, *The Refutation of the byshop of Winchesters derke declaration of his false articles* (London: John Herford, 1546)

Joye, George, *Our sauiour Jesus Christ hath not ouercharged his chirche with many ceremonies* (Antwerp: Catherine Van Endhoven, 1543)

Kaczerowsky, Klaus, *Sebastian Franck Bibliographie* (Wiesbaden: Pressler, 1976)

Käsemann, Ernst, *New Testament Questions of Today*, trans. by W. J. Montague (London: SCM Press, 1969)

Kertelge, Karl, *Rechtfertigung bei Paulus* (Munster: Aschendorf, 1967)

Ketley, Joseph, ed., *Two Liturgies with other Documents of King Edward VI*, Parker Society 29 (Cambridge: University Press, 1844)

King, John, *English Reformation Literature: the Tudor Origins of the Protestant Tradition* (Princeton: University Press, 1982)

King, John, *Tudor Royal Iconography* (Princeton: University Press, 1989)

Kingdon, Robert M., *Geneva and the Coming of the Wars of Religion in France, 1555-1563*, THR 22 (Geneva: Droz, 1956)

Bibliography

Kipling, Rudyard, *The Sussex Edition of Kipling's Works*, 35 vols (London: Macmillan, 1937-9)

Koepplin, Dieter & Tilman Falk, *Lukas Cranach*, 2 vols (Basel: Birkhäuser 1974)

Köhler, Hans-Joachim, *Flugschriften als Massenmedium der Reformationszeit* (Stuttgart: Klett-Cotta, 1981)

Kronenberg, M. E., *Nijhoff-Kronenberg Nederlandsche bibliografie van 1500 tot 1540* ('s Gravenhage: Martinus Nijhoff, 1923-71)

Kupperman, Karen Ordhal, *Roanoke: the Abandoned Colony* (Totowa, NJ: Rowman & Littlefield, 1984)

Kuppermann, Karen, *Settling with the Indians: the Meeting of English and Indian Cultures in America, 1580-1640* (Totowa, NJ: Rowman & Littlefield, 1980)

Kyle, Richard G., *The Mind of John Knox* (Lawrence, KS: Coronado Press, 1984)

Laing, David, *The Works of John Knox*, 6 vols (Edinburgh: Bannatyne Club, 1846-64)

Latré, Guido, 'The Place of Printing of the Coverdale Bible', *The Tyndale Society Journal*, 8 (November 1997)

Lawler, Thomas M. C., *The Complete Works of St Thomas More*, Germain Marc'Hadour & Richard C. Marius, vol. 6, part 1 (New Haven & London: Yale University Press, 1981)

Lawton, David, *Faith, Text and History: the Bible in English* (New York & London: Harvester Wheatsheaf, 1990)

Lefevere, Andre, ed., *Translation/History/Culture: a Sourcebook* (London: Routledge, 1992)

Léonard, Émile G., *Histoire générale du protestantisme* (Paris: Presses universitaires de France, 1982)

Lewis, John, ed., *The New Testament of Our Lord and Saviour Jesus Christ: Translated out of the Latin Vulgate by John Wiclif* (London: Thomas Page, 1731)

Luther, Martin, *Auslegung der Evangelien vom Advent bis auff Ostern sampt viel anderen Predigten* (Wittenberg: G. Rhaw, 1528)

Luther, Martin, *The Bondage of the Will*, trans. by J. I. Parker & O. R. Johnson (London: James Clarke, 1957)

Luther, Martin, *Lectures on Galatians*, Luther's Works, vol. 26 (St Louis: Concordia Publishing House, 1963)

Luther, Martin, *Lectures on Romans*, ed. & trans. by W. Pauck, Library of Christian Classics, vol. XV (London: SCM Press, 1961)

Luther, Martin, *Roemerbriefvorlesung*, ed. by Johannes Ficker, vol. 56 (Weimar: Boehlau, 1938)

Lyotard, Jean-François, *The Postmodern Condition: a Report on Knowledge* (Minneapolis: University of Minnesota Press, 1984)

MacCullough, Diarmid, *Thomas Cranmer: a Life* (New Haven & London: Yale University Press, 1996)

Maltby, William S., *The Black Legend in England: the Development of Anti-Spanish Sentiment, 1558-1660* (Durham, NC: Duke University Press, 1971)

Marshall, W., *A Prymer in Englyshe, with certeyn prayers and godly meditations, very necessary for all people that understonde not the Latyne tongue* (London: J. Byddell for W. Marshall, 1534)

Martin, Gregory, *A Discoverie of the Manifold Corruptions of the Holy Scriptures* (Rhemes: J. Fogny, 1582)

Mason, Roger, *John Knox and the British Reformations*, St Andrews Studies in Reformation History (Aldershot: Ashgate, 1998)

McCrie, Thomas, *Life of John Knox*, 5th edn (Edinburgh: W. Blackwood, 1831)

McDonald, Christie V., *The Ear of the Other: Otobiography, Transference, Translation*, trans. by Peggy Kamuf (New York: Schocken, 1985)

McKerrow, R. B. & F. S. Ferguson, *Title-page Borders used in England and Scotland, 1485-1560* (London: Printed for the Bibliographical Society at the Oxford University Press, 1932)

Bibliography

Memmi, Albert, *The Colonizer and the Colonized*, trans. by Howard Greenfield (New York: Orion, 1965)

Meyer, Carl, ed., *Sixteenth Century Essays and Studies* (St Louis: Foundation for Reformation Research, 1971)

Moeller, Bernd, 'Was wurde in der Frühzeit der Reformation in den deutschen Städten gepredigt?', *Archiv für Reformationsgeschichte*, 75 (1984)

Monceaux, H., *Les Le Rouge de Chablis, calligraphes et miniaturistes, graveurs et imprimeurs, part II* (Paris: A. Claudin, 1896)

Morison, Samuel Eliot, *The European Discovery of America: the Northern Voyages, A.D. 500-1600* (New York: Oxford University Press, 1971)

Moxey, Keith, *Peasants, Warriors and Wives* (Chicago: University of Chicago Press, 1989)

Mozley, James Frederick, *Coverdale and his Bibles* (London: Lutterworth Press, 1953)

Mozley, James Frederick, *John Foxe and his Book* (London: SPCK, 1940)

Mozley, James Frederick, *William Tyndale* (Westport, CN: Greenwood Press, 1937)

Mulier, E. O. G. Haitsma & G. A. C. Van der Lem, *Repertorium van geschiedschrijvers in Nederland* (Den Haag: Nederlands Historisch Genootschap, 1990)

Müller, Josef, *Rheinisches Wörterbuch* (Berlin: Erika Klopp Verlag, 1944)

Neale, J. E., *Queen Elizabeth I* (Garden City, NY: Doubleday, 1957)

The newe testament [sic] both in Latin and English after the vulgare texte (London: F. Regnault for R. Grafton & E. Whitchurch, 1538)

Newth, Samuel, *Lectures on Bible Revision* (London: Hodder & Stoughton, 1881)

Norton, David, *A History of the Bible as Literature*, 2 vols (Cambridge: University Press, 1993)

David Norton, 'John Bois's Notes on the Revision of the King James Bible New Testament: a New Manuscript', *The Library*, 6th series 18.4 (December 1996)

Norton, David, ' "Proofs of Holy Writ" ', myths of the Authorised Version: Kipling and the Bible', *Kipling Journal* 63 (December 1989)

Oberman, Heiki A., *Masters of the Reformation: the Emergence of a New Intellectual Climate in Europe*, trans. by D. Martin (Cambridge: University Press, 1981)

Olsen, V. Norskov, *John Foxe and the Elizabethan Church* (Berkeley: University of California Press, 1973)

L'Ordre et maniere d'enseigner en la Ville de Geneve au College (Geneva: Jean Girard, 1537)

Oswald, Hilton C., *Lectures on Romans: Glosses and Scholia*, Luther's Works, vol. 25 (St Louis: Concordia, 1977)

Paine, Gustavus S., *The Men Behind the King James Version* (Grand Rapids, MI: Baker Book House, 1959; repr. 1977)

Parker, John, *Books to Build An Empire* (Amsterdam: N. Israel, 1965)

Parshall, Linda & Peter Parshall, *Art and the Reformation, an Annotated Bibliography* (Boston: G. K. Hall, 1986)

Patrides, C. A. & Joseph Wittreich, eds, *The Apocalypse in English Renaissance thought and literature* (Manchester: University Press, 1984)

Pearson, George, ed., *Remains of Myles Coverdale* (Cambridge: University Press for the Parker Society, 1846)

Pelikan, Jaroslav, ed., *Martin Luther: Lectures on Galatians, Chapters 1-4* (St Louis: Concordia, 1963)

Pelikan, Jaroslav, *The Reformation of the Bible, The Bible of the Reformation*, ex. cat. (New Haven & London: Yale University Press, 1996)

Percy, Eustace, *John Knox*, 2nd edn (London: Hodder & Stoughton, 1954)

Pettegree, Andrew, *Emden and the Dutch Revolt. Exile and the Development of Reformed Protestantism* (Oxford: Clarendon Press, 1992)

Bibliography

Pettegree, Andrew, *Foreign Protestant Communities in Sixteenth-Century London* (Oxford: Clarendon Press, 1986)

Pidoux, Pierre, *Le psautier huguenot du XVIe siècle, Mélodies et documents*, 2 vols (Basel: Éditions Baerenreiter, 1962)

Pollard, Alfred W., *The Holy Bible: a Facsimile ... of the Authorized Version ...* (Oxford: University Press, 1911)

Pollard, Alfred W., ed., *Records of the English Bible* (Folkestone: Dawson, 1974)

Pollard, A. W. & G. R. Redgrave, *Short Title Catalogue of Books printed in England, and of English Books printed abroad, 1475-1640*, 2nd edn rev. & enlarged by K. F. Pantzer *et al.*, 3 vols (London: Bibliographical Society, 1976-91)

Pollock, Frederick, ed., *Table Talk of John Selden* (London: Quaritch, 1927)

Prescott, William H., *History of the Conquest of Peru* (London: Bickers, 1878)

The primer, set foorth by the kynges maiestie and his clergie (London: E. Whitchurch, 1545)

This prymer of Salysbery use bothe in Englyshe and in Laten (London: R. Redman, 1535)

Quinn, David Beers, *England and the Discovery of America, 1481-1620: From the Bristol Voyages of the Fifteenth Century to the Pilgrim Settlement at Plymouth: The Exploration, Exploitation, and Trial-and-Error Colonization of North America by the English* (London: Allen & Unwin, 1974)

Quinn, David Beers, ed., *The Hakluyt Handbook*, 2 vols (London: Hakluyt Society, 1974)

Quinn, David Beers, ed., *The Roanoke Voyages, 1584-1590: Documents to Illustrate the English Voyages to North America under the Patent Granted to Walter Raleigh in 1584*, 2 vols (London: Hakluyt Society, 1955)

Rabinow, Paul, ed., *The Foucault Reader* (New York: Pantheon, 1984)

Raleigh, Walter, *The discoverie of the large, rich, and beautifull Empire of Guiana* (London: R. Robinson, 1596)

Reinitzer, Heimo, *Biblia deutsch: Luthers Bibelübersetzung und ihre Tradition*, ex. cat. (Wolfenbuttel: Herzog-August Bibliothek, 1983)

Rennie, Neil, *Far-Fetched Facts: the Literature of Travel and the Idea of the South Seas* (Oxford: Clarendon Press, 1995)

Reuchlin, John, *De Rudimentis Hebraicis* (Pforzheim: T. Anselm, 1506)

Richardson, W. C., *Stephen Vaughan, Financial Agent of Henry VIII: A Study of Financial Relations with the Low Countries* (Baton Rouge, La.: Louisiana State University Studies, 1953)

Richmond, Legh, ed., *The Fathers of the English Church* (London: John Hatchard, 1807-12)

Ricoeur, Paul, *Freud and Philosophy: An Essay on Interpretation* (New Haven & London: Yale University Press, 1970)

Robinson, Mairi, ed., *The Concise Scots Dictionary* (Aberdeen: University Press, 1985)

Robinson-Hammerstein, Helga, ed., *The Transmission of Ideas in the Lutheran Reformation* (Dublin: Irish Academic Press, 1989)

Rosier, Bart A., *The Bible in Print: Netherlandish Bible Illustration in the Sixteenth Century*, 2 vols (Leiden: Foleor, 1997)

Rouzet, Anne, *Dictionnaire des imprimeurs, libraires et éditeurs des XVe et XVIe siècles dans les limites géographiques de la Belgique actuelle* (Nieuwkoop: De Graaf, 1975)

Rupp, Gordon, *The Righteousness of God: Luther Studies* (London: Hodder & Stoughton, 1963)

Sanders, Edward P., *Paul and Palestinian Judaism* (Philadelphia: Fortress Press, 1977)

Sanders, Edward P., *Paul, the Law and the Jewish People* (Philadelphia: Fortress Press, 1983)

Schleiner, Louise, *Tudor and Stuart Women Writers* (Bloomington, Ind.: Indiana University Press, 1994)

Schmidt, Heinrich Richard, *Reichstädte, Reich und Reformation. Korporative Religionspolitik*

Bibliography

1521-1529/30 (Stuttgart: Steiner Verlag Wiesbaden, 1986)

Schmidt, Philipp, *Die Illustration der Lutherbibel, 1522-1700* (Basel: F. Reinhardt, 1962)

Schnucker, Robert V., ed., *Calviniana. Ideas and Influence of Jean Calvin*, Sixteenth Century Essays and Studies Series: 10 (Kirksville, MO: Sixteenth Century Journal Publishers, 1988)

Scribner, Robert, *For the Sake of Simple Folk: Popular Propaganda for the German Reformation*, new edn (Oxford: Clarendon Press 1994; first published Cambridge: University Press, 1981)

The Septuagint ... with an English Translation by Sir Launcelot Lee Brenton (London: Bagster, n.d.)

Shaw, W. A., ed., *Three Inventories of the Years 1542, 1547, and 1549-50 of Pictures in the Collections of Henry VIII and Edward VI* (London: Allen & Unwin, 1937)

Sheppard, A. L., 'The Printers of the Coverdale Bible, 1535,' *The Library*, Quarterly Review of Bibliography, Transactions of the Bibliographical Society, ed. by Ronald B. McKerrow, 2nd series, 16 (1936)

Sheppard, Leslie, 'The Printers of the Coverdale Bible', *Library*, 16 (3) (1935)

Shirley, John, ed., *Thomas Harriot: Renaissance Scientist* (Oxford: Clarendon Press, 1974)

Smith , G. Gregory, ed., *Elizabethan Critical Essays* (Oxford: Clarendon Press, 1904)

Staehelin, D. E., ed., *Das Buch der Basler Reformation.Zu ihrem vierhundertjaehrigen Jubilaeum im Namen der evangelischen Kirchen von stadt und Landschaft Basel* (Basel: Helbing & Lichtenhahn, 1929)

Steiner, George, *After Babel: Aspects of Language and Translation*, 2nd edn (Oxford: University Press, 1992)

Steinmetz, David C., *Luther in Context* (Grand Rapids, MI: Baker Books, 1995)

Stendahl, Krister, *Paul among Jews and Gentiles* (London: SCM Press, 1977)

Stowers, Stanley K., *A Re-reading of Romans: Justice, Jews and Gentiles* (New Haven & London: Yale University Press, 1994)

Strachan, James, *Early Bible Illustrations* (Cambridge: University Press, 1957)

Strachey, William, *The Historie of Travell into Virginia Britania* (1612), ed. by Louis B. Wright & Virginia Freund (London: Hakluyt Society, 1953)

String, Tatiana C., 'Henry VIII and the Art of the Royal Supremacy' (unpublished Ph.D. Dissertation, University of Texas at Austin, 1996)

Strong, Roy, *Holbein and Henry VIII* (London: Routledge & Kegan Paul, 1967)

Tacke, Andreas, *Der katholische Cranach* (Mainz: P. von Zabern, 1992)

Taffin, Jean, *Of the markes of the children of God, and of their comforts in afflictions* (London: T. Orwin for T. Man, 1590)

Taylor, E. G. R., ed., *The Original Writings and Correspondence of the Two Richard Hakluyts* (London: Hakluyt Society, 1935)

Thys prymer in Englyshe and in Laten is newly translatyd after the Laten texte (Rowen: N. le Roux[?], 1536)

Tyndale, William, *The Obedience of a Christian Man* (Antwerp: J. Hoochstraten, 1528)

Tyndale, William, *The Obedience of a Christian Man and how Christen rulers ought to gouerne* (1528) ([Antwerp: H. Peeterson van Middelburch?] 1535) repr. in The English Experience 897, facsimile repr. (Amsterdam: Theatrum Orbis Terrarum; Norwood, NJ: Walter J. Johnson, 1977)

Urbach, Susanne, 'Eine unbekannte Darstellung von "Sündenfall und Erlösung" in Budapest und das Weiterleben des cranachschen Rechtfertigungsbildes', *Niederdeutsche Beiträge zur Kunstgeschichte*, 28 (1989)

Valkema-Blouw, Paul, 'Early Protestant Publications in Antwerp, 1526-30: the Pseudonyms Adam Anonymus in Basel and Hans Luft in Marlborow', *Quaerendo*, 26-2 (Spring 1996)

Valkema-Blouw, Paul, 'The Van Oldenborch and Vanden Merberghe Synonyms, or Why Frans Fraet Had to Die', Part One, *Quaerendo*, 22/3 (Summer 1992)

Bibliography

Van der Stock, Jan, *Antwerp: Story of a Metropolis* (Antwerp: Hessenhuis, 1993)

van Meteren, Emanuel, *Historie des Neder-landscher ende haerder Na-buren oorlogen ende geschiedenissen* ('s Gravenhaghe: Hillebrant Iacobsz, 1614)

Venaeus, John, *A notable Oration, made by John Venaeus a Parisien in the defence of the Sacrament of the aultare*, trans. by John Bullingham (London: John Cawood, 1554)

Venuti, Lawrence, ed., *Rethinking Translation: Discourse, Subjectivity, Ideology* (London: Routledge, 1992)

Venuti, Lawrence, *The Translator's Invisibility: a History of Translation* (London: Routledge, 1995)

Vervliet, H. D. L., *Sixteenth-Century Printing Types of the Low Countries* (Amsterdam: Menno Hertzberger, 1968)

Verwijs & Verdam, *Middelnederlands woordenboek* ('s Gravenhage: Martinus Nijhoff, 1899)

Visser, C. Ch. G., *Luther's geschriften in de nederlanden tot 1546* (Assen: Van Gorcum, 1969)

Vogel, Paul Heinz, 'Der Druckermarken in den Emdener Niederländischen Bibeldrucken, 156-1568', *Gutenberg Jahrbuch* (1962)

Vogel, Paul Heinz, 'Der niederländische Bibeldruck in Emden, 1556-1568', *Gutenberg Jahrbuch* (1961)

Wandel, Lee Palmer, *Voracious Idols and Violent Hands: Iconoclasm in Reformation Zurich, Strasbourg and Basel* (Cambridge: University Press, 1995)

Warnke, Martin, *Cranachs Luther: Entwürfe für ein Image* (Frankfurt: Fischer, 1984)

Watson, Francis B., *Paul, Judaism and the Gentiles: A Sociological Approach* (Cambridge: University Press, 1986)

Weigle, Luther A., *The New Testament Octapla. Eight English Versions of the New Testament in the Tyndale-King James Version* (New York: T. Nelson, [1962])

Wijnman, H. F., 'De Antwerpse hervormings-gezinde drukker Mattheus Crom en zijn naaste omgeving', *De Gulden passer*, 11 (1962)

Wijnman, H. F., 'Grepen uit de geschiedenis van de Nederlandse emigrantendrukkerijen to Emden', *Het Boek*, 36 (1963-4)

Willey, Basil, 'On translating the Bible into modern English', *Essays and Studies*, n.s. 23 (1970)

Wilson, Charles, *Queen Elizabeth and the Revolt of the Netherlands* (London: Macmillan Press, 1970)

Wing, Donald, *Short-Title Catalogue of Books Printed in England, Scotland, Ireland, Wales, and British America and of English Books Printed in Other Countries, 1641-1700* (New York: The Modern Language Association of America, 1998)

Wood, Christopher S., *Albrecht Altdorfer and the origins of landscape* (London: Reaktion, 1993)

Woolfson, Jonathan, 'English Students at Padua, 1480-1580' (unpublished Ph.D. thesis, University of London, 1995)

Worth, Valerie, *Practising Translation in Renaissance France: the Example of Etienne Dolet* (Oxford: Clarendon Press, 1988)

Wright, David F., ed., *The Bible in Scottish Life and Literature* (Edinburgh: St Andrew's Press, 1988)

Wright, Rosemary Muir, *Art and Antichrist in Medieval Europe* (Manchester: University Press, 1995)

Young, Robert, *Colonial Desire: Hybridity in Theory, Culture and Race* (London: Routledge, 1995)

INDEX

Index

Index